CONTENTS

PREFACE

NOT more than a decade ago the fields of general experimental psychology and child psychology were quite distinct. Rarely did the experimentalist use children as subjects, and equally rarely did the child psychologist employ experimental methods. In recent years, however, considerable attention has been given to the integration of these two fields. Stimulated by the success of the application of experimental techniques to education through programmed instruction, research workers have been increasingly turning to the experimental analysis of child behaviour and development.

This book is intended partly as a contribution to the traditional field of behaviour theory, and partly as a contribution to this new field of experimental child psychology. It sets out, first, to develop a theory or "model" of the discrimination process, and second, to relate this theory to certain features of the cognitive and perceptual development of the child.

As a result of this dual aim, parts of the discussion will seem out of place to the learning theorist. More will look out of place to the child psychologist. But the author firmly believes that this new field of inquiry has something to offer both sides. It should, for example, stimulate the experimentalist, preoccupied with rat and student learning, to venture into the field of development where there are a host of theoretical and practical problems requiring careful analysis. It should also emphasize to the child psychologist the relevance of traditional behaviour theory for an understanding of critical developmental issues.

This book should be useful for psychology graduate students who are looking for an area of research less constricted than conventional learning theory, and more relevant to pressing practical problems. It should also help educationally oriented students to find research problems outside the normal area of developmental study. The book might also be used to supplement more general texts in undergraduate cognition and learning courses.

Finally, I should like to thank Dr. Frank George of Educational

and Scientific Developments Ltd. and Mr. Peter Powesland of the University of Bristol Department of Psychology for their helpful advice and encouragement during the preparation of this book. I am also grateful to Professor Howard H. Kendler and to the American Psychological Association for permission to reproduce Figs. 12.1 and A.1, respectively.

July 1966.   BRIAN J. FELLOWS

CHAPTER 1

INTRODUCTION

THE DISCRIMINATION PROCESS

In this book the word "discrimination" will be used to refer to *the process by means of which an organism responds to differences between stimuli*. This process is assumed to *begin* with the exposure of the organism to a task situation involving stimuli to be discriminated and to *end* with the occurrence of a discriminatory response. In an attempt to clarify the interrelationships of the various operations we shall endeavour to develop a cybernetic *model* of the process.

The concept of a model in psychological theorizing is not unusual. It involves describing a process or system in terms of units with definite functional properties. Each unit receives input which it analyses in some way and produces an output which may provide the input for a further unit. The model is usually presented as a flow-diagram with arrows between the units indicating direction of influence. A point which is often made is that a model does not involve any assumptions about the technical nature of its components (Deutsch, 1960). The model is of the nature of a *blueprint* for a machine in which it is left to the engineer to choose the most suitable materials. Thus, in a model of behaviour no specific physiological explanation need be given. However, as Hebb (1949) demonstrated, "physiologizing" can be a valuable means to the clarification of function and can act as a powerful stimulus to further research. In the present study there will be no deliberate attempt to exclude physiological evidence. Nevertheless, it is primarily a behavioural study, and will therefore develop the model primarily on behavioural evidence.

Let us now attempt a rough sketch of the discrimination process before we go on to look at the details. *In ordinary language* to discriminate usually means the ability to detect differences between objects in our environment. This usage emphasizes the central feature of the process which is *the perception of stimulus differences*.

But to *detect* differences is one thing, to *respond* to them is another. To the psychologist studying discrimination experimentally it is difficult to conceive a discrimination as having been made unless a final discriminatory response occurs. For the perception of a difference is a private event, and so cannot be observed by anyone but the subject. This makes employing direct perception as a datum a very uncertain affair, as a study of some of the work of the early introspectionist psychologists will illustrate.

To exemplify this general point consider an imaginary whisky-taster who claims to be able to discriminate different brands of Scotch. To test this claim we may observe his behaviour "in the field" to see whether he exhibits what is normally accepted as discriminatory behaviour towards different brands of whisky. Alternatively, we may experimentally test his ability by arranging a variety of brands in neutral containers and asking him to identify them. If his behaviour is such that it could not have reasonably occurred on the basis of chance then we may conclude that the claimed ability exists, for it is difficult to conceive of successful discriminatory behaviour in the absence of perceptual discrimination. If, however, our studies revealed *negative* findings the interpretation would not be so simple. The subject may still claim that he can discriminate. He may refuse to accept the test results. He may argue, for example, that he cannot translate his ability into behaviour when he is the subject of study. Nevertheless, he remains convinced of his ability for, after all, he is the best judge of what he perceives. Or is he? The strict behaviourist would argue that the man was deluded. Yet, as we shall see in subsequent chapters, the issue is not simple. It is possible to distinguish *perception* and *response*, not only introspectively, but also through the differential effects that other factors exert on these operations.

For example, in discussing the detection problem in contemporary psychophysics Galanter (1962) points to a number of experiments showing how the behaviour of a subject during the determination of sensory thresholds is influenced not only by the strength of the stimulus (as has been classically held), but also by the expectations and motives of the subject and the background stimulation. The important point here is that *behaviour* during a detection task *is a function of perceptual and response variables*. Perceptual detection itself is primarily a function of stimulus strength. But the response, which is what we observe, is influenced not only by perception, but

also by factors, such as, presentation probabilities and outcome structures. These latter factors combine to produce *response bias,* which is a characteristic of behaviour largely unrelated to the perceptual aspects of the task.

Galanter (*op. cit.*, p. 111) presented his conclusions in the form of a model of stimulus detection behaviour. Figure 1.1 shows a model similar to Galanter's but modified to emphasize the distinction between perception and response.

This model shows the influence of expectations and motives upon the response operation. Perception is assumed to be subject only to the incoming stimuli set against a background of environmental and perceptual "noise". It may be noted that the evidence which

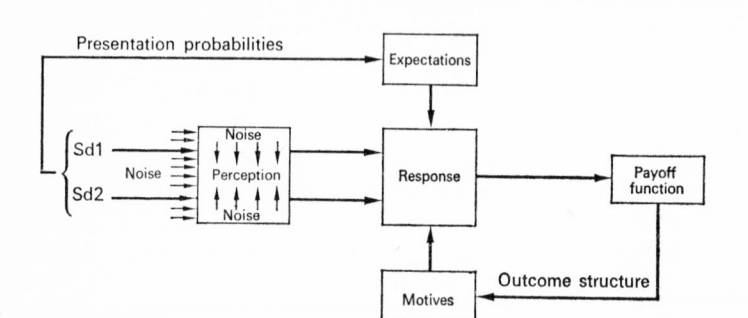

Fig. 1.1. A preliminary model of discrimination (based on Galanter, 1962).

apparently contradicts this assumption (e.g. Bruner and Goodman, 1947; Bruner and Minturn, 1955) is not without ambiguity and may be interpreted in terms of response bias. For a more detailed discussion of motivational variables, which will not be dealt with in this book, the reader is referred to Hebron (1966).

THE PROCESS OF PERCEPTION

The next stage in this preliminary analysis of discrimination concerns the nature of the operation labelled "perception". Perception may be defined as *the process by means of which an organism receives and analyses sensory information.* Thus, it seems to divide into two operations: reception and analysis.

Let us first consider *reception.* Clearly, both perception and discrimination require that the organism's receptors are exposed to the

environmental stimulus. In the case of vision this would involve activities, such as, moving the head and eyes to fixate the stimulus, scanning its contours, and the involuntary scanning activity called "physiological nystagmus" (Marshall and Talbot, 1942). In the present book we shall concentrate on the nature and functions of the two voluntary reception processes: orienting and contour scanning.

Orienting may be operationally defined as any response that serves to expose the organism's receptors (i.e. the retinas) to the sensory input. Though orienting is clearly very necessary for visual input, as we shall see, it is a skill which has been unduly neglected in theories of learning and behaviour until relatively recently. One point that should be made is that the stimulus for orienting is not necessarily the discriminative stimulus. In fact, as Lawrence (1963) indicates, the organism in a discrimination task usually has to learn to orient the appropriate stimulus and that this learning connects the orienting response with the invariant features of the task situation (see Chapter 8). Alternatively, as Berlyne (1960) has emphasized, the stimulus may have the novelty, intensity or complexity to attract an orienting response without any learning.

Scanning may be defined as the movement of the eyes while observing or orienting a stimulus. This scanning will produce a corresponding movement of the image on the retina. We may distinguish two types of scanning. First, there are the small *involuntary eye tremors*, which are physiological in origin and unrelated to the pattern of stimulation being observed. Much work has been conducted in the past decade, or so, into discovering the function of these nystagmus movements by stabilizing the retinal image (Ditchburn and Ginsborg, 1952; Riggs *et al.*, 1953; Pritchard *et al.*, 1960; Evans, 1965). Under these conditions patterns are perceived to fade and fragment according to certain laws. In general the fragmentation is digital (though not always so) with simple lines and meaningful entities comprising perceptual units. Thus, nystagmus movements are functionally important in the maintenance of perception, and by counteracting them it seems we may be able to learn much about the way the perception of a pattern is built up.

The second type of *scanning movement* is to a large extent in humans under voluntary control, though it usually occurs without awareness. These scanning movements are normally larger than nystagmus and are guided by the stimulus pattern being observed. One's own eye movements can easily be observed through the movement

of an after-image (Woodworth and Schlosberg, 1954, p. 497). These scanning movements, of course, formed an important element in Hebb's (1949) cell-assembly theory of pattern perception. Hebb likened eye movements to the hand of the builder whose function was to construct form perceptions, using lines and angles as bricks and the primitive unity of the figure as mortar (*op. cit.*, p. 83). Considerable attention will be given in later chapters to the role of this type of scanning in perception and its development. It may suffice at this point to note that effective perception of relatively simple figures is seriously disturbed in tachistoscopic presentation. The fact that some figures are perceived without eye movements may be due to the "internalization" of scanning with learning (see Chapter 20).

As Hebb (1949) and many others have stressed the sensory input is only the beginning of perception. Stimuli are not passively absorbed and transmitted by the perceptual system; rather they are *analysed and transformed* by the autonomous, on-going, activity of the system. Let us now try to develop a general picture of what happens after the stimulus has been received.

The *analysis* of sensory information has been the main field of inquiry in the experimental study of perception. It seems to involve two operations, which we might call "attention" and "organization". The main characteristic of *attention* is selection. The orienting response selects the sensory input from the myriad environmental stimuli impinging on the organism. Attention seems to perform a further selection of the input thus received. It selects, as it were, from the stimuli impinging on the receptors those which are to control the organism's behaviour. It may be noted here that perception and attention are treated as processes. The conscious awareness that accompanies both is assumed to be a non-functional by-product.

The selective process of attention seems to have two main parts. First, attention may be conceived as a *mediating process which supports certain sensory inputs* (Hebb, 1966, p. 96). That is, attending to a stimulus magnifies its influence. Second, attention also serves to *reduce the influence of competing stimuli*. The inhibitory aspect of attention is well illustrated by the blocking of the cochlear nucleus response to a click stimulus in the cat through attention to more significant visual and olfactory inputs (Hernandez-Peon *et al.*, 1956). The evidence points to the reticular system as a likely mechanism underlying attention (Magoun, 1963).

In addition to this gross stimulus selection activity, attention also

operates *to isolate certain characteristics* of the input. Thus, attention enables the organism to respond not only to the whole of a stimulus pattern, but also to certain features of it, such as, its form, its colour and its size. As we shall see, this abstraction, or stimulus dimension selection process figures large in many interpretations of animal and human discrimination learning.

Attention as we have presented it is primarily concerned with selection; the information actually getting through is not changed by this process, but only reinforced or inhibited. It is clear from the work on visual illusions, shape and depth perception, and size and shape constancy that this cannot account for all we know about perception. In addition, the basic input is supplemented and transformed by the existing characteristics of the perceptual system. This "perceptual work" is performed by what we might call the *organization operation* Its concern is not so much with selection as with the organization of the input so as to produce a useful and consistent picture of the environment the organism has to live in.

The most coherent account of perceptual organization offered prior to 1949 was Gestalt theory (Köhler, 1929; Koffka, 1935; Wertheimer, 1923). This proposed that perception was immediate and unlearned, and subject primarily to the Law of Pregnance or "Good Form". Hebb's attack on the Gestalt position in *The Organization of Behaviour* proved to be a watershed in thinking about perception. For Hebb, perception was essentially an additive process in which complex perceptions were constructed through learning from simple perceptual units. The microelectrode studies of Hubel and Wiesel (1959) have given considerable physiological support to this type of model in which perceptions are developed through a *hierarchy* of operations. The manner in which the perception of a stabilized image breaks down also gives substance to this conception, though this work does point to a possible reconciliation between the Gestalt and Hebbian positions. What is needed is a re-examination of the concept of "Good Form" in the light of the evidence about the simple units, and an attempt to describe the molar "field force" effects in molecular terminology. As Hebb (1966, p. 277) has recently indicated, the simple digital model of perception needs some modification, particularly in view of gradual fading of certain stabilized images. For a recent attempt to develop a model of perception in terms of a hierarchical organization the reader is referred to Forgus (1966).

As we shall see, in most interpretations of the discrimination process it has not been considered necessary to make a sharp distinction between the selective and the organizational aspects of perception. Usually, all that is required of the perceptual operation is for it to generate distinctively different outputs for the two discriminative stimuli. To a large extent this operation could be performed by what has been described above as attention. If, however, the stimuli are complex, or the discrimination is difficult, then some higher-order operation must be assumed. In the present book some attention is given to examining the factors involved in a difficult discrimination—*the discrimination of differently orientated forms*—in order to exemplify the interrelationships of the selective, organizational and judgemental variables. In emphasizing *the perceptual part of the process* this represents a break with the conventional approach to discrimination. But, as Lawrence (1963) and Dodwell (1964) have indicated, it is the stimulus that has been so neglected in previous work. By considering the role played by perception we should, it seems, arrive at a more satisfactory model of the discrimination process.

JUDGEMENT AND RESPONSE

Figure 1.2 shows the framework of a basic model of discrimination which will serve to guide us through the present study.

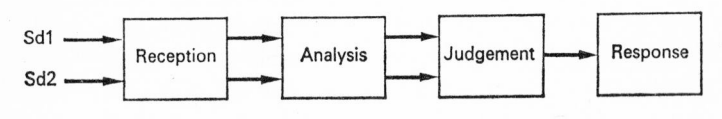

Fig. 1.2. A basic model of the discrimination process.

The model shows four main operations or "units". The first ensures the *reception* of the discriminative stimuli (Sd's). The second labelled *Analysis* refers to the processing of the sensory input through attention and perceptual organization. The third and fourth represent the final distinction to be made in this preliminary analysis. *Judgement* mediates between the perception and the response. It is an internal, cognitive, operation. This distinguishes it from *Response* which is directly responsible for the observable behaviour. Introspectively, the distinction is easy to make. It is also clear that in Galanter's psychophysical experiments it is the judgement operation that is affected by

the factors producing response bias. The work on "insight", "expectations" and "hypotheses" in animals (Köhler, 1925; Tolman, 1932; Krechevsky, 1932) suggests that the same distinction may be made in animal behaviour. This and related questions will be dealt with in later chapters.

DISCRIMINATION LEARNING

A convenient method of studying the discrimination process is through the acquisition of a discrimination. As we shall see, most of the work in this area has involved animals, though experiments employing children as subjects are on the increase (Bijou and Baer, 1960). Animals and children are particularly suitable for study since many of the component skills of discrimination performance are not present in their behavioural repertoires and hence have to be learned during the experiment. Since much of the work reviewed in this book employs the discrimination learning paradigm a few comments about *methodology* and techniques might be of value.

The classical discrimination learning experiment employs two discriminative stimuli (Sd's), one of which is positive (Sd+) and the other negative (Sd−). In order to promote learning, responses (R) to Sd+ are reinforced. Responses to Sd− are not reinforced and may be punished. The discrimination is said to have been learned when the organism consistently responds to Sd+ and avoids Sd−. Alternatively, the subject may be required to make two different responses, one to each stimulus.

In the *simultaneous* discrimination learning procedure both Sd's are presented simultaneously to the subject on every trial. In the *successive* procedure the Sd's are presented successively, one on each trial. In both procedures care has to be taken in the manner in which the Sd's are presented to control for *sequential and position effects*. For example, in the simultaneous procedure the Sd's are usually presented in certain positions. To prevent better than chance performances occurring as a result of some method of responding based on the relative positions of the Sd's rather than on the Sd's themselves, and also to prevent any accidental differential reinforcement of position hypotheses (see Appendix), it is necessary to randomize the positions occupied by the Sd's from one trial to the next. Such sequences have been prepared by Gellerman (1933c) and are widely used and also recommended for use (Hilgard, 1951, p. 533; Bijou

and Baer, 1960, p. 170; Sutherland, 1961a, p. 23). But in the light of recent work on the analysis of hypotheses in discrimination performance these sequences have needed revising (Fellows, 1967).

Matching-to-sample and *oddity learning* are two other useful discrimination tasks. As we shall see, these are particularly informative procedures for use with children and the higher primates, though their cognitive complexity has usually ruled them out in animal work. These tasks are discussed in detail in Chapter 13. Concentrating on the discrimination process in children, the model we shall attempt to develop is of the matching task, though most of the operations will also apply to the other tasks.

A great variety of discrimination learning apparatus has been used, depending largely on the capacities of the organism and the objectives of the experimenter. The *Lashley Jumping Stand* (Lashley, 1930) was popular in the 1930's and 1940's for experiments with rats. In this the rat was placed on a stand and trained to jump across a small gap to one of two cards on which were printed the Sd's. If the rat jumped to Sd+ the card fell back revealing food. If, on the other hand, Sd— was jumped at the card remained firm, the rat bumped its nose and fell into a net.

The Jumping Stand involved a large number of problems and now has been superseded by more sophisticated techniques. For example, Sutherland (1961c) describes a discrimination training apparatus for rats in which drinking nozzles containing milk project through the centre of stimulus shapes. Approaching Sd— causes a bell to ring and a small current to pass through the nozzle of Sd— which would shock the animal's mouth should it attempt to drink. Other methods for training animals are described by Woodworth and Schlosberg (1954, Chapter 20) and Sutherland (1961a).

The *Wisconsin General Test Apparatus* (Harlow, 1949) was a popular method during the 1940's and the 1950's for discrimination work with monkeys. It consists essentially of a tray containing two or more foodwells each of which is covered by a stimulus object. The experimenter places food under Sd+ and pushes the tray up to the animal who then attempts to locate the food. Usually the situation is so arranged that the monkey may make only one response at a time. Under these conditions monkeys show themselves capable of a great variety of relatively complex cognitive and perceptual skills. This apparatus has also been successfully used with normal and mentally retarded children (e.g. House and Zeaman, 1958).

The study of discrimination learning in children is dealt with in some detail in later chapters of this book. A useful method which has been employed by Holland (1962), Bijou (1962), Hively (1962a, b) and Fellows (1965) is to display the stimuli in windows which the child is required to press on to indicate his choice (see Fig. 17.2).

DISCRIMINATION AND DEVELOPMENT

Throughout this study special attention will be given to the developmental aspects of the discrimination process. We shall see that the experimental analysis of child development is a rapidly growing and very fruitful field of investigation, and one which has been unduly neglected by learning theorists. Foremost in this movement is the work of Bijou and his colleagues at the University of Washington in Seattle (Bijou, 1955, 1957, 1958a, b, c, 1961, 1962; Bijou and Baer, 1960, 1963; Bijou and Orlando, 1961; Bijou and Sturges, 1959; Baer, 1961; Orlando and Bijou, 1960). For other work in this area the reader is referred to Lipsitt and Spiker (1963, 1965), Wright and Kagan (1963), Stevenson (1963) and Hoffman and Hoffman (1964).

This book has two main *aims*: first, to develop a model showing the operations involved in the process of discrimination; and second, to investigate the developmental features of these operations. To fulfil the latter we shall examine in detail the discrimination performance of the young child and try to isolate and identify the various operations. In particular, we shall attempt to distinguish the perceptual and the motor aspects of the performance. Our investigation will spotlight the matching-to-sample task. This is cognitively quite a complex task and one which a young child (4–5 years of age) cannot consistently cope with. Hence we should be able to observe the component skills more readily than with a simpler task. To illustrate the perceptual part of the process a detailed analysis will be made of the visual discrimination of differently orientated forms. In this the young child shares with many species of animal an apparently basic perceptual problem: a disposition to treat differently orientated forms as equivalent. This is reflected, for example, in the problem of reversals in reading and in mirror writing.

In the main we shall be guided by *three questions*. First, what is involved in terms of skills or operations in the successful performance on a task, such as matching which demands a discrimination on the

basis of the orientation of forms? Second, in the event of an unsuccessful performance, what went wrong? What difficulties does a child face on such a task? And how well equipped is he to deal with them? Third, what can be done in terms of instruction or training programmes to improve a poor performance?

To answer the first question we shall examine the theoretical and experimental work relating to the learning and performance on visual discrimination tasks and try to develop a "paper and pencil" model on the lines of the analysis outlined above. In the course of this we shall be looking for features of the child's cognitive behaviour which will help us to answer the second question. The latter part of the book (Chapters 15–20) is primarily concerned with the perceptual process involved in the discrimination of orientation. Why is this discrimination so difficult? To answer the third question we shall examine the possibility of developing suitable training programmes to establish the necessary cognitive and perceptual skills.

CHAPTER 2

CLASSICAL THEORIES OF DISCRIMINATION LEARNING

PRIOR to the publication of Lashley's *Brain Mechanisms and Intelligence* in 1929, the learning of a discrimination problem by an animal was usually regarded as an unavoidable nuisance, preliminary to the investigation of its sensory capacities. The interest of experimenters such as Bingham (1913, 1914) and Fields (1928, 1929, 1931, 1932) was chiefly centred upon the ability of different animals to make different sorts of discriminations. Their interest in the task itself was largely limited to making *ad hoc* adjustments to apparatus and procedure in order to speed up the learning. Very largely as a result of a suggestion by Lashley there was a definite shift of interest, and the discrimination experiment came to be employed in the study of the learning process, *per se* (Spence, 1936).

PRE-SOLUTION BEHAVIOUR

Lashley (1929) objected to the Watson–Thorndike description of the pre-solution behaviour of an animal learning a task as random. On the contrary, Lashley argued, at least in normal animals, there is a certain kind of *order* or *system* about the way an animal tackles a new task. It does not, typically, rush into the task situation, making a number of wild and blind responses. Rather, it appears to "... experiment with many solutions" (*op. cit.*, p. 135). This experimentation is manifested in systematic, but incorrect, ways of responding. Thus, the animal may persist in responding to one position, or it may alternate its responses, or it may respond to cues from the movements of the experimenter. All these are seen by Lashley as "*attempted solutions*", which tend to precede the acquisition of the correct discriminatory behaviour.

These observations were confirmed in a series of experiments performed by Krechevsky (1932a, b, c, d, 1933a, b, 1935, 1938), in

which he showed, by an appropriate analysis of individual records (see Appendix for his method of analysis), that the behaviour of the rat prior to the attainment of criterion performance on a two-choice discrimination learning task, was very definitely not a chance affair. On the contrary, the pre-solution behaviour was characterized by a number of systematic methods of responding, position perseveration, position alternation, etc., which Krechevsky called "*hypotheses*".

NON-CONTINUITY THEORY

Both Lashley and Krechevsky argued that these observations were evidence that a rat's acquisition of a discrimination does not take place gradually over a period of trials in which the correct and the incorrect responses are being differentially strengthened by the reinforcing contingencies, as the trial and error theory of learning would have us believe (Hull, 1930a). Rather, in the words of Krechevsky (1932c),

> Learning consists of changing from one systematic, generalized, purposive way of behaving to another and another until the problem is solved. The learning process at every point consists of a series of integrated, purposive behaviour patterns. [p. 532.]

According to this interpretation, therefore, the rat apparently learns nothing in acquiring a discrimination. All it does is spontaneously *try out* one method of responding after another. When it hits on the method labelled by the experimenter as "correct", the experiment usually stops and, as far as the experimenter is concerned, the rat has learned.

But does this mean that the rat's selection of behaviour is not guided at all by the outcome? For example, if we left the rat on the experiment after it had learned would it go on experimenting? The work on overlearning, in which training continues after the usual criterion of acquisition has been passed, certainly indicates that once the correct method of responding is adopted then the subject will persist in it and abandon his pre-solution-type behaviour (Mackintosh, 1962, 1963a, 1964).

Another problem for the Lashley–Krechevsky theory is accounting for the *switches* in hypotheses in the pre-solution period. What makes the rat change its method of responding? Krechevsky, at least, regards these switches in hypotheses as being partly, but not wholly, a function of the outcome. The hypothesis testing, for Krechevsky, is

purposive; its aim is to realize the attainment of the goal object. Hence, hypotheses will be tested and discarded until the correct one comes along, at which point, having achieved its objective, the animal ceases experimentation.

But the outcome, for Krechevsky, is not the only determinant of hypothesis behaviour.

> When we say that an individual has an 'hypothesis' we imply that the individual is contributing something to the situation. His behaviour is not something forced upon him by the immediately presented stimuli . . . . An 'hypothesis' is the individual's interpretation of the data, it is not a phenomenon deriving from the presented data alone. [*Op. cit.*, pp. 531–2.]

CONTINUITY THEORY

That is the main point of issue between the Lashley–Krechevsky view and the widely held theory that the learning of an animal is entirely a function of the differential reinforcing effects of trial and error practice. That systematic response tendencies do occur in the pre-solution period is a well-established experimental fact (Hamilton, 1911; Yerkes, 1916; MacGillivary and Stone, 1930). A major difference exists, however, as to the interpretation of these tendencies. According to Krechevsky's theory, which he subsequently called the "non-continuity hypothesis" (Krechevsky, 1938), hypothesis behaviour represents insightful, intelligent, attempts at solution, which are only guided by the outcome; that is, the outcome has only *informational* value. On the other hand, the *continuity* theory, which is represented mainly by Spence (1936, 1937a, b, 1939, 1940, 1941, 1945, 1951, 1952, 1955, 1960), holds that these systematic pre-solution behaviours are quite in accordance with the expectations of a trial and error view of learning. According to the latter theory no extra assumptions need to be made about possible non-observable, intervening or mediating, variables to give a comprehensive account of the whole of discrimination performance.

Spence (1936) indicates that neither the early crude versions of the trial and error theory (Thorndike, 1898; Watson, 1914), nor the later more sophisticated versions (Hull, 1930a), held that the organism came to the learning task with a clean sheet, or a *tabula rasa*. Rather, the behaviour exhibited on a task will depend to a large extent upon previously acquired skills and associations and any innate or inherited responses. The effect of the conditions of the task and the reinforcing contingencies is to *re-shape* the behaviour, which the

organism brings to the situation and which is most likely quite inappropriate, so as to make it conform to the experimenter's requirements.

There is, however, one implication of the non-continuity theory which, on the face of it, is less easy to reconcile with the continuity hypothesis. Since this concerns the role of attention, it is of immediate interest.

ISSUE OF PERCEPTUAL SELECTIVITY

Krechevsky (1938) criticized Spence's (1936) account of the discrimination learning process in that it said nothing about the selectivity of animal's perception and learning. According to the continuity theory all the R's made in the task are differentially strengthened to all the S's present in the situation. Krechevsky, on the other hand, argued that any learning or strengthening that does take place only involves those aspects of the situation which the animal is attending to at the time of response. The existence of a hypothesis implies selection, and selection implies that certain aspects of the situation will not be conditioned to excitatory and inhibitory response tendencies, at least so long as the hypothesis lasts. In the words of Lashley (1929), the learning performance of the individual animal

> . . . strongly suggests that the association is formed very quickly and that both the practice preceding and the errors following are irrelevant to the actual formation of the association. [p. 135.]

SPENCE AND RECEPTOR ORIENTING ACTS

The way Spence (1940) deals with this criticism is very relevant to the development of a model of the sequence of events involved in discrimination behaviour, and so it will be considered in some detail.

Spence's main point is that Krechevsky obtains the results he does because he requires his animals to learn, in addition to the instrumental approach–avoidance R, a response which serves *to expose them to the appropriate S aspects of the task*. Spence emphasizes that in his own experiments the discrimination apparatus was so designed that the animal could not help receiving the two discriminative stimuli (Sd's). In most of Spence's experiments the animal was required to discriminate two brightnesses. But in most of Krechevsky's

experiments the animal was required to discriminate between two visually presented forms. It is Spence's point that using forms as Sd's does not ensure that the animal will automatically receive discriminably different retinal stimulations from them. He argues,

> In these instances the animal is required to learn, in addition to the final selective approaching response, the appropriate (perceptual) response which leads to the reception of the relevant stimulus aspects. That is to say, the animal must learn to orient and fixate its head and eyes so as to receive the critical stimuli. [Spence, 1940, p. 276.]

Therefore, according to Spence, and his views have not radically altered (see Spence, 1951), the organism, in learning a two-choice pattern discrimination task, has, in fact, to learn a chain of *two* R's. The first, which may be called a "receptor-orienting act", serves to expose the organism's receptors to the relevant Sd's. The second is the approach–avoidance instrumental R, which is made to the Sd's and which serves to produce the outcome contingencies.

So, when an animal exhibits a position hypothesis, this is presumably a sign that it has yet to learn the appropriate receptor-orienting activity which will serve to expose it to the relevant Sd's. Its behaviour is still largely guided by kinesthetic information, to which it may be innately predisposed to attend. The purpose of the discrimination learning task is to suppress this tendency and replace it with an Sd-guided hypothesis.

Therefore, at least in a pattern discrimination task, it is not the case, as the "pure" continuity hypothesis would have it, that all the S's in the situation are differentially conditioned to all the R's made. There is in fact a selection process operating, which means that only those S's *actually impinging* on the organism's receptors around the time of the R will be involved in the conditioning process.

It is not likely, however, that Krechevsky would have been satisfied by this interpretation of his findings. Though he may have agreed that some receptor-orienting activity has to be learned, he would probably have argued that this would not be sufficient to explain the sort of selection that actually occurs. For though looking at and receiving a S are necessary conditions for making R's to it, they are not sufficient; we may look without seeing. This distinction would be brought out by an experimental design in which the relevant Sd and the locus of R were spatially contiguous. Assuming that the organism looks where it responds this should ensure the orienting R to the Sd. But would it guarantee that Sd learning took place? We shall see in

some of the subsequent chapters that mere contiguity of Sd and R does not ensure a discrimination; in addition, some covert, post-retinal, selection must be assumed to take place. This is presumably what Krechevsky would be tempted to label "attention".

Ehrenfreund (1948) modified the Lashley Jumping Stand discrimination apparatus in an attempt to exercise some experimental control over the orienting behaviour of the rat. In the original version of this apparatus (Lashley, 1938a) the rat was required to jump to the *base* of the stimulus cards displaying the discrimination figures. Since Lashley himself noticed that the rats had a tendency to discriminate in terms of the lower half of the Sd's, Ehrenfreund hypothesized that maybe, if he got the rats to jump to the *centre* of the S card, their discriminatory behaviour would be more likely to be controlled by the whole S than by part of it.

Ehrenfreund decided to use this design to test Spence's explanation of Krechevsky's (1938) failure to find any adverse effects on reversal learning of a little pre-solution practice on a discrimination task. According to Spence's version of the continuity hypothesis, provided the relevant Sd's are impinging on an organism's receptors, then any R's the organism makes, which are rewarded, will be conditioned to these Sd's. This means that even a little trial and error practice, even though the performance is still around chance level, will be enough to differentially reinforce the approach–avoidance R's to the Sd's. This implies that if, after a little such practice, the values of the Sd's are reversed, then learning the reversal will be more difficult than the learning of the original discrimination would have been; for the now negative Sd has some positive attraction which will have to be overcome before the appropriate associations are established.

Spence argued that Krechevsky's failure to find this effect was the result of his rats not having learned, in the practice allowed to them, the appropriate receptor-orienting R's. This interpretation is supported by the fact that some of Krechevsky's rats which were given double the pre-solution training were in fact retarded on the reversal task.

Ehrenfreund found that those rats which were required to jump to the centre of the card (appropriate orienting R) in the pre-solution training were retarded on the reversal task; but those rats which were required to jump to the base of the card (inappropriate orienting R, there being no differences between the lower portions of the Sd's) were not retarded. This was interpreted as supporting Spence's

explanation of Krechevsky's findings. The training given to the base-jumpers was presumably not enough to ensure that the appropriate orienting R was acquired and, therefore, there could be no differential Sd learning.

CONCLUSION

What may we conclude from this discussion of the classical continuity versus non-continuity controversy which will be of help in our objective of identifying the operations involved in the performance on a discrimination task? The most valuable information on this score is clearly Spence's modification of the continuity theory to include receptor-orienting acts. But it is quite obvious that Spence's two-element chain is not sufficient to describe all the characteristics of discrimination behaviour. We have noted that, in addition, we shall most probably need some implicit, post-retinal, selection mechanism to account for the selectivity of visual discrimination behaviour. Also, as Dodwell (1964) has recently argued, the main fault of these early accounts of discrimination learning was their *neglect of the perceptual factor*. Spence, by means of his receptor-orienting acts, shows some recognition of the role played by perception in learning, but, as we shall see in subsequent chapters, not nearly as much as it deserves. As the theory of Sutherland (Chapter 8) clearly indicates, Spence's fears about the danger of relapsing into mentalism by considering perception as a determining variable are not realistic.

CHAPTER 3

ORIENTING ACTIVITY IN DISCRIMINATION IN ANIMALS

IN THIS chapter we shall look at some other sources of information about the role of orienting behaviour in discrimination performance of animals.

WYCKOFF'S OBSERVING RESPONSE

A very similar account of the nature of discrimination learning to that of Spence has been proposed by Wyckoff (1951, 1952, 1954). He arranged a task, using the Skinner-box, in which pigeons were required to execute a chain of two R's in order to obtain reinforcement. The first R consisted of the pigeon stepping on a pedal fixed to the floor of the box. This had the effect of lighting up two translucent keys with colours. The final instrumental R required was a discriminatory peck at one or the other of the keys that was showing the positive colour. So the presentation of the Sd's, and therefore the reinforcement, was contingent upon the occurrence of a pedal R. This pedal R, Wyckoff called an "observing response" (Ro). An Ro was defined as ". . . any response which results in exposure to the pair of discriminative stimuli involved" (1952, p. 431). So Spence's receptor-orienting acts are, by this definition, Ro's.

Wyckoff's main concern in his experimental work (1951, 1952) was to identify the source of strengthening of the Ro. By making the Ro discrete and measurable Wyckoff had considerably simplified his task. As we would expect, the probability of Ro was higher under differential than under non-differential reinforcement (reinforcement of pecking irrespective of Sd's). The problem is that only 50 per cent of Ro's in fact lead to reinforcing conditions. Spence (1936, 1940) argued that the Ro is probably strengthened by being succeeded after a short interval of time by the final goal R. But if this only follows 50 per cent of the time we would not expect Ro to be very firm, which in fact it is.

Wyckoff (1952) argued that the presentation of the Sd's acquires secondary reinforcing value through being associated with the reinforcement. Berlyne (1960, p. 205) proposes an alternative explanation. According to this the Ro is strengthened and maintained as a result of its role in the reduction of conflict or uncertainty in the task. Thus, while the keys are white, pecking has only a 50–50 chance of being rewarded. The pedal R eliminates the ambiguity from this situation, reduces the uncertainty.

In his theoretical work Wyckoff (1952, 1954) has included this Ro in a comprehensive model of discrimination behaviour in which he attempts to quantify the relationships between Ro and the other variables in the performance. This model has provided the stimulus for more detailed and sophisticated versions in recent years (Atkinson, 1958, 1959, 1961, 1963; Zeaman and House, 1963). But in the present context, Wyckoff's most important contribution was in confirming the role of orienting in discrimination behaviour, and in demonstrating how it can be made overt and measurable, and hence, in principle, controllable.

GOODWIN–LAWRENCE DIMENSION ORIENTING RESPONSE

Goodwin and Lawrence (1955) interpret their results in a very similar manner to Spence and Wyckoff. They report, in accordance with a similar study by Lawrence and Mason (1955), that once a discrimination has been established in rats on two cues of one stimulus dimension, it is not broken down or extinguished when the animal is required to learn a discrimination on two cues of a different stimulus dimension, even though during this latter training the animal was being randomly reinforced and non-reinforced on each of the two cues of the original discrimination.

This finding they argue is not what would be expected from a continuity theory. This, in its "pure" form (see Chapter 2), would predict that the random outcomes during the learning of the second discrimination would tend to weaken, and ultimately extinguish the differential approach–avoidance tendencies acquired during the first discrimination task. As an alternative Goodwin and Lawrence propose a non-continuity mechanism which bears a very strong resemblance to Spence's receptor-orienting R, though they fail to acknowledge it.

According to the Goodwin–Lawrence theory an organism in a discrimination task has to learn *two* things. First, it must learn to orient the relevant S dimension; and second, it must learn to approach S+ and avoid S—. In presenting their theory Goodwin and Lawrence make the assumption that the two S dimensions are spatially separate. This means that the orienting R they postulate will be an overt R, like those of Spence and Wyckoff. But, the fact that in their experiment the two dimensions, brightness and hurdles, were not separated, clearly, indicates that this assumption is not necessary. For presumably, in the experimental set-up, the same selection occurred even though a single orienting R would be sufficient to expose both dimensions. In this sense, the Goodwin–Lawrence orienting R does differ from those of Spence and Wyckoff, in that it takes place *after the reception* of the Sd's by the subject. Goodwin and Lawrence prefer to call this implicit dimension-orienting ". . . the identification of and reaction to a dimension or set of stimuli . . ." (*op. cit.*, p. 442).

In order to explain the fairly prompt switch from one dimension to another Goodwin and Lawrence were obliged to assume, further, that the orienting R *extinguishes more rapidly*, following the withdrawal of reinforcement, than the preference built up for the Sd+ over the Sd—. This means that when hurdles become the relevant dimension, orienting the brightness dimension quickly extinguishes and is replaced by orienting hurdles. The preference for the light Sd over the dark Sd, however, extinguishes less quickly. When the brightness orienting R is switched out the brightness Sd's are no longer being received by the subject and hence are not affected by the reinforcement contingencies. So, the original discrimination will be maintained at the strength it was when the orienting R changed during the learning of the hurdle discrimination. When brightness again becomes the relevant dimension, the orienting R quickly switches back to this dimension where it finds the original preferences just as strong as when it was switched out.

There is one fairly clear and testable prediction from the Goodwin–Lawrence theory about the differential extinction rates of orienting and discriminative R's. Since the orienting R extinguishes quickly when the full measure of reinforcement is withdrawn, learning the reverse of a discrimination should be more difficult than learning another discrimination. This has been confirmed by Kelleher (1956) using rats, and Kendler *et al.* (1960) using nursery school children. However, as Kendler and Kendler (1962a) indicate, this only appears

to be the case when the learning is *non-mediational*; in older children and adults the situation is reversed, and reversal learning is easier (see Chapter 11).

It may be noted here that the discrimination model of Sutherland and Mackintosh, discussed in Chapter 8, proposes that the process of learning which stimulus analyser to switch-in occurs comparatively slowly, but once established it is less susceptible to extinction than is the overt discriminatory R. This assumption is considered necessary to account for the facilitatory effect of overtraining on reversal learning (Mackintosh, 1962, 1963a). The effect of overtraining is to switch-in the appropriate analyser firmly enough to resist the period of intermittent reinforcement during which the connections between the overt R's and the outputs from the analyser are being switched-over when the Sd values are reversed.

If we assume that there is some similarity between the Goodwin–Lawrence dimension identification or orienting R and Sutherland's switching-in of a stimulus analyser, then there appear to be two divergent opinions about extinction rates. But maybe they can be reconciled. If we assume that in the Goodwin–Lawrence non-reversal learning experiments the training on the initial task was not sufficiently extensive to enable the orienting R to be firmly switched-in, then, in terms of the Sutherland–Mackintosh theory, it is to be expected that it would extinguish quite rapidly. Some support for this reconciliation comes from the findings of Mackintosh (1962) that overtraining actually interferes with non-reversal learning.

PRE- AND POST-RECEPTION RESPONSES

To summarize, the orienting behaviour as proposed by Spence and Wyckoff involves some sort of overt change in the relationship between the Sd's and the subject's receptors. This change is such as to expose the subject's receptors to the Sd's. Hence, the Sd's will be received by the subject's perceptual apparatus as sensory input.

The orienting-identification R as proposed by Goodwin and Lawrence also involves overt orienting to expose the Sd's. But, in addition, it involves some sort of *post-reception analysis* which serves to isolate one stimulus dimension from another. Thus, though both S dimensions are technically received by the subject, only one serves to control the subject's behaviour.

A similar distinction has been made by Berlyne (1960). Berlyne identifies two classes of processes that subserve selective attention. Firstly, there are

> ... control processes which influence the fate of sensory information after it has left the sense organs and while it is passing through the nervous system on its way to the effectors. [*Op. cit.*, p. 78.]

Secondly, there are

> ... other processes which intervene earlier and affect the nature of the stimulation reaching the sense organs.

These latter R's, which alter the stimulus field, are called "exploratory behaviour" by Berlyne. Clearly, the Spence–Wyckoff orienting R's fall into this latter class. The Goodwin–Lawrence identification R, on the other hand, seems to fit better in the first class. We shall see in future chapters that this distinction will serve us well in the differentiation of the orienting and the perceptual aspects of discriminatory behaviour. Though it will be clear that the perceptual part is not always implicit.

VICARIOUS TRIAL AND ERROR

A frequently observed form of behaviour in the discrimination performance of animals which seems to have many features in common with the sort of orienting activity discussed above is vicarious trial and error. Tolman (1932) was the first to call attention to the characteristic *vacillation* behaviour that occurs when a rat is faced with a choice between two alleyways in a maze. The animal is seen to waver back and forth, first looking in one direction, then in the other, sometimes making feints towards one alley or the other. Tolman suggested that such abbreviated "runnings-back-and-forth" served to verify and strengthen the differentiation of the critical cues, after the relevant S dimensions had been isolated. It was actually Muenzinger (1938) who called this behaviour "vicarious trial and error" (VTE); "vicarious" because the animal goes through the motions of trying the alternative R's without actually completing them.

That VTE facilitates the learning of a maze and a discrimination is indicated by the following observations. Peaks in VTE are usually correlated with improvements in performance. Anything that encourages VTE also improves performance. Brain-damaged animals show less VTE and poorer learning than normal animals. The fact

that once a discrimination is acquired VTE falls off indicates that it is not necessary for the maintenance of the habit. The more difficult the discrimination the more VTE (Muenzinger, 1938; Tolman, 1932, 1939, 1948; Tolman and Minium, 1943; Tolman and Richie, 1943; Goss and Wischner, 1956).

VTE is certainly not identical with what we have been referring to as an orienting R. VTE seems to be a sort of orienting *strategy*. It is a way of behaving in a choice situation which involves a number of rapid alternating orienting R's to each of the Sd's. As we shall see in our model presented in Chapter 14, this sort of rapid alternation will greatly facilitate the comparison of the two Sd's and this is probably part of the explanation of the facilitatory effect of VTE on the acquisition of a discrimination. In terms of the model VTE would seem to be controlled by the Response Strategy unit.

CHAPTER 4

ORIENTING AND ATTENTION IN CHILDREN

In this and the next two chapters we shall be concerned with experimental and theoretical studies which tend to emphasize the role of orienting and attentional processes in the discrimination performance of young children. These discussions will be interested more in the motor side of the performance than the perceptual, though, as will be seen, this distinction is not always easy to maintain.

KURTZ'S OBSERVING RESPONSE

A very similar account of orienting in children to that of Spence, Wyckoff and Goodwin and Lawrence has been offered by Kurtz (1955) to account for the positive transfer effects resulting from stimulus pretraining in children. He found that training young children to respond with the words "same" or "different" according to whether the two stimuli presented were identical or not, facilitated the subsequent acquisition of specific verbal labels for these stimuli. Kurtz hypothesized that the pretraining enabled the children to acquire *observing responses* which transferred to the labelling task and facilitated the children's performance on it. Kurtz's definition of an observing response was

> ... any response which, when made to one or the other of a given pair of stimulus complexes which are different, consistently results in distinctive stimulation from those two stimulus complexes. [*Op. cit.*, p. 290.]

Kurtz also thought that the facilitatory effect of verbal labelling on motor discrimination (Rossman and Goss, 1951) could also be explained in these terms.

Kurtz's definition of observing R is very similar to Spence's definition of orienting R. Both emphasize that the R functions so as to produce distinctively different stimulations from the two Sd's.

But there are two possible ways of interpreting the phrase "*distinctively different stimulations*". In one sense, which is what Spence appears to mean, it may merely refer to the existence of two different patterns of excitation on the subject's receptors. But this, of course, does not ensure that the two Sd's will be operationally distinctive. For Spence's mechanistic S–R theory, however, this difference is enough. But Kurtz seems to imply that his observing response is sufficient to guarantee, not only that the subject's receptors will be exposed to different patterns of excitation, but also that they will be differentially responded to. In other words, for Kurtz the phrase "distinctively different stimulations" is operationally defined in terms of the subject's ability to indicate in some way that he can discriminate them. Such an interpretation implies that it is very likely that bound up with the observing R is some sort of implicit, post-receptor, operation which serves to make the Sd's different for the subject orienting them.

It is perhaps unfortunate that Kurtz did not make this distinction clear. For, on the face of it, his interpretation implies that a child's discrimination of two Sd's can be ensured merely by making sure that he observes them. G. N. Cantor (1955) showed that though S pretraining involving pointing at the Sd's did facilitate the subsequent acquisition of other overt, motor, discriminatory R's, the effect was much less than if the child was trained to name the Sd's, and no better than if the child was trained to name other Sd's than those involved in the final discrimination (i.e. irrelevant S pretraining).

Clearly, this finding seriously weakens Kurtz's case. Observing, *per se*, is not all that is involved in a discrimination. Kurtz's same–different pretraining must have enabled some *implicit discriminatory operation* to be performed on the Sd's which meant that other R's in the future would be much more easily associated with them.

Partly on the basis of Cantor's findings, Spiker (1956) proposed, in contrast to Kurtz's theory, that there was something about the *learning of names, per se*, that facilitated subsequent discriminations. If this were the case we would expect Cantor's labelling procedure to be a more effective pretraining technique than Kurtz's same–different procedure. This was confirmed by Norcross and Spiker (1957). In a second study Spiker and Norcross (1962) found that whether the Sd's in the same–different procedure were presented simultaneously or successively the result was the same, the superiority of naming.

One difference between the Kurtz experiment and these latter ones may help to indicate an explanation of the different results. It will be remembered that Kurtz used names as the final discriminatory R's. So it may be argued that though naming may serve as a useful predifferentiation technique for establishing subsequent motor R's, in some cases the subject may have difficulty in attaching the appropriate labels and may need some suitable observing R training. We shall see that this sort of situation arose in Jeffrey's (1958a, b) experiments in which young children were unable to attach verbal labels to differently oriented stick figures and musical notes. Jeffrey found that this naming was considerably facilitated by some observing R pre-criterion training (see Chapter 17 for Jeffrey's work and Chapter 9 for differentiation technique).

ZEAMAN–HOUSE ATTENTION DEFICIENCY THEORY

House and Zeaman (1960a) proposed a similar mechanism to that of Kurtz to account for the positive transfer effect from a discrimination task employing objects as Sd's to one employing two-dimensional patterns having the same relevant cues as the objects. In a later paper, Zeaman and House (1963) include the observing R in a comprehensive model of discrimination performance in retarded children. They criticize the classical S–R approach to discrimination learning for failing to pay sufficient attention to the *perceptual* aspects of a performance. They argue that far from sampling all the relevant S's on every trial, the subject comes to the task with certain *observing strategies* which seriously curtail the S's he receives and responds to. If these habits coincide with the ones required by the task then learning will be quick. If, however, the habits the subject brings with him are not appropriate he will have to extinguish them and learn to attend to the relevant stimulus aspects.

Zeaman and House (1963) propose that in acquiring a discrimination a subject has to learn *two* things. First, he has to learn to attend to the relevant stimulus dimension; and second, he has to learn to respond to the positive cue on that dimension. This is identical to the Goodwin–Lawrence proposal, except that Zeaman and House prefer to use the term "attention" to describe the dimension-selection process.

This two-factor theory of discrimination learning arose out of work with retarded children. A number of investigators have reported that

retardates are particularly slow in learning a simple discrimination, slower even than normal children of similar MA (Stevenson and Iscoe, 1955; House and Zeaman, 1958, 1960b; Girardeau, 1959). Zeaman and House, through an appropriate analysis of the individual learning curves, suggested the cause of this deficiency. They noticed that the curves differed only with respect to the length of the initial *flat* portion. Once the curve began to rise, it rose at about the same rate for all subjects. The more retarded a child, other things being equal, the longer the initial flat portion of the curve.

According to Zeaman and House the length of the flat portion of the curve reflects the length of time it takes the subject to attend to the relevant dimension. Once this attention has occurred the learning with respect to which cue to respond to was the same for all subjects. Hence, the deficiency of retardates on a discrimination is not due to any inability to develop the appropriate S preferences, i.e. is not a learning deficiency; rather the retarded child is defective on the attentional side, he takes a long time to observe the relevant S dimension.

This theory, of course, has far-reaching practical implications. It stresses the need in remedial education to look for ways by which we may be able to exercise control over the variables affecting the child's attention. In some subsequent chapters we shall discuss the possibility of "externalizing" the operations involved in the selection of dimensions in much the same way as Wyckoff externalized the observing R in pigeons. This may, perhaps, be achieved by making the presentation, i.e. exposure to the subject, of the relevant S dimension contingent upon the occurrence of an appropriate overt and observable attention response.

ATTENTION-CONTROLLING TECHNIQUES

One way of establishing control over the postulated attention R is demonstrated in the House and Zeaman (1960a) study already referred to in which training in the discrimination of objects differing along a certain dimension facilitated the subsequent discrimination of patterns differing on the same dimension. In terms of the proposed model what presumably happened here was that the appropriate attention R, which served to isolate the relevant S dimension, was established on the *easy* object-discrimination task and then transferred to the *difficult* pattern-discrimination task. The object discrimination

is basically easier than the pattern discrimination probably as a result of all the extra three-dimensional cues the subject has to base his discrimination on. There is, of course, a chance that the appropriate attention R will not be maintained following the abrupt withdrawal of these extra cues. To guard against this some sort of "fading" programme may be inserted to make the transition and the withdrawal of prompts more gradual (see Chapter 10).

There is a more general point here that has not received its full due of recognition in traditional discussions of learning, though it has recently received much more attention from investigators in programmed learning (Lumsdaine and Glaser, 1960). This is that a subject will generally perform much better on a difficult task if he is first given some training on a simpler task of the same type. This qualification "of the same type" stresses that the essential skills on the difficult task must be present on the easy task (see Chapter 9).

Attention may also be controlled by some of the *attention-getting* characteristics of stimuli tabulated by Berlyne (1960). Orienting responses, which serve to increase the strength of the sensory input, are elicited by intense, or meaningful, or novel, or unusually complex stimuli. So presumably if we wish to increase the probability of an observing R occurring to the relevant dimension we would be well advised to give the dimension in question one of these characteristics. As we shall see in Chapter 10, intensity is often used to prompt the appropriate orienting R in discrimination work. Zeaman *et al.* (1958) demonstrate how the introduction of a new, unexpected S, in place of either Sd+ or Sd− in a discrimination learning task will bring about a relatively sudden rise to criterion performance; another demonstration of control over attention.

With regard to maintaining attention over a fairly extended discrimination learning session, House *et al.* (1957) and White (1964) find that varying either the Sd+ or the Sd− produces good results.

CHAPTER 5

ATTENTION, STRATEGIES AND AGE

IN THE present chapter we shall review and discuss some recent experimental work conducted by S. H. White into the role of attentional and other mechanisms in the discrimination learning of the young child, together with the findings from a recent study by the author.

EYE MOVEMENTS DURING DISCRIMINATION LEARNING

In order to obtain some *direct* information about exactly what sort of orienting activity young children indulge in when they are faced with the task of learning a discrimination, White and Plum (1962) photographed their eye movements. The films thus obtained were scored to give a measure of the number of times the fixation point of the eyes shifted back and forth from one Sd to the other during the course of a single presentation.

White and Plum found that on the first one or two trials of a new discrimination problem the eye movement score was high, perhaps five to ten shifts between the Sd's. This was followed by a relatively quiet period of only one or two fixations per trial. This pre-solution stage was marked by *visual position habits*, which were invariably accompanied by the corresponding position habit in instrumental behaviour. During this period the learning curve was flat. The onset of correct responding was typically marked by a sharp increase in the eye movement score. If the discrimination was overtrained eye movements again decreased.

These findings show a remarkable correspondence to the peaks and troughs of VTE during the acquisition of a discrimination by a rat as demonstrated by Tolman and Minium (1942) (see Chapter 3). A similar trend was noticed by White and Plum during the development of a learning set, from one discrimination problem to the next; but only when the discriminations were easy. When the discriminations

were difficult the eye movements remained fairly constant throughout the experimental session.

WHITE'S ACCOUNT OF DISCRIMINATION LEARNING

On the basis of this and various other studies (White, 1958, 1962,
1963, 1964b, c; White and Grim, 1962; Grim and White, 1964) White
(1964a) proposed an account of the mechanisms which appear to
underlie the acquisition of a discrimination by a young child. As in
all the other accounts, with the possible exception of the extreme
non-continuity theory, White sees the development of an association
between the Sd+ and the discriminatory R as a necessary part of
discrimination learning. But he is careful to stress that, at least for
children, acquiring this association is not *the problem*. Either the
child acquires the discrimination immediately, in which case there
is no progressive development of positive and negative R tendencies,
or he tries out one or two other methods of responding before
switching abruptly to the correct habit. In this latter case, the rapid
acquisition of criterion performance clearly indicates that there is no
problem in building up the appropriate S preference. As Zeaman and
House found with their retardates (Chapter 3), the main problem
facing the child seems to be to "get the hang of the task", to find out
just what it is the experimenter wants him to do. White agrees that
this is a function of some attentional mechanism.

POSITION HABITS

White's most important contribution from our point of view was
the emphasis he placed upon the role of the position-responding
tendency as an interfering error factor in the child's acquisition of a
discrimination. It will be remembered from Chapter 2 that most
experimenters, whatever their theoretical standpoint, agreed on the
observation that most subjects in learning a discrimination go through
a pre-solution period in which, though they are responding randomly
with respect to the Sd's, are in fact responding systematically with
respect to the relative positions of the Sd's. White argues that this
position-guided behaviour represents a kind of "floor" behaviour
in choice responding.

This primitive method of responding also affects the choice
behaviour of young children. White reports that he has found it

extremely difficult to teach a discrimination problem to a child of $2\frac{1}{2}$–3 years, for they exhibit strong and usually quite unbreakable position habits. However, children seem to grow out of this tendency. With increasing age, position habits are less powerful and affect the learning curve to a less extent; i.e. the initial flat portion gets progressively shorter.

White also reports that the *type* of position-guided behaviour changes with age. The very young prefer straight position perseveration habits, the slightly older ones simple alternation, and the still older a strategy based upon the outcome of the position responses, such as win–stay, lose–shift. This transition, for White, represents a transition from behaviour which is predominantly controlled by proprioceptive and kinesthetic stimulation to behaviour in which these sources combine with visual and auditory stimulation from the environment.

HIERARCHY THEORY OF SENSE MODALITIES

Therefore, White envisages an age shift in the relative control over behaviour afforded to stimulation from *near* receptors and stimulation from *distance* receptors. His general thesis is that

> ... cognitive development proceeds from a phase where behaviour is primarily organised around near receptors (tactual, kinesthetic, proprioceptive and visceral interoceptors) to a later phase when it is much more dependent upon distance receptors (visual and auditory exteroceptors). [*Op. cit.*, p. 29.]

This idea receives some support from Piaget and Inhelder (1956) and Birch and Lefford (1963) who report an improvement in the integration of haptic and kinesthetic information with visual information with increasing age.

White quotes a doctoral study by Schopler (1964) which demonstrates that between the ages of 3 and 8 years there is a progressive increase in the proportion of time spent in visual play (e.g. looking at a display of colourful toys, playing with a kaleidoscope) as opposed to tactile play (e.g. placing hands in box to feel a toy, playing with plasticine). However, Schopler's finding that retarded children prefer visual play as much as normal children of the same age seems to indicate that the progression is more closely related to CA than to MA.

The concept of a hierarchical structure of sensory systems, in which the dominance of the interoceptive and visceral sensations in the

young child gradually gives way, first to tactile and kinesthetic and then to visual and auditory information, is also suggested by Renshaw (1930), Zaporozhets (1961), Birch (1962) and Hermelin and O'Connor (1964).

The remaining variable which White emphasizes could influence the acquisition of a discrimination by a child, but in fact rarely does, is the *discriminability* of the Sd's. It has been noted in previous chapters that this is an aspect of the task often neglected, particularly by those theorists in the classical S–R tradition (e.g. Bush and Mosteller, 1955; Restle, 1955a, b; Shepard, 1957, 1958). It has been the custom to use easily discriminable Sd's so that the learning process, *per se*, is highlighted. One of the questions we must consider is what happens when the discrimination is made a difficult one? Also we want to know, with particular reference to the discrimination of orientation by children, what we can do to control it? These questions will be considered in more detail later. Here we are concerned with the variables influencing the acquisition and maintenance of a discrimination habit and with finding out how they work and how we can exercise control over them.

One of the implications of White's position tendency hypothesis is that one way to make the acquisition of a discrimination habit easier would be to arrange the task set-up so as to discourage the development of a position habit.

CONTROL OF POSITION HABITS AND AGE

Usually the experimenter is content randomly to vary the position of the Sd+ from one trial to the next, probably using a Gellerman (1933c) series to determine the actual sequence. However, all this does is ensure that no method of responding except for the correct one will receive maximum reinforcement. But since, as Skinner (1961) demonstrates, intermittent reinforcement is often a very potent control schedule, this randomizing of the position of the correct R is unlikely to be particularly effective in eliminating position responding.

A potentially more effective method was employed by White (1964). Instead of using just two windows for presenting the two Sd's, as is usual, he decided to use *three*, in a triangular formation. This meant that he could now vary from one trial to the next the windows used to present the two Sd's. The subject had to make his choice by pressing on one of the windows displaying the Sd's. This arrangement would

clearly make very difficult the maintenance of a consistent position habit, for the subject will not be able to respond to the same two windows throughout, since on a random third of the trials any given window is not operating.

White's results show an *age factor*. Though the position variation benefited a group of 7–9-year-olds in the acquisition of criterion performance on an easy discrimination, as compared with non-variation, it produced a deterioration in the corresponding performance of a group of 5–7-year-olds. Just what effect the variation condition had upon the behaviour of the younger children could possibly be ascertained from an examination of the individual records. Unfortunately White did not provide this information.

In an attempt to promote *orienting R's* White (1964) employed a procedure in which either Sd+ or Sd− was varied from one trial to the next. Since novelty or S change is said to elicit orienting activity (Berlyne, 1960) and since peaks of orienting are correlated with correct responding (White and Plum, 1962), we might expect such an S variation procedure to facilitate the acquisition of a discrimination. This expectation was not confirmed for any age of child within the range tested (4–9 years). The S variation conditions were found to positively hinder the discrimination learning of the 4-year-olds as compared with no variation. With increasing age this interference effect was progressively reduced, though it was never transformed into a facilitatory effect.

To account for the relative success of position variation as against stimulus variation, White suggests that the changes introduced by the former condition are extrinsic to the informational content of the Sd's, and hence are easier to filter out. The ability to ignore distracting irrelevant cues is presumably a function of age.

AGE SHIFTS AND THE REGRESSION HYPOTHESIS

As we shall see in Chapter 11, similar age shifts to those noted by White have been found with respect to the mediational nature of learning (Kendler and Kendler, 1962) and the participation of language in regulating behaviour (Kuenne, 1946; Luria, 1961a, b). Such changes, White thinks, probably stem from a common maturational process, crystallizing at about 6 years. But the pre-shift mode of behaviour does not disappear. Rather it is inhibited and may appear as a *regressive* or disinhibitory effect of stress or frustration. Thus, if a task

is difficult, a post-shift child may regress to operating in a pre-shift manner, the main characteristic of which, as we shall see in Chapter 11, is the gradual build up of excitatory-inhibitory response tendencies, as postulated by the classical S–R accounts of learning. In mature organisms this regression is marked by a sharp decrease in the latency of R's to the presented task Sd's. This *impulsive* characteristic of a young child's behaviour has recently received some attention by Kagan *et al.* (1963). The young child, like the lower animals, has a distinctive tendency to respond *without thinking*. This it seems is the ideal situation for the operation of the differential reinforcement contingencies of classical S–R theories.

HYPOTHESIS REGRESSION DURING MATCHING-TO-SAMPLE

In a series of experiments employing 100 4- and 5-year-old children the present author has observed a number of instances of what might represent regression in task hypotheses or strategien (Fellows, 1965). In these experiments, which used a procedure and apparatus very similar to that of Hively (1962a, b) (see Fig. 5.1), as

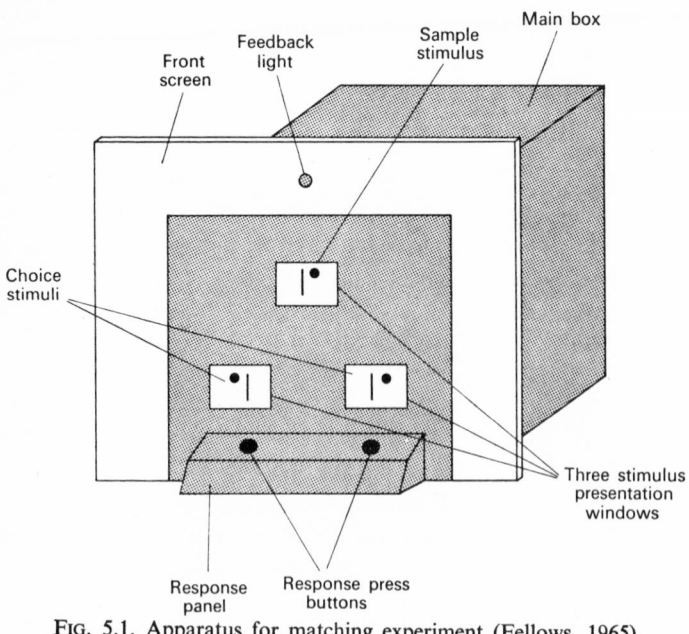

FIG. 5.1. Apparatus for matching experiment (Fellows, 1965).

analysis was made of the strategies exhibited in a two-choice matching to sample task. The method of analysis is described in detail in the Appendix. Briefly, the procedure was first to give the child practice in matching with differential reinforcement on a task involving a relatively simple form discrimination (e.g. square versus circle). This was continued until the child had attained a certain level of accuracy (say, 9 correct out of 10 consecutive choices). At this point the child was immediately transferred to a more difficult discrimination task, involving figures differing only in the spatial orientation of a common form (see Chapter 15). On this he was given a set amount of practice (e.g. 48 trials), again with differential reinforcement of matching. A non-correction procedure was used. The feedback usually comprised a small light coming on for correct responses. Responses were made to buttons under the stimuli.

It was found that the transition from the easy to the difficult discrimination task produced some interesting effects on the behaviour of the subjects. Unless the transition was made gradually (by interpolating a discrimination task of intermediate difficulty) in the majority of cases the established matching habit would break down on exposure to the difficult discriminations. In most of these, by using the hypothesis analysis technique outlined in the Appendix, it was possible to detect the strategy which replaced matching.

There were a number of instances of *matching* being replaced by its converse *oddity* responding. Instead of choosing the matching stimulus the child would now respond to the non-matching, or odd, stimulus. Since oddity responding is, cognitively speaking, a simpler method of responding than matching (see Chapter 13 for more discussion on this point), this switch in hypotheses might be interpreted as regression.

It was interesting to observe that in at least five cases the matching hypothesis was readopted after a short period of oddity responding. One way of interpreting this would be to argue that the regression to oddity responding represented an attempt to relieve the pressure on the cognitive operations while the perceptual mechanisms learned to cope with the new and difficult discriminations. Once this perceptual learning had taken place the system might once more be able to bear the extra burden involved in matching. An example of this type of performance is presented in the Appendix (Fig. A.2).

There were also a large number of instances of matching being replaced by one of the position habits (see, for example, Fig. A.3

in the Appendix). But here there was only one clear example of a return to matching. This suggests that once the appropriate orienting response is switched out it does not readily reassert itself, at least under conditions of differential reinforcement of the final response. (The orienting response in matching and oddity responding is the same. See Chapter 14. Also compare this conclusion with the findings of Kendler in Chapter 12.)

If we look at the hypotheses on a matching task in terms of their intrinsic complexity, age trends and the effects of increases in discrimination difficulty or of learning, then a picture of a hierarchy of hypotheses emerges ranging from simple position perseveration or alternation responding at the bottom, through the outcome hypotheses (win–stay lose–shift, etc., with respect to position), to oddity responding, and finally to matching. This is very much in line with White's position.

There is some evidence that regressions in task behaviour are accompanied by sharp reductions in the latency of responses (Bijou, 1962). This suggests that performances might be maintained in the face of increases in task difficulty, i.e. regression prevented, through the exercise of control over the S–R latency. Thus the child may be prevented from making his response until the stimulus he is observing has been exposed for a certain length of time. Luria (1961a) suggests ways of achieving this (see Chapter 11).

CHAPTER 6

ORIENTING AND PLANNING

IN THE present chapter we shall be looking primarily at the work of Zaporozhets (1957, 1961) and various other Soviet psychologists on the role of orienting behaviour in the efficient execution of a learning task. The relationship between these findings and ideas of Zaporozhets and those of Western psychologists, particularly with respect to the role of *plans* in behaviour, will also be discussed.

The past decade or so has witnessed a rapid growth in the interest taken by Western psychologists in psychological research being conducted in the U.S.S.R. This is reflected in a large number of general surveys of Soviet work (McLeish, 1955; Mintz, 1958, 1959; Razran, 1961; Berlyne, 1963a, b; Pick, 1963; Brozek, 1964; Lynn, 1966) and in the translation into English of important books (Luria, 1961a; Vygotsky, 1962) and papers (Wortis, 1950; Simon, 1957; O'Connor, 1961; Gray, 1964; *Problems of Psychology*, 1960, unfortunately discontinued).

THE ORIENTATION REACTION

A study of the available literature reveals a very strong interest by Russian psychologists in the nature and the functions of orienting behaviour. This interest stems chiefly from the work of Pavlov (1927) on the orientational or "what-is-it reflex" and Bekhterev (1933) on the "concentration reflex". These reflexes involve such overt receptor-adjusting R's as turning the head and eyes towards the source of a S, pricking up the ears, etc. These R's together with their recently discovered covert accompaniments (EEG changes, physiochemical changes in sense organs, muscle tonus) are now usually referred to as the "orientation reaction" (Lynn, 1966). This has two main features: (1) it serves to increase the organism's capacity to extract information from the environment; and (2) it prepares the organism to respond on the basis of what it receives (Berlyne, 1960).

ZAPOROZHETS AND ORIENTING BEHAVIOUR IN CHILDREN

Zaporozhets (*op. cit.*) has been chiefly concerned with investigating the role that such orienting behaviour performs in the general development and learning of children. He makes the same distinction as that of Wyckoff (1952) between *executive behaviour* (e.g. pressing a key, pushing a toy car along a maze) upon which the goal is contingent, and *orienting-investigatory activity* (e.g. touching the keys, feeling the paths of the maze with the fingers, turning the head towards signals, following the movements of the experimenter during a demonstration), which prepares the subject for the executive actions.

Zaporozhets reports that the *spontaneous* orienting behaviour (OB) of a child faced with a learning task is different at different ages. The younger the child, the greater the tendency he shows to explore the features of the task with his hands. With increasing age manipulation becomes less important and the child is more content to explore with his eyes. Schopler (1964) has confirmed this (see Chapter 5).

With respect to White's (1964) regression hypothesis, discussed in the last chapter, we may note that Zaporozhets (1961, p. 280) reports an experiment by Boguslavskaya in which it was demonstrated that when the complexity of the task objects was increased there was a tendency for an older child to supplement his visual activity with *manual* exploration. It is as if the movements of the fingers serve to guide and to reinforce the information gained from looking.

As we would expect from the Zeaman–House attention deficiency theory of retardate learning (Chapter 4), the OB in children of low MA is primitive and unstable (Luria, 1961b).

Zaporozhets (1957) also reports that the amount of spontaneous OB engaged in by the child is directly related to the efficiency of the final performance (EB). This being the case it suggests that EB can be improved by encouraging OB. Zaporozhets found that verbally instructing a child to engage in OB on a tactual maze, before attempting EB, considerably improved the performances of 5-, 6- and 7-year-olds as compared with matched groups engaging in only EB (i.e. trial and error activity). A number of other examples of the heuristic value of OB in improving EB performances are given by Zaporozhets (1961).

Zaporozhets (1957) noticed that the effectiveness of *verbal instructions* in establishing OB varied with the age of the child. The 3-year-old

will follow the verbal instructions only if, while he is listening, he simultaneously looks at the features of the task referred to. With advancing age the instructions, *per se*, become able to set up an *image* of the activity required in the absence of the direct perception of the task; and this image will serve to guide the child's OB when the task is eventually presented. The effects of this age shift are also to be seen in the effects of verbal tuition in establishing matching-to-sample behaviour in young children. (For further discussion, see Chapter 11.)

The *passive movements* method, actually moving the child's limbs in the appropriate manner, was also found by Zaporozhets (1961) to be an effective way of getting the child to perform correctly. The classic study of the role of guidance in learning by Carr (1930) also indicates the value of manual guidance in promoting the acquisition of a stylus maze skill, provided the guidance is given early in training and does not continue for too long. This guidance presumably is useful in preventing the development of incorrect strategies which, as we have seen, tend to occur early on in training; but it is important that the subject does not become dependent on it for his correct responding. A more effective method of ensuring this than Carr's abrupt withdrawal of guidance would be to *fade* it gradually (Chapter 10).

Zaporozhets found that learning by observing a demonstration was not efficient until about the age of 6 or 7 years. Though the children were fully able to follow the movements of the demonstrator before this age they appeared to lack the necessary ability by which to develop a visual image of the activity required which would serve to control their own behavionr. This finding needs further confirmation.

HOW ORIENTING BEHAVIOUR FACILITATES DISCRIMINATION

Summarizing his work on orienting behaviour Zaporozhets (1961) writes,

> ... its main function is in the formation of the sensory part of the elabora-ted motor system, in the preliminary analysis and synthesis of the afferent stimuli in the system. [p. 281.]

With regard to the analytic aspects of OB, he draws attention to the *intensification of sensation*, which

> ... is a factor of considerable importance for the separation of stimu-lations of a certain type from the general mass of agents acting on the analysers. [*Op. cit.*, p. 281.]

Thus OB serves to clarify the relevant aspects of the task, or make them more distinctive, which will, in turn, serve to facilitate the establishment of associations between them and the appropriate executive R's. But how does it achieve this?

In his translated work Zaporozhets is not too clear about this. However, it does appear that more is involved than the mere selection of S dimensions, which is the main function of the Goodwin–Lawrence and Zeaman–House orienting operations. The Zaporozhets OB does not just consist of a "look at" R; it also comprises "look around" R's. One possible result of this is the *visual image* of the task. Another is the provision of distinctively different kinesthetic feedback stimulations from the Sd's in the task. In terms of the Dollard and Miller (1950) hypothesis, to be discussed in Chapter 9, this feedback stimulation from the OB may become attached to the sensory input from the task Sd's, thus accentuating their physical differences (giving them *acquired distinctiveness*). In this sense OB has more in common with the orienting activity presumed to participate in the perception of the Sd's, than with the purely task-orienting activity of the sort that serves to expose the Sd's. This will be discussed in more detail in Chapter 20.

In addition to this analytic function, OB, as Zaporozhets conceives it, also has a *synthetic* function. This operates by ". . . giving expression to the relationships between stimuli . . ." (1961, p. 283). In terms of the model presented in Chapter 14, this synthetic function of OB appears to embrace the operation of the comparison of the two Sd's as processed. The term "orienting" in this book is not used in this wide sense. Here it will refer to the operation by means of which the Sd's are exposed to the subject's receptors; and, in a slightly different context, to the overt manifestations of the activity of the subject's visual apparatus involved in the perception of the Sd's.

NATURE OF VOLUNTARY BEHAVIOUR

Zaporozhets' main objective is to give some sort of account of the development of voluntary behaviour as a child grows up. His views are remarkably similar to those of White (Chapter 5) and Kendler (Chapter 11).

Voluntary behaviour is behaviour which is *emitted*. That is, it is not forced upon the subject by the task conditions. In man it is under

conscious control and, usually, *planned*. Like Krechevsky's (1932) hypotheses it originates to some degree from within the subject.

The maze learning behaviour of the *very young* child does not exhibit these voluntary features. Zaporozhets observes that the 3-year-old will typically immediately grasp the toy car, which has to be manoeuvred through a maze, and quite blindly attempt to push it through without regard for blind alleys and wrong turnings. Eventually, with practice, he will learn, and his performance curve will tend to exhibit the negatively accelerating form predicted by classical S–R theories of Thorndike (1913, 1932, 1935, 1949), Guthrie (1935, 1938) and Hull (1930a, 1943, 1951).

With increasing age the child will be found to "look before he leaps". His reaction to the task is slower, more "thoughtful". He will tend to look around the maze and eliminate false turnings before he actually comes to them. As a result his learning will be fairly abrupt and, unless the maze is a very complex one, conform to the *insight* paradigm proposed by the Gestalt theorists (Koffka, 1924, 1935; Köhler, 1925, 1929, 1940).

To Zaporozhets these observations meant that whereas the older child *plans*, the younger child does not. Kendler, as we shall see (Chapter 11), prefers to say that the older child's learning is *mediated* whereas that of the younger child conforms to the single unit S–R paradigm of learning, and is un-mediated. This planning involved building up an *image* of the activity to be performed. According to Zaporozhets this image consisted of ". . . a representation of the situation and the action which had to be performed in relation to it" (1961, p. 284).

We see from this quotation that an image has *two* parts. Firstly, it is a *representation of the situation*. This seems to correspond to what Tolman (1948) called a "cognitive map". This is a representation of the environment concerned with routes, paths, relationships, and so on; it consists of signs and significates, what-leads-to-what, or S–S associations. Tolman considered such a map as adequate to account for behaviour. However, as Guthrie's (1935) cogent criticism illustrates, a map is a map, and is neutral about what route one should actually take.

> In his concern with what goes on in the rat's mind, Tolman has neglected to predict what the rat will do. So far as the theory is concerned the rat is left buried in thought; if he gets to the food-box at the end that is his concern, not the concern of the theory. [Guthrie, 1935, p. 172.]

Zaporozhets is not open to this criticism. For, in addition to representing the situation, an image indicates the *action* which has to be performed in relation to it. What is represented in the image then is an *internalized* version of the required executive behaviour. How did it get there?

The answer to this question appears to depend, at least partly, on the age of the child. In the very young child it is put there by a slow process of trial and error learning. In the older child it is put there by the orienting behaviour; and it probably is an abbreviated version of this OB, which can be detected as small changes in muscular tension (Jacobsen, 1932; Max, 1935, 1937). The big difference, however, between these two ages is that the younger child does not get a proper plan of the activity; for his behaviour is determined by relatively specific S–R habits.

PLANS AND IMAGES IN BEHAVIOUR

Recently, Miller *et al.* (1960) have proposed a general theory of behaviour that has much in common with Zaporozhets' account of voluntary behaviour. They try to see behaviour in terms of the formation and execution of plans and the development of an image. The plans correspond to the internalized OB and the image to the cognitive map. However, since plans are learned they become part of the image, and since knowledge must be incorporated into the plan, images form part of the plan. A plan is like a computer programme; it consists of a set of instructions which control the order in which a sequence of operations is to be performed. The image is like the memory store of a computer; it consists of bits of information and instructions which have come into it from the outside world; it comprises, as it were, a store of internalized S–S associations.

According to Miller, what a subject has to learn in a task is a plan, which the experimenter initially has but the subject has not. The learning experiment therefore is seen in terms of a teacher–pupil relationship; the purpose of the experiment is for the teacher to communicate a certain plan to the pupil. If the pupil is human and reasonably mature the plan can be communicated verbally. But this is usually only the beginning; for having a plan (knowing what) does not imply its execution (knowing how). Miller *et al.* argue that though the *strategy* is communicable, the *tactics* have to be learned through practice (*op. cit.*, p. 83).

With animals and pre-verbal children (i.e. no verbal mediation) plans cannot be communicated verbally, and so have to be learned through practice. Miller makes the same point as has been made above that such training seldom enables the subject to acquire a total plan; the strategy remains in his trainer or in the mechanical substitute (*op. cit.*, p. 88). But, what is not clear, is how we can tell the difference between a subject who behaves according to a plan and a subject who behaves *as if* he had a plan. Miller suggests that we discover the difference if we pull away one or two of the environmental supports of the latter's plan. Thus, Clever Hans would not have been so clever without Van Osten (Katz, 1953), nor Skinner's ping-pong playing pigeons without the reinforcing contingencies. But would not the so-called "intelligent" behaviour of mature humans be similarly affected by the withdrawal of such environmental supports?

It is difficult to accept Miller's implication that the only sort of planning is verbal planning. Though the possession of internalizable vocal behaviour ensures mediation it is not necessary for it. Zaporozhets has argued that orienting behaviour may be the basis of plans, and orienting behaviour is not.specific to man. Harlow's (1959) report that a wide variety of animals are capable of acquiring complex learning sets attests to the existence of non-verbal mediation.

There is it seems a constant danger of extrapolating from what is to what must be. The way an organism learns depends partly on the organism, on its sensory and neural apparatus, and partly on how it is taught. The fact that we cannot communicate our plans to animals verbally does not mean they are incapable of receiving plans. As Ferster (1964) has convincingly demonstrated the extent of an animal's capacity to reason is largely a function of our own ability to speak its language.

CHAPTER 7

S–R SPATIAL CONTIGUITY AND ORIENTING

IN THE present chapter a further source of information relating to the role of orienting activity in discrimination performance will be considered. It was argued in Chapter 2 with reference to experiments by Lashley (1938a) and Ehrenfreund (1948) that what a rat learned on a Lashley Jumping Stand depended partly on the *locus* to which it jumped. If the rat was forced to jump to the base of the stimulus cards, as in Lashley's experiments, then it would tend to discriminate on the basis of the lower portions of the Sd's. But if the apparatus were so arranged that the rat was forced to jump to the centre of the stimulus cards, as in Ehrenfreund's experiment, then it would be more likely to discriminate on the basis of the whole Sd. This meant that the discrimination of complex patterns, which was very difficult to establish with the former procedure, would be greatly facilitated. Spence interpreted this facilitation effect as being due to the latter design encouraging the appropriate receptor-orienting acts which served to expose the animal to discriminably different stimulations from the two Sd's.

S–R SPATIAL DISCONTIGUITY EFFECT

A similar way of describing essentially the same effect has arisen from recent work on the S–R spatial discontiguity effect, particularly in monkeys. This refers to the effect upon the acquisition of a discrimination, or a discrimination learning set, of the spatial separation of the *position occupied by the Sd* and the *locus to which the animal's R is to be made*. In general, it has been found that the greater the S–R spatial discontiguity the more difficult it is for monkeys to learn a discrimination (Gellerman, 1933a; Jenkins, 1943; McClearn and Harlow, 1954; Murphy and Miller, 1955, 1958; Schuck, 1960; Meyer et al., 1961; Stollnitz and Schrier, 1962; Miller and Murphy, 1964;

Polidora and Fletcher, 1964; Wunderlich and Dorff, 1965; Polidora and Thompson, 1965). A similar effect has been reported in the learning of the rat and the dog (Lashley, 1949) and the pigeon (Ferster and Skinner, 1957, pp. 527–9).

The effect has also been reported in children. For example, Murphy and Miller (1959) found that 5 out of 8 9-year-olds failed to transfer a learned pattern discrimination from one task in which the S and R were contiguous to another in which there was a 6 inch separation. Also 6 out of 9 children failed to learn the discrimination under the discontiguous conditions. So S–R discontiguity affects both the establishment of a discrimination and its maintenance or performance. Polidora and Fletcher (1964) confirmed this conclusion with monkeys.

The practical implication of these findings was emphasized by Murphy and Miller (1959). They suggested " . . . that some attention to the spatial relationships in learning situations would perhaps permit learning in otherwise unlearnable situations" (p. 488).

In the terminology of Spence (1940), by arranging the task situation so that the subject actually orients and thereby receives the relevant discriminative aspects of the stimulus figures, we should be able to raise considerably the general level of discrimination learning performance. The chief contribution of the S–R discontiguity research is in indicating just how the task situation is to be arranged so as to ensure the appropriate orienting R. Its advice is to use the locus of R, or, in the case of monkeys and children, the fingers of the subject, to control the fixation. The premiss is that an animal will literally "look before it leaps", or at least look at the place where it is going to leap. The monkey and the child will look where they point.

It will be seen in later chapters that this connection between the locus of the fingers and the fixation of the eyes can also be used as an extremely valuable "heuristic" perceptual technique for the analysis of complex visual shapes. Here we shall restrict ourselves to considering its implications for the control of the orienting behaviour which we have seen is so essential for an efficient discrimination performance.

Murphy and Miller's findings with children have recently been confirmed by Jeffrey and Cohen (1964). They assessed the relative difficulty of learning a discrimination under five different conditions of S, R and reward spatial contiguity. They found that the learning of 3–4-year-olds was relatively poor only on those tasks in which the S and the R were separated.

A brief look at some of the apparatus that has been used in the study of a child's discrimination learning reveals an implicit recognition of the S–R spatial contiguity principle. For example, the child has been required to open a drawer immediately beneath a S (Hunter, 1952), open a door with a S printed on it (Alberts and Ehrenfreund, 1951), press on a glass window displaying a S (Long, 1940; Holland, 1962; Bijou, 1962; Hively, 1962a, b), point to a stimulus object (Hicks and Steward, 1935), push a button beneath a S (Shepard, 1956; Lipsitt, 1958), move a box with a S printed on it (Spiker, 1956), and move a S object to obtain a reward (House and Zeaman, 1958).

Though *spatial S–R contiguity* facilitates the acquisition of a discrimination it apparently *is not absolutely essential*, for a number of studies have demonstrated learning and performance under extremely discontiguous conditions. Jenkins (1943) reports that three of his chimpanzees exhibited a high standard of discrimination performance even with a 6 inch S–R separation. McClearn and Harlow (1954) found that some of their monkeys were able to learn a black–white discrimination with a 4 inch separation. Murphy and Miller (1958) found one monkey who negotiated a contiguous–discontiguous transfer to a 7 inch separation with no breakdown in performance. Stollnitz and Schrier (1962) reported that two out of six monkeys maintained their performance through a gradual transition from S–R contiguity to an 18 inch separation. In another experiment they found that two out of five monkeys learned a discrimination with a 7 inch separation and then successfully transferred to an 18 inch separation.

Clearly, S–R discontiguity does have an overall significant effect upon the acquisition of a discrimination. But what still remains to be explained is why certain subjects were apparently not affected.

DOUBLE RESPONDING ON DISCONTIGUOUS TASKS

One possible explanation is suggested by an observation by Murphy and Miller (1958) that some monkeys when faced with an S–R discontiguity discrimination task will spontaneously engage in "double-responding". This consists of *touching or nearly touching the S before making the instrumental R to the remote site*. This observation was confirmed by Polidora and Fletcher (1964), who also found that the double-responders performed much more efficiently than those

monkeys which did not engage in this behaviour. Therefore, double-responding seems to be a technique which certain subjects spontaneously adopt to enable them to overcome the potentially disrupting effect of the separation of S and R.

How does this double-responding technique work? How does it in fact facilitate discrimination learning? In the light of the discussions in the previous chapters the most obvious explanation is in terms of orienting behaviour. What these monkeys do is learn *two* responses. They learn to orient the S, an activity which is guided by an overt pointing R to the S. And, secondly, they learn to make the choice R to the remote S. This, as we have seen, is what a subject probably has to learn in any discrimination task, but the S–R discontiguity task brings out the difference much better than if the R is actually made directly to the S.

A similar explanation is contained in Schuck's (1960) *visual sampling gradient hypothesis*. This emphasizes the existence of

> ... a spatial gradient in the visual sampling domain of the monkey, with a maximum at the region of the monkey's hand position during the response. [p. 254.]

In other words the monkey receives most strongly those aspects of the S which are nearest to its hand at the time of R. That means it will tend to discriminate on the basis of these aspects. The further away from the locus of R the S is the less the control it exercises over the behaviour.

POLIDORA–FLETCHER THREE-STAGE MODEL OF DISCRIMINATION LEARNING

Polidora and Fletcher (1964) suggest on the basis of their findings that

> ... the focal point of the sampling gradient is at the centre of the area viewed *before* the instrumental response is performed ... [and that] ... a discriminative stimulus can be perceived only during a sampling response which can only, but does not necessarily, occur during an orienting response. [p. 229.]

According to this view discrimination performance consists of a chain of *three* responses. First, the *orienting R* which serves to expose the organism's receptors to the Sd. This is Spence's receptor-orienting R and Wyckoff's observing R. It is

> ... any response which results in receptor orienting exclusively to one of the discriminative stimuli (by looking at, listening to, or touching it) .... [*Op. cit.*, p. 229.]

Second, there is the *sampling R*. This is defined as

> ... the perception of at least some element of that discriminative stimulus (by seeing, hearing, or feeling it). [p. 229.]

This sampling R seems to correspond with the Goodwin and Lawrence "identification response" (Chapter 3). It involves the selection of some aspect of a S which is not spatially separated from other aspects and so cannot be isolated by an overt orienting R. It involves, therefore, a *post-reception* selection mechanism. The definition given by Polidora and Fletcher is not very satisfactory. For a sampling R is not "the perception" of a S; rather it is a process or operation which probably results in the perception of a S. It would probably be as well to keep the term "perception" out of such definition altogether. A more satisfactory definition of a sampling R is to see it as an implicit post-reception operation which has the effect of selecting certain non-spatially separated features of the S for association with the final overt instrument R's. Perception as a conscious introspection is assumed (maybe incorrectly) to be a mere by-product of this operation.

The third response in the chain is the overt, instrumental, *choice response* upon which the reinforcement is contingent.

So, according to this interpretation, the double-response technique facilitates discrimination learning and performance under S–R spatial discontiguous conditions by ensuring that the S is oriented and thus received by the subject before the overt choice R is made. The most obvious sort of double-R consists first of a pointing or touching R to the S followed by the choice R to the manipulandum. But of course this pointing or touching is only a "heuristic"; it is not in itself necessary for a successful performance, it merely prompts or guides the appropriate receptor-orienting R.

Polidora and Thompson (1965), by observing the eye movements of the monkeys engaged on a discrimination task, found that sophisticated monkeys (which had been frequently used on similar experiments before) often did not execute S-pointing or S-touching double-R, but instead performed a *visual* double-R. This consisted merely of a quick look at the S before making the R. This then is the "true" or "pure" orienting R envisaged by Spence. These highly-trained monkeys had clearly learned to do without the overt"heuristic"component of the double-response. In other words, the prompting or cueing R had spontaneously "faded" (see Chapter 10).

Similar visual double-responding in monkeys has also been observed by Stollnitz and Schrier (1962), Schrier *et al.* (1963) and Davis *et al.* (1964).

This model proposed by Polidora and Fletcher (1964) has many features in common with the model to be presented in Chapter 14. It is the first model we have discussed in which *the orienting and the dimensional selection operations are differentiated.* In the next chapter we shall consider Sutherland's account of the discrimination process. In this the emphasis is placed on the dimensional selection or stimulus analysing operation.

CHAPTER 8

SWITCHING-IN STIMULUS ANALYSERS AND CODING RESPONSES

WE HAVE seen in previous chapters that at least two operations intervene between the presentation of a discrimination problem to a subject and his response. The subject must first orient or look at the Sd's in order to receive them as stimulus input. Secondly, he must learn to select and respond to the relevant features of this input. In the present chapter we shall be looking at two recent models or theories about discrimination performance, both of which develop the second of these operations.

SUTHERLAND–MACKINTOSH TWO-STAGE THEORY OF DISCRIMINATION LEARNING

First, let us look at the model developed by Sutherland and Mackintosh which incorporates the idea of an implicit *stimulus analysing mechanism* (Sutherland, 1959a, 1963e;·Sutherland *et al.*, 1963a, b; Mackintosh, 1962, 1963a, b, 1964, 1965a, b; Mackintosh and Mackintosh, 1963, 1964). According to this account, in acquiring a discrimination a subject has to learn *two* things. He has first to learn *to switch-in the appropriate S analyser.* Then, he has to learn *to attach the appropriate instrumental R's to the outputs from this analyser.*

Therefore, as far as this model is concerned the reception of the Sd by the subject is assumed. That is, the subject is assumed to be in a position to receive the relevant Sd's without having to make any particular orienting R. It will be remembered that Spence (1936) also made this assumption. But it will also be recalled that this assumption does not hold for all discrimination tasks; in some, such as Krechevsky's (Chapter 2), and those in which S and R are discontiguous (Chapter 7), an orienting R is required.

So, according to the Sutherland–Mackintosh theory, the incoming S is analysed or processed and the results of this operation fed into a

response unit which connects the S-as-analysed to the appropriate overt R. The process by which the S is analysed will be dealt with in detail later. Here we may note that *the function of the S analyser is to generate distinctively different outputs for the two Sd's*. This is one of the things that has to be learned in making a discrimination. The subject has to learn to switch-in the analyser which will do this. Each of the two Sd's may comprise a number of different stimulus dimensions, such as colour, brightness, size and orientation. The subject is assumed to have an analyser appropriate for differentiating cues along each of these. However, usually the experimenter arranges the task so that the Sd's differ only along one dimension. Since only one analyser can be used at a time (an assumption, though not a necessary one, of the model) this means that the subject has to discover which analyser will serve to generate distinctively different outputs from the two Sd's, by trying one after the other. Eventually, the analyser will be switched-in that serves to differentiate cues along the relevant dimension, on which the two Sd's differ.

The second thing that has to be learned is to attach the appropriate R's to these outputs. The model assumes that there are two R's which the subject is set to make. The point is which does he make to each output? This is largely controlled by the reinforcement contingencies. If the experimenter has decided to reinforce R1 to Sd1 and R2 to Sd2, and not to reinforce R2 to Sd1 or R1 to Sd2, then the former connections will be the ones to be made by the subject.

It has already been noted, in connection with the Goodwin and Lawrence theory (Chapter 3), that the present model also assumes *differential acquisition and extinction rates* for these two skills. It is assumed that learning which analyser to switch-in occurs comparatively slowly; but once established the analyser is not easily extinguished. On the other hand, learning which R to connect to which analyser output occurs quickly, but is quickly extinguished.

This model is clearly in a good position to make predictions about *reversal and non-reversal learning*. It predicts, for example, that the more training given on a problem the easier it will become to learn the reversal. For, the more training that is given, the stronger becomes the S analyser. So, when the S values are reversed the S analyser, which is still appropriate, is not easily extinguished by the sudden cessation of maximum reinforcement. But the R connections, which have been little affected by the extended training, are quickly extinguished, and remade to the other S outputs. Therefore, after

overtraining on a problem (training past a given learning criterion) the subject is able to reverse his R's to the analyser outputs, following a reversal of S values, before the appropriate analyser is switched out. This prediction has received much experimental confirmation (Reid, 1953; Pubols, 1956; Capaldi and Stevenson, 1957; Mackintosh, 1962).

It follows from this that since the effect of overtraining is to cause the S analyser to become very firmly switched-in, we would expect that the ease of learning to discriminate in terms of another dimension (non-reversal learning), which would involve switching-out the existing analyser and switching-in a different one, would be inversely proportional to the extent of practice given on the original problem. Mackintosh (1962) confirmed this expectation. He found that whereas overtraining rats on a brightness discrimination facilitated them learning of its reversal (as compared to rats trained to criterion), it positively hindered their learning of a vertical–horizontal pattern discrimination (again as compared with rats trained to criterion on the original).

There is an important general principle involved here, that *overlearning leads to inflexibility*. Gilhousen (1931) demonstrated how rats which were overtrained to take a certain path in a maze which included a difficult jump would continue to take that path even when more economical ones were available. This sort of behaviour reminds us strongly of the fixations reported by Maier (1949) as arising from frustration. There are many examples from human behaviour that are very clearly the result of overlearning during childhood and schooldays. Holt (1931) and Murphy (1947) provide many instances of fixed and highly artificial ways of doing things which seem to result from "canalization" in childhood. Luchins (1942) and Wertheimer (1945) stress the dangers of drill and overtraining in school learning, which lead to the pupil being blinded to new ways of looking at things.

The Sutherland–Mackintosh model would also predict that the overtraining effect on reversal learning would be more pronounced the more *irrelevant dimensions* differentiating the Sd's. For, the more irrelevant dimensions there are competing for attention the more likely the non-overtrained animal will switch over to one of them following the reversal in Sd values. This prediction has been confirmed by Mackintosh and Mackintosh (1963).

Harlow's (1959) *error-factor theory* would also predict this though for different reasons. Since irrelevant dimensions are the sources

of error factors we would expect their presence to increase the effect of overtraining. It will be remembered that learning for Harlow's theory consists solely of the suppression of incorrect S–R associations (error factors). However, whereas Harlow's theory demands the irrelevant cues be present during training, the present model does not. The Sutherland–Mackintosh model predicts that even if introduced after training the irrelevant cues would have little effect on an over-trained discrimination, for what is learned is not, not to respond to the irrelevant cues (i.e. not to switch-out incorrect analysers), but to respond to the irrelevant cues (i.e. to switch-in the correct analyser). Mackintosh (1963b) confirmed the latter prediction by showing that where there were two irrelevant cues, overtraining had a greater facilitatory effect on reversal learning than when there was only one, whether or not the second cue had been present in the original learning.

The Sutherland–Mackintosh model can also account for the pheno-menon known as *the transfer of a discrimination along a continuum* (Lawrence, 1952). This refers to the fact that a difficult discrimination is more easily acquired if training is begun on an easier discrimination of the same type than if all the training is given on the difficult discrimination (see Chapter 9). Sutherland (1961b) and Sutherland *et al.* (1963a) confirmed this with octopuses. The interpretation is that training on the widely different Sd's enables the correct analyser to be firmly switched-in. But training from the outset with Sd's lying close together on a certain dimension may mean that the correct analyser never gets properly switched-in, because, even when it is switched-in, some mistakes will be made due to the similarity in its outputs, and the resulting non-reinforcement may cause it to be quickly switched-out again.

There is one small point about this interpretation which has relevance for our own model. It will be noticed that as well as selecting which R's are connected with the analyser outputs, the R unit of Sutherland's model also has a *discriminatory role* to play. For, if the outputs are similar, we see that the operation does not work so well as when they are different. In the Chapter 14 model these two functions are clearly separated. The outputs from the analyser pass first to a *comparison* unit whose responsibility is to say whether they are the same or different. This information is then presumed to pass to a *response strategy* unit which serves to direct the response selection unit as to which response to make to the Sd's.

What is not so easily explained by the Sutherland–Mackintosh model is the phenomenon known as *the transfer of a discrimination across two continua* (Terrace, 1963b). In this, learning a difficult discrimination is facilitated by prior training on an easier discrimination of a different type (see Chapter 10). Thus, the transfer is from one dimension to another. It is not easy to see how the switching-in of one analyser can facilitate the switching-in of another. What possibly happens is that the original training enables the appropriate orienting behaviour to become well established, and it is this that transfers to the second task. But the fact that to be really effective the transition has to be made gradually, by progressively fading-out the original Sd's, suggests that some implicit switching-over has to take place as well.

ISSUE OF PERCEPTUAL LEARNING

A final word on the Sutherland–Mackintosh model. Like most other discrimination learning models there is no real provision for any learning which may take place on the perceptual side. Learning to switch-in an analyser is a rather primitive form of perceptual learning. But the S analysers themselves are assumed to be laid on, immediately ready to be switched-in to the incoming stimuli. Later some attempts will be made to show how, even in relatively short-term experiments, the way a stimulus is analysed can be controlled, and improvements in perception can be demonstrated.

Dodwell (1961) acknowledges this shortcoming in his own shape coding system and suggests a coupling of the output from the coding system to a *classifier* or recognizer of the sort proposed by stocastic and cybernetic models (Dodwell, 1964). Perceptual learning can be accounted for by building into the classifier a *memory system*, which becomes self-organizing in terms of the stimulus regularities of the environment (Uttley, 1956, 1958, 1959). The conjunction–disjunction counting system proposed by George (1961, Chapter 5), called an association or *belief net* could also be coupled to a stimulus classifying mechanism to allow for perceptual learning.

Clarke and Blakemore (1961) proposed that the large improvements made on a discrimination task by 9-year-old imbeciles were attributable to three processes. There is a general know-how about the task, which they suggest is a learning set. The second is what they call "... a sharpened and improved perceptual discrimination ..."

(*op. cit.*, p. 131), and the third "a sharpened conceptual discrimination". These proposals, though rather vague and imprecise, do appear to acknowledge the existence of a perceptual learning factor in the acquisition of a discrimination. Using an Itard (1932) type of perceptual training programme, Clarke and Cookson (1962) have demonstrated how imbeciles can benefit from *sense training*. The recent work with the Marianne Frostig Developmental Test of Visual Perception seems to have much promise in this field (Frostig, 1961, 1963; Frostig *et al.*, 1961, 1964; Frostig and Horne, 1964; Maslow *et al.*, 1964).

LAWRENCE'S CODING RESPONSE HYPOTHESIS

The other major account of discrimination behaviour to be considered in this chapter is that of Lawrence (1963). Like Sutherland and Dodwell, Lawrence is very concerned with the nature of the stimulus in a discrimination task. We have seen, that as a result of the shift in interest following Lashley's (1929) suggestion about the role of "attempted solutions" in discrimination learning (see Chapter 2), there was a neglect of the stimulus. The original continuity theory (Spence, 1936) and its more recent statistical counterparts (Bush and Mosteller, 1955; Restle, 1955a, b; Shepard, 1957, 1958) make certain assumptions about the stimulus. They talk of a homogeneous population of more or less discrete stimulus units which is sampled from trial to trial. But different stimuli are analysed in many different ways. Unless we know how the stimulus is analysed we cannot know the effective stimulus input.

Lawrence (1963) is particularly concerned to explain the influence of variables which have been variously referred to as set, insight, attention, etc. Lawrence points out that Spence's (1940) revision of the continuity position overlooks the fact that if receptor-orienting acts are to account for the sudden shifts in S–R correlations, that is, account for the apparently non-continuous nature of discrimination learning, then these acts must be under the control of stimuli that are relatively independent of those controlling the instrumental R's. A similar point is made by Mackintosh (1962) in his criticism of the Reid (1953) and Pubols (1956) "response of discriminating" hypothesis. Since Sd's are the product of the orienting R, this R cannot be evoked by them. Therefore, there must be two functionally distinct parts to the visual task environment. One part, the Sd,

controls the instrumental R's. Another part controls the orienting behaviour. This distinction will be maintained in our Chapter 14 model.

As a development of the stimulus substitute theory of discrimination learning (see Chapter 9) Lawrence proposes a *coding-response hypothesis*. Following Hebb (1949) and Gibson (1963) he assumes that learning takes place within the S and the R components of an association. Like its parent theory, this hypothesis assumes that the S–R connection is mediated. According to Lawrence, the coding R is the mediating process. It functions in a very similar manner to the Sutherland–Mackintosh stimulus analysing mechanism. The coding R is an implicit process that operates upon the sensory input producing a new event, which Lawrence calls the *stimulus-as-coded*, or *s.a.c.* Hence, it is the s.a.c. and not the Sd that is directly associated with the instrumental R.

According to this theory, therefore, the naïve subject, at least, has to learn *two* things in making a discrimination. On the stimulus (or decoding) side, an appropriate coding R must be made; one which produces s.a.c.'s which are correlated with the same aspects of the sensory input as are the reinforcement contingencies in the environment. On the response (or encoding side), the appropriate R's have to be attached to the s.a.c.'s.

Besides the terminology, there is an important difference between the Sutherland–Mackintosh and the Lawrence models. This concerns *the controlling stimulus of the analysis or coding operation*. According to Lawrence,

> ... once the appropriate coding response is elicited and consistently followed by reinforcement, it would tend to become associated with the contextual or unchanging aspects of the task situation . . . . [*Op. cit.*, p. 191.]

From this it seems that in addition to eliciting the overt receptor-orienting R's, the stable or unchanging aspects of the task are also responsible for controlling the coding operation.

Though Lawrence does not make it clear, it would seem best to distinguish the *stable aspects of the task situation*, which serve to evoke the appropriate orienting R's, from the *stable aspects of the Sd's*, which serve to evoke the appropriate coding R's. This distinction is necessary since the effect of the orienting R's is to switch the stimulus input received by the subject from the contextual aspects of the task to the Sd's, which means that the former cannot be responsible for

eliciting the coding R, which is made after the orienting R. This distinction is made clear in the model to be presented in Chapter 14.

Though the Sutherland–Mackintosh model does not make this distinction, it does acknowledge that the analysing operation is under the control of the stimulus input. As we have seen, what it fails to do is to provide an interpretation of how the organism gets the S input in the first place. The Chapter 14 model both clarifies the Lawrence model by distinguishing the unchanging aspects of the task from the unchanging aspects of the Sd's, and makes up this deficiency in the Sutherland–Mackintosh model by proposing a receptor-orienting operation to expose the Sd's to the subject.

CHAPTER 9

DISCRIMINATION TRAINING AND THE ACQUIRED DISTINCTIVENESS OF CUES HYPOTHESIS

IN THE present chapter we shall be considering two discrimination training techniques, the effectiveness of which, as compared with trial and error practice, has important implications in our analysis of the nature of the cognitive and perceptual operations that take place in the making of a discrimination. The two techniques we shall be discussing are *the transfer of a discrimination along a continuum* and *stimulus predifferentiation.* In the following chapter some modifications of these basic techniques will be considered. Also in the present chapter we shall discuss some possible explanations for the effectiveness of these training methods, with particular reference to the *acquired distinctiveness of cues hypothesis.*

TRAINING A DIFFICULT DISCRIMINATION

William James (1890, vol. 1, pp. 505–15) proposed two techniques by means of which the acquisition of a very difficult discrimination may be facilitated. First, a fine discrimination may be established by "progressively ordered practice". In this training is begun with an easy discrimination, which is gradually made more and more difficult as training progresses. Eventually, a discrimination is reached which was impossible to establish by trial and error practice.

James' second method was to begin training by establishing two distinctively different R's to the two Sd's. After some practice has been allowed on this task two other R's, much less different than the original pair, have to be associated with the same Sd's. The assumption is that the training with the distinctive R's helps, in James' words, to "drag the stimuli apart", thus facilitating the association of other R's to the two Sd's, as compared with trial and error practice solely with the two similar R's.

In the light of Lawrence's (1963) theory, discussed in the preceding chapter, these two techniques can be seen as facilitating the decoding (making the right coding R) and the encoding (making the right instrumental R's) operations, respectively.

TRANSFER OF A DISCRIMINATION ALONG A CONTINUUM

The training value of the former of these techniques was recognized by Pavlov (1927). He found that the normal method of differential reinforcement was often quite inadequate to establish a very fine stimulus discrimination in dogs.

> But if we proceed to establish a differentiation of a remoter stimulus, working up gradually through finer differentiations until the very closely allied stimulus is again reached, it is found that this latter differentiation is now very rapidly established. . . . [*Op. cit.*, p. 121.]

Schlosberg and Solomon (1943) also found that rats were able to acquire a difficult simultaneous discrimination involving two narrowly separated greys as Sd's without any errors if the two Sd's were *gradually changed* through the task from white and black to the final greys. Lawrence (1952) confirmed this finding under conditions in which the total amount of practice allowed both to the transfer and to the trial and error groups was the same.

Baker and Osgood (1954) found that the same effect occurred in pitch discrimination tasks. However, they observed one peculiarity which the previous investigations had failed to notice. They noticed that too much practice with large differences between the Sd's actually *increased* the difficulty of detecting smaller differences, unless mediated by a graduated series of changes. It is as if the subject becomes adapted to the easy level of discrimination, and so becomes less well equipped to deal with small differences (cf. Helson's, 1947, 1959, *theory of adaptation level*). Another way of interpreting this would be in terms of the *stereotyping effect of overlearning* (see Chapter 8). But it must be noted that the stereotyping does not appear in the direction predicted by the Sutherland–Mackintosh model, for this would seem to predict that overtraining would facilitate such transfer by switching-in the appropriate analyser more firmly. Alternatively, what may happen is that the extra practice on the original easy discrimination strengthens the R connections with the specific analyser outputs to such an extent that when the Sd's are changed these

connections are lost. This seems to be in line with the common observation with regard to narrowing or "canalizing" effect on behaviour of overtraining (Murphy, 1947).

As well as brightness and pitch continua, both of which are physically well defined, transfer of a discrimination has also been demonstrated along *shape* continua. Pavlov (1928) demonstrated the establishment of a circle–ellipse discrimination in dogs by progressively altering the shape of the ellipse to make it more and more like the circle. Sutherland *et al.* (1963a) demonstrated the same technique with a square–parallelogram discrimination in octopuses. As we shall see in Chapter 17, Bijou (1962) attempts to use a variation in children. In this the form of a non-matching figure is progressively changed so that it approximates more and more the mirror-image of the sample in a matching-to-sample task. Children were also shown to respond well to the transfer along a continuum procedure by Spiker (1959) on a brightness discrimination task.

The success of this technique in facilitating the acquisition of a discrimination seems a little puzzling when viewed from a classical trial and error learning theory standpoint. The fact that it pays to train a subject on a discrimination other than the one he finally has to perform on does not appear to be in accordance with a theory which sees learning as the gradual strengthening of specific S–R bonds, and transfer as a function of the number of *identical elements* (S–R's) in the two tasks (Thorndike and Woodworth, 1901; Thorndike, 1903). According to this theory, the most effective training will be that which is done on an identical task to the one on which the final performance has to be made.

It seems that in order to explain this effect some *mediating process* between the physical S and the physical R must be postulated. As we have seen in the preceding chapter, Sutherland (1963e) proposed that training with widely separated Sd's enables the appropriate *analyser* to be firmly switched-in, as a result of the generation of distinctively different outputs for them both; and this analyser remains switched-in when the Sd's are brought closer together. Training solely on the narrowly separated Sd's may not enable the appropriate analyser to be firmly switched-in due to the possibility of the two outputs being confused by the R selection operation.

Spiker (1959) suggested that the easy discrimination training enabled the appropriate *orienting responses* to be learned. These

then transferred to the difficult task and thus facilitated the subjects' performance on it. If Spiker means by this an overt receptor-orienting R, then this is a possibility. For the subject trained solely on the difficult task, just as he will not have the appropriate analysers reinforced, so he will not have the appropriate orienting R's strengthened. Hence, he will switch his observation to other features of the task; and, particularly if there is any S–R spatial discontiguity, may well fall into a position habit.

As an alternative explanation, Spiker (1959) suggested that maybe the effect of the initial easy task was to keep at a low level any *frustration* that may accompany failures on the difficult task. On its own it seems unlikely that this will be sufficient to explain the facilitatory effect. For it would predict that any sort of easy preliminary training, no matter what the task, would facilitate any difficult task. Nevertheless, there is probably a grain of truth in it. Failure-produced frustration certainly will not facilitate learning, and the easy task may help to raise the subject's morale and confidence.

So far we have dealt only with James' first discrimination training technique. The phrase "transfer of a discrimination along a continuum" was coined by Lawrence (1952) to describe it. The main theory to be considered in this chapter also attempts to give an account of James' second technique which is now usually referred to as "stimulus predifferentiation" (Gagne and Baker, 1950; Arnoult, 1953, 1957; Cantor, J. H., 1955).

STIMULUS PREDIFFERENTIATION

Most of the work on stimulus predifferentiation has employed children as subjects. Usually the child is given preliminary practice in discriminating two Sd's by means of two distinctively different R's. The most popular R for this pre-criterion training is a verbal label. After the child has learned this task to a required criterion he is transferred to another task in which the Sd's are the same as in the first, but the R's are different. Motor R's, such as pressing a button or moving a box, are usually used in this second task.

As we shall see in Chapter 17, the stimulus predifferentiation paradigm has been used to very good effect in the establishment of a difficult orientation discrimination in children. Just as Bijou (1962) simplified the orientation discrimination task by manipulating the

stimuli, so Jeffrey (1958a) simplified it by changing the *response*. The strategy is, if one sort of R cannot be established in a discrimination task, go on trying others until one is found which will serve to differentiate the Sd's, and then return to the original R, preferably in easy stages.

The effectiveness of using verbal labels in the predifferentiation task has been widely confirmed, and, as we have seen (Chapter 4), this has led Spiker (1956, 1963) to propose that there is perhaps something special about naming which facilitates the acquisition of subsequent motor R's to the Sd's named.

ACQUIRED DISTINCTIVENESS OF CUES HYPOTHESIS

Let us turn now to consider the acquired distinctiveness of cues hypothesis. The basic idea is that through learning the relevant stimulus acquires distinctiveness which makes it functionally (and maybe perceptually too) *stand out* from the rest of the stimuli in the task situation. James' two training techniques work by encouraging this process.

This idea has its roots in Hull's (1930b) speculation about *pure stimulus acts*. These are implicit responses ". . . whose sole function is to serve as stimuli for other acts" (*op. cit.*, p. 515). These pure stimulus acts are assumed to become associated through learning with a certain stimulus input. In this way they are added to the input to produce a new and more distinctive pattern of stimulation. It is this modified stimulus that is eventually connected to the overt R through learning.

So far this looks very much like the Sutherland–Mackintosh and Lawrence models presented in Chapter 8; the pure stimulus act being equivalent to the stimulus analyser or the coding R. However, in the way Hull's suggestion was developed by Miller and Dollard (Miller and Dollard, 1941; Miller, 1948; Dollard and Miller, 1950) there emerges an important distinction. Whereas the former models assume that the stimulus input is actually operated upon and *transformed* in the process, the latter theory assumes merely that the input is added *to*. Thus Dollard and Miller (1950) write,

> Part of the effectiveness of verbal labels probably comes from the non-verbal cue-producing responses which are attached to them in the course of extensive social learning. [p. 103.]

This, then, is the essence of the acquired distinctiveness of cues hypothesis which was formally presented by Lawrence (1949, 1950) in order to account for the transfer of a discrimination, without breakdown, in rats, from a simultaneous to a successive presentation task. Since the R's required on these two tasks are different the experiment involved stimulus predifferentiation. As already noted Lawrence (1952) went on to demonstrate the transfer of a discrimination along a continuum effect in rats.

How does the acquired distinctiveness of cues hypothesis explain these two effects? In the *stimulus predifferentiation* experiment the training with distinctive R's enables the *feedback stimuli from these R's to become attached to the Sd's* thus making them, to the subject's response selection unit, more distinctively different than they were before this training. This means that it will be easier to attach other, probably not very distinctively different, R's to these Sd's than it would have been without this predifferentiation training.

There is one clearly *testable prediction* from this explanation. It implies that the transfer effect will be a direct function of the distinctiveness of the R-produced stimulation. Assuming that the similarity of R's is correlated with the similarity of the S's they produce, we would expect that the *more* different the R's used in the predifferentiation training the *greater* will be the transfer effect. Thus Miller (1948) argued that

> ... learning to respond with highly distinctive names to similar stimulus situations should tend to lessen the generalisation of other responses from one of these situations to another since stimuli produced by responding with the distinctive names will tend to increase the differences in the stimulus patterns of the two situations. [p. 174.]

This prediction was tested and confirmed by Norcross (1958). She found that children asked to learn to attach very similar verbal labels to two Sd's, learned to attach motor R's to these same Sd's much less well than children who had been instructed to attach distinctively different labels to the Sd's in predifferentiation training. However, the reliability of this finding has been questioned by Pfafflin (1960) who found that more distinctive labels do not produce greater transfer. It has also been reported that some transfer occurs even when the same label is attached to each Sd (Hake and Erikson, 1955; Robinson, 1955).

From our knowledge of the sequence of behaviour required by a discrimination these apparently conflicting results are not unexpected.

For the facilitatory effect of predifferentiation training is probably attributable to a number of factors, of which acquired distinctiveness is but one. For example, one of the effects of predifferentiation training would undoubtably be to strengthen the appropriate orienting and processing activity required in the discrimination of the two Sd's. This would tend to occur even when the R's made in pre-criterion training were not very distinctively different.

Spiker (1956), as we have already mentioned, thought that *labelling, per se*, had some training value, apart from its role in providing added distinctiveness to the Sd's or in enabling the appropriate orienting and processing activity to be established. Just what this value is was suggested to Spiker by his observation that children trained to label the Sd's in predifferentiation training bridged the gap in a subsequent delayed reaction task between the presentation of the Sd's and the R, by saying out aloud the name of the correct Sd. Hence, Spiker hypothesized that one factor in the predifferentiation effect using verbal labels is that these labels enable the subject to *rehearse* the correct Sd during the interval between the tasks, and thus, as it were, "keep it fresh in his mind" (cf. Broadbent, 1958, p. 226).

There seems to be a strong similarity between the use of names to rehearse and Sd and the *double-responding* technique which animals and children have been observed to engage in in a S–R spatially discontiguous task (see Chapter 7). In each case there is a gap to be bridged between looking at the stimulus and making a R. The fact that subjects tend to carry over from one task to another *abbreviated versions* of skills acquired on the first, which seem to facilitate the performance on the second, is a common observation, and may provide some clue as to the nature of the mediating mechanism in discrimination learning. See, for example, Jeffrey's (1958a) observation of the shoulder-raising heuristic R which some children used to help them discriminate differently orientated stick figures (Chapter 17). It seems possible that any response can be used as a mediator, provided that it works and does not get in the way of the acquisition of subsequent discriminatory R's. As we shall see in Chapter 11, *verbal R's* are particularly suitable as mediators. They are readily "internalizable" and overlap hardly at all with any other response mechanism.

Finally, let us consider the acquired distinctiveness of cues hypothesis account of the effectiveness of James' other discrimination

training technique, called *the transfer of a discrimination along a continuum*. What happens here is that the initial training on the discrimination with the widely separated Sd's intensifies their distinctiveness by adding to them the feedback stimulation from the R's made. When the Sd's are moved towards each other along the continuum this added distinctiveness remains with them, and so the performance on the final discrimination will be better than if this initial training had not been allowed. For the trained subjects the final Sd's are functionally, at least, more distinctive than they are to the non-trained (trial and error) subjects.

CHAPTER 10

PROGRAMMING A DISCRIMINATION

IN THE preceding chapter we have seen how a discrimination, which was difficult, if not impossible, to establish under normal conditions of differential reinforcement, could be established by beginning training with a task in which either the required discrimination, or the responses were simplified. Thus, training given on a task with widely separated Sd's will facilitate the learning of a subsequent task in which the Sd's are close together, and hence difficult to discriminate (transfer of a discrimination along a continuum). Also, training given on a task requiring the acquisition of distinctively different discriminatory R's will facilitate the learning of a subsequent task in which two less distinctively different R's have to be made to the same Sd's as in the first task (stimulus predifferentiation).

In both these procedures there is an *element of risk*. There is a danger that the transition from the pre-criterion training task to the main criterion task will not be negotiated without a breakdown in the discrimination performance. The procedures to be discussed in this chapter may be used to reduce this risk. They refer primarily to how a transition may be made from one task to another so as to reduce the chance of breakdown in performance. They refer, in other words, to how the relatively *abrupt* transitions envisaged by the techniques discussed in the last chapter can be *smoothed out*.

These procedures will be called *programming procedures*. The term "programming" will be used, as it is in the field of programmed instruction (Lumsdaine and Glaser, 1960), to refer to the arrangement of items in a task into a graduated sequence in such a way that the final, or criterion, task is approached through a series of small steps. Programming, then, is a form of training, but not the only form. For a subject may be trained on a task in which there is no sequencing of items, as, for example, in Harlow's (1949) learning set procedure.

Programming procedures are very much better adapted to dealing with transitions involving a change in the stimuli than those involving

changes in the responses. This is chiefly due to the fact that whereas the stimuli are directly under the control of the experimenter the responses are not. But there are other reasons which will emerge in the following discussion.

RESPONSE PROGRAMMING BY SHAPING

The most widely known method of response programming is shaping. This refers to the differential reinforcement of *successive approximations* to the required form of behaviour (Skinner, 1953, Chapter 6; Holland and Skinner, 1961, Part 4). So, instead of waiting patiently for a certain R to occur in an experimental situation, such as a rat pressing a lever in a Skinner-box, the R may be *shaped*. In this R's are initially reinforced which are merely similar to the required R, or at least, not incompatible with it, such as the rat looking in the direction of the lever. Throughout the training the criterion of reinforcement is gradually changed, so that the rat not only has to look at the lever, but also move towards it, and then to touch it, and finally to press it, to obtain its reward. In trial and error practice, on the other hand, reinforcement is contingent from the outset on the occurrence of the final R.

According to Skinner (1953) the successive approximations procedure is an efficient way of establishing a R that has an initially low probability of occurrence because it cashes in on the essential *continuity of behaviour*. Lever-pressing does not merely consist of the discrete instrumental R that the experimenter records. This is only one R in a long chain of behaviour which begins with the rat being placed in the box. The first element in this chain is orienting, or looking towards, the lever. By reinforcing this the experimenter makes more probable a movement towards the lever, and by reinforcing this in turn makes more probable a touching of the lever, and so on.

This conception of behaviour clearly fits in very well with our model of discrimination. However, it is unlikely that Skinner would concur with our use of internal, and essentially unobservable, operations.

It is not quite clear just how the successive approximations method could be used in facilitating the transfer in a stimulus predifferentiation procedure, for this transfer usually involves the change from one pair of discrete discriminatory R's to another quite different pair.

Shaping has more relevance to the actual establishment of the R in the first place, which is usually taken for granted in work with children.

The most suitable programming procedure for the stimulus predifferentiation technique would seem to be some sort of *fading*, which is to be discussed in detail in a moment in connection with stimulus programming. Edfeldt (1959) demonstrated the effectiveness of a *response-fading* procedure in his work on the establishment of silent reading habits in children. The stages through which the fading went were: (1) reading aloud; (2) reading in whispers; (3) reading with pronounced lip movements but with no sound; and (4) reading with no observable movements or sounds. Our problem is not only to get rid of one R, but to introduce another without upsetting the performance. Where one response is vocal and the other motor, as is usually the case in stimulus predifferentiation (Chapter 9), the two R's can be made simultaneously, and the problem of transfer is greatly simplified. First, the one R can be established, then, the other faded-in, and finally, the original R faded-out. The fact that abbreviated versions of the original R remain after the transfer (Spiker, 1963; Jeffrey, 1958a), suggests that this sort of fading goes on spontaneously. If we are to use the stimulus predifferentiation training technique some attention must be given to the question of the method of transfer.

STIMULUS PROGRAMMING BY FADING

Turning to the transfer of a discrimination along a continuum technique, we notice that the James–Lawrence version did in fact employ a programming procedure. The transfer from the easy to the difficult discrimination was smoothed out by gradually changing the Sd's from one trial to the next.

A variation of this stimulus programming procedure is a technique in which the required behaviour is *prompted* and the prompts, then, gradually withdrawn or faded, leaving the behaviour as required. This technique utilizes S–R associations already in the subject's behavioural repertoire. The prompt is introduced, the problem is how to get rid of it without disturbing the behaviour it evokes. An efficient way of doing this is through fading.

Strictly speaking, there are two sorts of fading. *Fading-out* refers to the progressive removal of a S from a task, and *fading-in* refers to the progressive introduction of a S into a task. These two processes

can be seen as a form of the classical transfer of stimulus control paradigm.

An early recognition of the principle of fading is found in Thorndike (1913). Here, Thorndike attempted to modify his extreme identical elements theory of transfer (Thorndike and Woodworth, 1901) by means of the principle of *associative shifting*. The basic idea is that if a response can be kept intact through a series of changes in the stimulating situation, it may finally be given to a totally new stimulus. In this way we may ". . . get any response of which a learner is capable associated with any situation to which he is sensitive" (Thorndike, 1913, p. 15).

During fading-in, a *new*, non-controlling S is introduced into a task situation containing an established S–R relationship. The aim is to introduce this S without disturbing the relationship. The ultimate objective is to substitute this new S for the original one, while maintaining the R. The following table shows a paradigm for the fading-in of a *new* S (SN) into a situation containing an *old* S (SO). The suffixed figures refer to some measure of S magnitude.

Items	1		2		3		4	
Stimuli	SO3	SNo	SO3	SN1	SO3	SN2	SO3	SN3

This procedure has recently been employed by Terrace (1963a) as a part of a training procedure to establish a colour discrimination in pigeons. Each bird was trained to peck an illuminated key (SO3) and to ignore an adjacent, unlit, key (SNo). Terrace compared the efficiency of four different ways of introducing positive SN values into the situation. He found that the discrimination behaviour established on SO3–SNo was best maintained if SN was introduced early on in the training (with no overlearning on the original), and progressively. Thus, SN was gradually increased in intensity (SN, SN2, . . .) until it reached the same intensity as the SO colour. By the use of this fading-in of the Sd— Terrace demonstrated that a colour discrimination could be established in pigeons *without any errors* (no R's to Sd—).

In addition to demonstrating the effectiveness of this fading-in procedure in promoting an errorless acquisition of a discrimination, Terrace also noticed that subsequent performances on this and on other discrimination tasks were much improved. Therefore, the

standard of subsequent performances seemed to be a function of the number of errors made during learning. This suggested to Terrace that ". . . one of the effects of large amounts of responding to S— during the acquisition of a discrimination is the development of permanent faulty discrimination performance" (1963a, p. 24). This question will be returned to in a moment.

Let us turn now to *fading-out*. This refers to the progressive withdrawal of a controlling or prompting S from the task situation without interfering with the established R. The following table shows the fading-out of the *old* stimulus (SO) leaving the *new* stimulus (SN) alone and controlling the R.

Items	1		2		3		4	
Stimuli	SO3	SN3	SO2	SN3	SO1	SN3	SOo	SN3

Both the fading procedures taken together, we can see, provide a paradigm for the transfer of stimulus control from SO3 to SN3 over a certain R. The two procedures may be used in succession or they may be used simultaneously as the following table shows.

Items	1		2		3		4	
Stimuli	SO3	SNo	SO2	SN1	SO1	SN2	SOo	SN3

The fading-out procedure may be illustrated by a second study of Terrace (1963b). In this Terrace used fading-out to produce an *errorless transfer of a discrimination across two continua*. First, pigeons were trained, using the early-progressive introduction of Sd—, to discriminate two colours. Next, either a vertical or a horizontal line was superimposed on each colour. After a little practice, the two colours (SO's) were progressively reduced in intensity (SO3, SO2, . . .), while the vertical and horizontal lines (SN's) were maintained, until eventually the two colours had been completely faded-out (SOo).

Terrace found that whereas this procedure could establish the vertical–horizontal discrimination without errors, other procedures, such as trial and error practice on the line discrimination, colour

training with no superimposition, and colour training with super-imposition but no fading, produced a large number of errors. As in the previous study there was a positive relationship between the absence of errors in training and the efficiency of subsequent performance.

Terrace also reports that attempts to train the vertical–horizontal discrimination by fading-in the Sd— were not so successful as the transfer from the colour discrimination. A possible interpretation of this difference is suggested by the fact that fading-in the Sd— can be seen as a process of fading-out the differences on a certain stimulus dimension.

At the outset of Terrace's colour discrimination task the two Sd's differed in brightness as well as colour. It seems that the bird's behaviour was initially based on the brightness differences; in Sutherland's terminology (Chapter 8) the bird had the brightness analyser switched-in. By gradually increasing the intensity of Sd—, this brightness difference is faded-out, and the previously non-dominant dimension of colour comes to provide the most distinctive differences between the Sd's. (Physically, the colour differences are not faded-in since the wavelengths of the key-lights are not changed.) Therefore, the failure of the fading-in procedure in establishing the line discrimination without errors may be due to the relative difficulty of switching from a brightness to an orientation analyser as compared with switching from a brightness to a colour analyser. Terrace's (1963b) second study shows how the brightness-orientation switch can be mediated by the colour analyser. The best procedure appears to be as follows: (1) establish a brightness discrimination; (2) fade out the brightness difference, so leaving the colour difference; (3) fade out the colour difference, so leaving the orientation of the line difference.

HIVELY'S STIMULUS PROGRAMMING IN A MATCHING TASK

Let us turn now to consider some of the programming techniques used by Hively (1962a) in his study of *matching-to-sample* behaviour in young children.

Figure 10.1 shows the main features of Hively's training programme. The square boxes represent the upper and lower windows of the apparatus used to present the stimuli. The oblong upper window

displays the sample and the two lower windows the choices. The letters A and D stand for the two stimulus figures.

The programme began with *Series 2SCO*, which comprised the two items shown in the figure. In each case, there was no non-matching choice and each S always occupied the same position. All the child had to do here was press on the lower window displaying

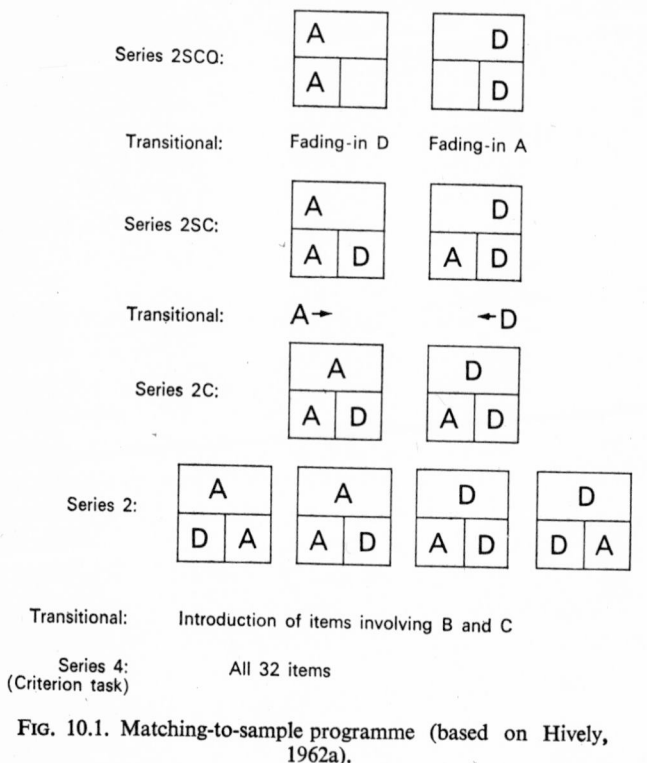

FIG. 10.1. Matching-to-sample programme (based on Hively, 1962a).

a S. In the *Transitional Series* the non-matching choice figures were gradually faded-in to produce *Series 2SC*. Clearly, the child can no longer rely on the strategy of pressing a window displaying a S, for now both windows contain S's. Now the strategy must be, at least, "Press the window which is underneath the pattern in the top window". In the next *Transitional Series* the basis of this strategy is removed by gradually moving the sample S towards the centre of the

upper window, so that it will be midway between the two lower windows. This takes us up to *Series 2C* in which the only non-matching strategy possible is "Press left window when A is sample and right window when B is sample". A genuine matching hypothesis would be supported by the constancy of the positions occupied by the two choice S's. *Series 2* removes this support and makes matching essential for correct performance. *Series 4* is the criterion task in which two other stimulus figures (B and C) are introduced.

Though Hively found this training programme quite effective in establishing a stable baseline of matching behaviour in his 6-year-old subjects it might be asked why this behaviour was not acquired immediately by means of *verbal instructions*. Considering the popularity of the matching method in assessing the young child's discriminative capacities (Gibson and Olum, 1960), it would be expected that this behaviour would be readily accessible to verbal instructions. If we look closely at Hively's procedure the explanation is clear. The fault lay in the incomplete and misleading nature of his initial instructions to the subjects. Not only did they fail to mention the discriminative stimuli or the need for matching, but they actively drew the child's attention to the response features of the task. As far as the child was concerned the game was merely to press the windows and make the lights change. One feels that the training programme would have been more successful had nothing been said.

This explanation was confirmed by an experiment conducted by the author in which the matching performances of two groups of 10 5-year-olds were compared (Fellows, 1965). One group which received the same instructions as Hively's subjects did not learn to match under conditions of differential reinforcement. Instead, as might be predicted, they adopted position habits. In the other group, which received instructions designed to activate the constituent skills, 8 out of 10 learned very quickly. The accessibility of the matching habit on a fairly easy discrimination task to verbal instructions in the majority of children between the ages of 5 and 6 years was confirmed in a number of other experiments. However, it is also clear that at this age the habit is not completely reliable, and tends to break down with an increase in the difficulty of the required discriminations, giving way to oddity responding and the more primitive response strategies (see Chapter 5). Whether Hively's training programme produces a more stable performance is a question for further research.

The whole question of the effectiveness of verbal instructions and the role of language as a mediator will be dealt with more fully in the next chapter.

ROLE OF ERRORS IN LEARNING

Like Terrace, Hively observed a relationship between the number of errors made in training and the proficiency of the final performance.

> The more errors the training procedure allowed the children to make, the more they tended to go on making. . . . There appears to be a progressive loss of control. After a bad programme has been tested, it can be revised, but the subjects must be thrown away. [1962a, p. 297.]

Just what do errors mean? There are no doubt a number of factors in the commission of an error. The child may be performing very well, but is suddenly distracted by something. He loses his "concentration", and produces what we call a "careless" error. Alternatively, in a discrimination task an error may be due to the child's inability to distinguish between two Sd's. Again, there are what Harlow (1950) calls *error factors*. These are manifested in systematic methods of responding on the basis of cues which are not correlated with 100 per cent reinforcement.

Why should errors in learning produce less stable subsequent performance? One way of looking at this is to see errors as indicators of loss of experimental control. The subject is doing something that he should not, and this is the fault of the programme. This goes counter to a widely held educational hypothesis that a child learns from his mistakes. But, we may ask, what does he learn? Does he learn to eliminate these errors and respond in the way the teacher wants him to? Or are these errors in some way reinforcing for incorrect habits? In the two studies just discussed it seems that the latter is the case. A possible explanation may be that errors are a sign that the subject has a tendency to respond on the basis of some incorrect habit which may be strengthened by the intermittent reinforcement it receives. It seems likely that differential reinforcement on its own is not a very effective way to eliminate predispositions which the subject brings with him to the task.

CHAPTER 11

MEDIATIONAL PROCESSES AND LANGUAGE

IN A number of the preceding chapters it has been mentioned that there appears to be an *age effect* in the way a child tackles and learns a discrimination task. In Chapter 6, for example, with reference to the work of Zaporozhets, it was noted that very young children appear to go about learning a task in much the same way as rats learning a maze, or cats getting out of a puzzle box. Initially, their behaviour appears to be quite random, and learning takes place in much the way predicted by S–R theory. Older children, however, go about a task "more thoughtfully", their behaviour appearing to be under the control of stimuli emanating from elsewhere than the external environment. Hebb (1949) proposed a similar account. He argued that it was impossible to avoid the conclusion that both continuous and non-continuous types of learning occur, ". . . and that one is characteristic of the mature animal, and the other mainly of the infant" (p. 115). Harlow (1949) argued in a similar manner, but stressed the role of previous experience in establishing the appropriate learning sets, which the organism brings with it to a new task and which may enable it to learn without practice.

DEVELOPMENT OF LANGUAGE AS A MEDIATOR

In a series of investigations with children the Kendlers have observed much the same effect of age (Kendler and Kendler, 1956, 1959, 1961a, b, 1962a, b). Kendler *et al.* (1960) found that *3- and 4-year-olds* learned a non-reversal task much quicker than they learned a reversal task. This, it will be recalled (Chapter 2), is what the "pure" form of the continuity hypothesis would predict. On the other hand, Kendler and Kendler (1959) found that half the children between the ages of *5 and 7 years* learned the reversal task easier than the non-reversal, which is what a mediational theory would predict.

These findings together with others (e.g. Kuenne, 1946; Riess, 1946; Alberts and Ehrenfreund, 1951; Kendler *et al.*, 1961) indicated that very young children respond to problem-solving tasks in a concrete, unmediated manner. In the course of development they learn to make use of mediating behaviour, which considerably facilitates their learning.

What is the nature of this mediating behaviour? Kuenne (1946) suggests that it is closely connected with the development of the child's *verbal behaviour*. She writes,

> ... there are at least two developmental stages so far as the relation of verbal responses to overt choice behaviour is concerned. In the first, the child is able to make differential verbal responses to appropriate aspects of the situation, but this verbalisation does not control or influence his overt choice behaviour. Later, such verbalisations gain control and dominate choice behaviour. [*Op. cit.*, p. 488.]

Some confirmatory evidence for this came from Kendler *et al.* (1960) who observed that during the course of a reversal task it was not unusual for 4-year-olds to verbalize spontaneously the correct solution while they simultaneously made the incorrect R. This suggests that such children are at a stage in which, though readily available as instrumental choice R's, verbal R's do not easily function as mediators for other behaviour. Kendler and Kendler (1962a) interpreted this as indicating that verbal and motor operations are parallel in the young child, and do not interact.

Kendler and Kendler (1961a) found that instructing 4-year-olds to verbalize the relevant dimension on a reversal learning task did improve their performance as compared with children of the same age who did not receive this training. That the performance of 7-year olds was not improved by verbalization was to be expected, since they are at a stage when they would be able to provide their own verbal mediators.

This suggests that language is a relatively *closed-system* of behaviour. Intrinsically, vocal activity has no real connection with any other activity; any relationships that develop have to be learned. It is partly this *integrity*, and partly the *ease of internalization*, that seems to make vocal R's so useful as *mediators*. This is not to suggest, however, that vocal R's are the only mediators. As Harlow's (1959) work, in particular, indicates, animals, which possess the most primitive of vocal behaviour, manage a great degree of mediation. Any response can act as a mediator for any other response, provided

the one does not interfere with the other. The deaf and dumb person probably makes great use of internalized finger movements as mediatory behaviour. Clearly, behaviour which is internalized will have less interfering potential. At the very bottom there may be a subconscious pool of internalized activities, where they all interact with the greatest freedom. This is *pure thought*. Maybe it corresponds with what Vygotsky (1962) called the "sense-saturated" level of inner speech. This, for Vygotsky, is the source of original thought. To extend the metaphor, the pool of internalized actions is where we fish, or, more likely, dive into, for fresh ideas. The greatest problem is in translating these ideas into overt behaviour, i.e. *externalizing* them.

The work of Kuenne and the Kendlers has received confirmation from Luria (1957, 1961a, b) who has attempted, as it were, to externalize some of Vygotsky's ideas into experimental fact. His conclusions are very similar to those already expressed.

> In the early stages of child development speech is only a means of communication. . . . Subsequently it becomes also a means whereby he organises his own experience and regulates his own actions. So the child's activity is mediated through words. [1957, p. 116.]

Luria observes how the mediating speech R's gradually become abbreviated and internalized with increasing usage. The older child and adult habitually think in silence until faced with a complex problem, when this mediating activity tends to become overt, in the form of lip movements, whispers, or normal speech.

VERBAL CONTROL OF CHILD BEHAVIOUR

Luria (1961a) reports that the nature and extent of control that can be exercised by the experimenter over a child's behaviour is also a *function of age*. For the very young child ($1\frac{1}{2}$–3 years) verbal instructions have an *initiating or releasing function* on his behaviour. He will carry out instructions, such as "Squeeze the bulb", or "Give me the ball", only if he is set to do so. The instruction serves merely to release behaviour the child is ready to perform. This tendency means that long instructions tend to be responded to in a *piecemeal* fashion. If instructed to "Press the bulb when the light comes on", the child will very likely press the bulb immediately, without waiting for the light, particularly if he happens to have the bulb in his hand at the time. Paradoxically, the effect of the light coming on may be

to inhibit the pressing. This Luria attributes to external inhibition. In terms of our present conception of discrimination behaviour, this presumably means that the onset of the light elicits an orienting R to it, which has the effect of inhibiting the pressing R. If the instruction is changed to "When the light comes on press the bulb", the child will tend to look for the light, but is unlikely to press the bulb when it comes on. As was noted in Chapter 6, this seems to reflect an inability on the part of the child to build up an image or plan of the activity required merely on the basis of verbal communication.

Gradually, the child becomes able to respond to verbal instructions *conditionally*. Thus, the child of about 5 years will tend to wait for the light to come on before pressing, if instructed to do so. Luria concludes that before the age of about *$4\frac{1}{2}$–$5\frac{1}{2}$ years* ". . . it is absolutely impossible to elaborate in the child a stable system of motor reactions by means of verbal instructions only" (1961a, p. 60).

What this means is not that it is impossible to teach a child anything by verbal means, but that to be effective verbal instructions must refer to *immediately required responses* and to *corresponding events in the environment*. For example, it is clear from Luria's experiments that conditional statements, which include "if" and "when" clauses, and negatives cannot be guaranteed to work. Such statements, therefore, must be broken down into a number of simple, positive and categorical imperatives which are synchronized with the corresponding event in the environment. So the instruction "Press the bulb when the light comes on" can be broken down thus: (1) "Wait for the light." This serves to orient the child to the source of the light so that when it comes on he cannot help but see it. (2) The light comes on. (3) "Press the bulb." After a few repetitions of this the pressing response will probably become conditioned to the onset of the light and so the instructions can be dropped, or gradually withdrawn.

For Luria the child's main problem is the *lack of inhibitory mechanisms*, a deficiency which shows up particularly in the conditional type of task. The child must refrain from responding until the event mentioned in the instructions occurs. But there is a way of getting round this inhibition deficiency. Luria sees inhibition working by means of a *conflict of intentions*. So the tendency or impulse to do one thing is inhibited by the tendency to do something else. So instead of instructing a child not to do something we ask him to do something else which is incompatible with him doing the first thing.

A PROGRAMME FOR THE VERBAL CONTROL OF
MATCHING BEHAVIOUR

In some exploratory work with children aged 3–5 years the present writer has attempted to develop a verbal tuition programme to establish matching to sample behaviour by using these principles. The programme comprises a sequence of instructions such that each step in the task is prompted by the appropriate instruction.

1. "Put your hands on your knees." This employs the conflict of intentions technique to inhibit any premature responding when the stimuli are presented.

2. "Look at the upstairs window." The arrangement of presentation windows is shown in Fig. 5.1. One is at the top for the sample stimulus (upstairs), and the others immediately beneath for the choice stimuli (downstairs). This instruction directs the child's attention to the locus of the sample stimulus to ensure his reception of it when it appears. In the model presented in Chapter 14 this corresponds to $ro(TW)$.

3. The sample is presented. The child is instructed to "Look carefully at this pattern". This aims to encourage the *stimulus processing* operation. Pointing out the relevant features, or asking the child to name the pattern (Spiker, 1956) may also help. Probably the best way of promoting the analysis operation would be to suggest that the child traced around the pattern with his finger.

4. Unless a delayed matching procedure is employed there should be no cause to attempt to exert control over the *memory* operation. Nevertheless, an instruction to "Remember that pattern" will do no harm.

5. "Look at the downstairs windows." This serves to ensure that the choices will be received when they are presented.

6. In accordance with our Chapter 14 model it was considered best to present just one choice stimulus in the bottom window on the left. "Look at that pattern."

7. "Is it the same as the pattern in the upstairs window? Or is it different?" This attempts to control the *comparison* operation. This is the point where most difficulty was experienced in this experiment in maintaining control. It seemed that the verbal labels "same" and "different" did not mean the same to the children as they did to the experimenter. In cases of doubt, the other choice was also presented

and the child encouraged to compare the choices with the sample to find the one that was the same.

8. The next step was to control the *response strategy* operation. The instruction "Now point to the pattern that is the same and press the button underneath".

There are a number of practical problems associated with the administration of this programme. For example, asking a child to do something does not guarantee that he will do it. Even with the simple imperatives verbal control over behaviour is not perfect. But probably the most serious problem was caused by the child's tendency to jump ahead of the programme, to anticipate events and responses. This has the effect of disturbing the continuity, and hence, the effectiveness of the programme.

This programme was administered as a remedial measure only to those children who had failed to respond appropriately to normal conditional instructions for matching. It was found that of the sample of 27 children, within the age range 3 years 2 months to 5 years 1 month, 15 were in need of special treatment, and only one of these was over the age of 4 years 7 months. Conversely, only 4 out of the 12 acquiring matching behaviour with normal instructions were below this age (Fellows, 1965). These findings also suggest the age of $4\frac{1}{2}$ *years* as being a critical one in the use of language as a mediator.

CONCLUSION

In conclusion, there does seem to be some sort of mediational deficiency in young children which is closely connected with the ability to use speech to regulate behaviour. To what extent this is a function of the task conditions is a matter for empirical investigation. As Reese (1962) argues,

> If mediation is a "voluntary" process, . . . there may be a stage of development in which subjects have typically not yet learned to use it, and instruction in the use of the process should facilitate the learning of these subjects. [p. 507.]

As the preceding discussion has indicated, this instruction would involve the use of verbal and general orienting behaviour to mediate the performance of the child. This behaviour may then be internalized by some fading procedure.

CHAPTER 12

KENDLER'S MODEL OF DISCRIMINATION PERFORMANCE

In the present chapter we shall consider in some detail a recent model of the sequence of events involved in the performance on a visual discrimination task proposed by Kendler *et al.* (1961). This model contains many of the operations which have been seen in previous chapters to be necessary for such a performance. It resembles more closely than any the recent scheme put forward by Polidora and Fletcher (1964) which has been discussed in Chapter 7. This particular model is important since it provides the basic structure upon which the model to be presented in Chapter 14 is constructed.

Figure 12.1 shows a diagrammatic representation of the sequence of events involved in Kendler's model. According to Kendler's description the capital letters stand for directly observable events and the small letters for inferred events. The significance of the different connecting lines is not made clear by Kendler.

THE TASK

The task which was assumed to involve this chain of events was as follows. On each trial two figures were simultaneously flashed onto a screen in front of the subject. The short period of exposure (5 msec) combined with the spatial separation of the figures (29 inches) meant that the subject could not fixate more than one figure on any one trial. Immediately before presenting the stimuli the experimenter instructed the subject to get ready. This is the *Ready Signal* (S).

If the subject is to receive either of the stimulus figures, he must, in response to this signal, turn his eyes to one or the other of the positions on the screen where they are to be presented. This is the *Orienting Response* (r). Strictly speaking, it is not unobservable, as Kendler's model indicates, but in his experiment it was not recorded. There are two possible orienting responses: one to the left and one to

the right. The subject must learn to make one or the other in response to the ready signal if he is to receive either of the figures.

There were two different sorts of figures used in the task. One was a circle with a radius in one of four positions (12, 3, 6 or 9 o'clock), and the other a square with one of four patterns of stripes (vertical, horizontal, NW.–SE. oblique, or NE.–SW. oblique). The task was *concept learning*. There were two concepts: Horizontal–Vertical (HV)

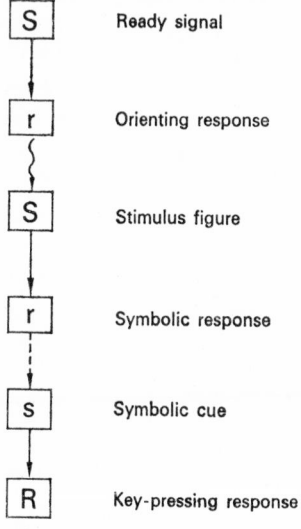

Fig. 12.1. A model of discrimination performance (from Kendler *et al.* (1961)).

and Straight–Oblique (SO). To learn the HV concept the subject was required to press one of two keys when the radius of the circle was vertical (12 or 6 o'clock) and the other when the radius was horizontal (3 or 9 o'clock). To learn the SO concept the subject was required to press one key when the stripes on the square were straight (horizontal or vertical) and the other when the stripes were oblique. So, to acquire the HV concept the subject must respond only to circles and to acquire SO concept he must respond only to squares.

On each trial both a circle and a square were presented in fixed positions, either on the left or on the right of the screen. This meant that a subject, having to learn a particular concept, will always have to make the same orienting response to receive the appropriate figure.

KENDLER'S SYMBOLIC RESPONSE

So, the observable sequence of events is ready signal, orienting response, presentation of figures and key-pressing. So far this is much the same as the models proposed by Spence (Chapter 2) and Wyckoff (Chapter 3). But, as we see from Fig. 12.1, it goes one step further in postulating operations mediating between the presentation of the figures and the occurrence of the instrumental response. We have seen in many of the preceding chapters that such operations are necessary in accounting for the apparent non-continuity of much discrimination learning. Goodwin and Lawrence suggested the identification response (Chapter 3), Zeaman and House attention (Chapter 4), White attention (Chapter 5), Polidora and Fletcher the sampling response (Chapter 7), Sutherland and Mackintosh switching-in of a stimulus analyser and Lawrence coding response (Chapter 8). Kendler's contribution to this list is the *symbolic response*.

The function of the symbolic response is much the same as that of the other postulated mediating mechanisms listed above. It serves to isolate those aspects of the stimulus figures that are correlated with reinforcement.

Let us now run through the assumed sequence of events involved in the acquisition of a particular concept. The first thing the subject has to learn is to make the appropriate orienting response, so as to receive the appropriate stimulus figure. Assume the concept to be learned is HV, and that the circles are always presented on the left of the screen. This means that the orienting to be made in response to the ready signal is looking to the left. If the subject looks to the right, or anywhere else, he will not be exposed to the stimulus cues correlated with reinforcement. It will be noticed that the orienting response in this situation serves, not only to expose the subject to a stimulus figure, but also to expose him to the correct one.

Having made the appropriate orienting response, and having been exposed to the circle stimulus, the subject's task now is to discover which of the aspects of the stimulus are relevant. Each circle has a radius in one of four positions. Kendler assumes that the subject will learn to make a symbolic response to these features of the stimulus, and that this will have the effect of yielding one of two distinctively different *symbolic cues for each circle*. Thus, when the radius of the circle is horizontal symbolic cue H may be produced, and when the radius is vertical symbolic cue V.

The final link in the chain is between each of these symbolic cues and an *overt key-pressing R*. This link should follow the reinforcement contingencies in the task. So, if, when the radius of the presented circle is horizontal, only responses to the left-hand key are reinforced, the connection between the symbolic cue H and the R to the left key will be strengthened. And if, when the radius is vertical, only R's to the right-hand key are reinforced, the connection between the symbolic cue V and the R to the right key will be strengthened.

THE FINDINGS

Let us now look briefly at the findings of Kendler *et al.* (1961) using this sort of task. They compared the effects of four types of transfer between two tasks. College students were employed as subjects.

One group were merely required to *reverse their R's* (reversal shift). This meant that if a subject learned in the first task to respond to the left key for the H concept and to the right key for the V concept, in the second task he would be required to respond to the right key for the H concept and the left key for the V concept. In terms of the model this involved a switch-round of the symbolic cue—overt R links. All the other operations between the two tasks are the same.

A second group, in addition to reversing their R's, also were required to make *new orienting responses*. So, on the second task the relevant figure was presented on the opposite side of the screen to where it was on the first task. But the link between the stimulus figure and the symbolic response was the same in both tasks.

The third and fourth groups were required to learn a *different concept* in the second task from that learned in the first. This meant that the link between the stimulus figure and the symbolic response established on the first task was of no use in the second. One of these two groups was also required to make a *different orienting response* in the second task.

Kendler found that the performance of the first group (reversal) on the second task was significantly better than that of any other group. The other three groups did not differ significantly. The performances of the second group (reversal plus orienting) seem to divide into two distinct types. Either the new task was learned very quickly, or it was learned very slowly. Kendler suggests that in the latter case the problem was learning to make the new orienting

response; but while this was being learned the appropriate symbolic response was being extinguished and this had to be relearned when the new orienting response was strong. In the light of the Sutherland–Mackintosh theory (Chapter 8) it would be very interesting to see the differential effects of overtraining on these various operations.

INTERACTION OF BEHAVIOUR CHAINS

How does Kendler account for the superior performance of the reversal only group? The obvious explanation is in the fact that for that group there was more in common between the two tasks, and therefore less to learn, than for any other group.   But there is one problem which has not been fully answered in previous accounts of reversal learning. Why does this reversal shift take place so rapidly? Kendler *et al.* (1961) proposed that this is due to "... the operation of a behavioural chain in addition to the one described" (p. 189). The first non-reinforcement, they argue, sets off a chain of behaviour, the consequence of which is the selection of the key other than the one that was previously correct. According to this there is a tendency *to respond to non-reinforcement by switching R's*. This is probably a learned tendency. It might correspond to what Harlow (1950) called the response shift error factor, or it may be a manifestation of the lose–shift strategy (see Appendix). In Kendler's view the first correct R on the second task is not the result of the subject "adopting the principle" of reversal shift. Instead processes appear to be operating which encourage the selection of the opposite R while the implicit symbolic cue appropriate to the correct concept is still present. The contiguous occurrence of the cue and the correct R, followed by the reinforcement, is enough to establish immediately this new association.

The hypothesis, therefore, is that the rapid reversal shift is due to "... the contiguous occurrence of an implicit cue and an overt response which are themselves segments from different behaviour chains" (*op. cit.*, p. 189). This *double-chain* theory of reversal learning, which is developed in more detail by Kendler and Kendler (1962a), provides an alternative account to the one proposed by Sutherland and Mackintosh, which involves differential effects on the switching and overt R mechanisms of non-reinforcement. It attempts to explain the effect more in a non-continuity framework, in terms of what skills the subject brings with him to the task. But questions

remain about the nature, origin and controlling variables of this separate chain. Are there other ways of detecting it? Is it learned? Could this be what is acquired on a reversal learning set task (Harlow, 1949)?

CHAPTER 13

THE MATCHING-TO-SAMPLE TASK

So FAR, we have been primarily concerned to give an account of the sequence of events assumed to take place when an organism performs on a simple two-choice discrimination task. This sort of task has been, by far, the most popular, both for the study of the learning in animals, and in the study of their discriminative capacities (Sutherland, 1961a). The matching-to-sample task has been less used due mainly to its cognitive complexity. There were two main factors determining the choice of matching as the task for analysis in this work.

ADVANTAGES OF MATCHING FOR ANALYSIS

First, it was felt that the classical single-problem discrimination learning procedure, though often used with children (Gibson and Olum, 1960), did not really test their cognitive capacities to the full. Matching is more demanding; errors may occur and some learning is usually necessary. This enables us to examine the constituent cognitive operations more easily. The classical type of discrimination task, on the other hand, is quickly, if not immediately, acquired by all but the youngest and most immature children; and the execution of the task is so simple that the performance is fairly insensitive to any changes that might be introduced into the task situation.

The second reason for choosing matching is that it allows one to make many more changes in the discriminative stimuli than would have been possible with a simple discrimination task. This is the chief disadvantage of using the latter task to assess discriminative capacities. Only two stimuli can be used in each task. The technique of transfer tests developed by Lashley (1930) and Kluver (1933) to some extent overcome this problem, but the limitation remains. A big improvement can be made by setting up a discrimination learning set in which the trials-per-problem can be cut to two (Harlow, 1949). But matching is still more economical since, once established, the

stimuli can be changed on every trial without disturbing the performance. This, of course, makes it possible to test many more discriminations in a given amount of time. As a consequence, the whole
performance is much smoother than it would be if the subject had to
relearn stimulus preferences on every change of stimuli.

In the present chapter we shall consider a few of the findings
which might help to throw some light on the nature of the operations
involved in matching. In the next chapter an attempt will be made to
develop a general model which will serve to describe the sequence of
events involved in the performance on a matching task.

LASHLEY'S WORK ON MATCHING IN RATS

Lashley (1938a, p. 175) failed to establish matching in either of
two rats despite 200 trials of differential reinforcement. He used the
jumping stand with three doors instead of the more usual two. On
the centre door, which was locked, the sample was presented. The
two choice S's were presented on the two side doors; the door displaying the matching S being open and leading to food, and the door
displaying the non-matching S being locked. So, to reach the food and
avoid bumping its nose the rat had to learn to jump to the side door
displaying the matching S and to avoid jumping at the non-matching
S. Since the S used as sample and the position of the matching S
were varied between trials, the rat had to learn to respond to a
stimulus relationship and not to a specific S, and this it seems was its
undoing. The fact that it was this task that was "the problem" for
the rat is indicated by the ease with which the figures involved were
discriminated in a normal approach–avoidance task.

Lashley hypothesized that the problem arose due to the rat's
inability to respond conditionally. For matching requires a conditional
response, the correct S being conditional upon the sample. However,
Lashley (1938a) reports a study by Borovski in which rats were shown
to be able to respond conditionally; but this was not on a matching
task. Lashley (1938b) confirmed this finding by demonstrating that
rats could be trained to choose an erect or an inverted triangle
according to whether the background were black or striped. This
clearly indicates that the rat's failure to acquire matching is not due to
its inability to respond conditionally.

To explain this discrepancy, Lashley (1938b) argued that in the
conditional R set-up "... the connexion of figure and ground is

sufficiently close to permit of a ready association between the differentiating (triangle orientation) and reversing (background) factors". On the other hand, in matching, the sample and the choices are, not only spatially separated, but also of "different significance". For, while the choices are things *to be jumped at*, the sample is solely something *to be looked at*. Since the sample is not jumped at it is not oriented, and therefore not received by the rat.

THE ORIENTING RESPONSE IN MATCHING

This explanation of Lashley's is very much in line with our own conception. As the work on S–R spatial contiguity indicated (Chapter 7), if the locus of R is removed from the S to be oriented then this will very likely interfere with learning. It is clearly essential that the sample is oriented and received, if it is to determine which of the choices is to be responded to. It is not easy to see how this sample-orienting could be guaranteed on the jumping stand.

One possible way around this problem would be to encourage a response to the stimulus relationships between the sample and the choices (identity or difference) by arranging the task set-up so that the response panels were situated midway between the sample and each of the choices. This would encourage the sort of behaviour the rats spontaneously engage in on a conventional approach–avoidance task, except that in this case the Sd's are *stimulus complexes* made up of the sample, and either the matching or the non-matching choice. According to Nissen *et al.* (1948), this is very likely the way an animal does tackle a matching task in any case. But, if this skill is to be generalizable to other stimulus figures, then some sort of *abstraction* must take place. The animal must learn to respond to the homogeneous part of the visual field irrespective of the actual S's used. Lashley (1938b) claimed to have demonstrated that rats, having learned a conditional problem, were in fact responding to the stimulus elements and not to the whole Gestalt. This implies, in this situation, post-reception selection of dimensions (cf. Goodwin and Lawrence, Chapter 3).

Ferster (1960) demonstrated how an initial *orienting response to the sample* could be made part of the whole chain of behaviour involved in matching. He trained pigeons to peck an illuminated centre key. This had the effect of lighting up two side keys and extinguishing the centre one. Reinforcement was contingent upon a R to

the key of the same colour as the centre key. The colours used for the sample and the position of the correct key were varied from one trial to the next, so the task was truly a matching-to-sample one. Since the sample was not present when the choice R was made it was a "delayed" matching task. Berryman *et al.* (1963) also found that this procedure was very effective for establishing matching behaviour in pigeons. Nevin *et al.* (1963) increased its efficiency by demanding five responses to the centre (sample) key before the choice keys were illuminated, and by leaving the sample key lighted during the choice R.

This work supports what was argued above that provided an orienting response to the sample stimulus was ensured, matching behaviour could probably be established in rats. In Ferster's procedure the pecking R presumably takes with it an orienting R. Ehrenfreund's (1948) work suggests that the rat's orienting could be similarly controlled (Chapter 2).

Weinstein (1941) found it necessary to use a *preliminary tutoring procedure* to establish matching in two children aged 2:10 and 3:1 and two rhesus monkeys. He found that the main problem was to get them to look at the sample object. His method of obtaining this response resembles Ferster's. He first trained the subject to displace the sample object in order to obtain a reward underneath. When this behaviour was well established, two other objects were placed by the side of the sample, one identical to the sample, the other different. A reward was placed under the matching object. After a little practice all four subjects learned to displace both the sample and the matching object and to ignore the non-matching object, irrespective of its position. The next step was to stop rewarding R's to the sample object. Now only R's to the matching choice object were rewarded. This as expected caused a rapid decline in R's to the sample, but the matching behaviour remained quite firm. Since an orienting R must be made to the sample for the correct choice to be made, we must conclude that the heuristic, overt, sample R was spontaneously faded, leaving only the necessary orienting R.

In a later study in which he actually filmed the behaviour engaged in by monkeys on a matching task, Weinstein (1945) found that an efficient performance was marked by a quick glance at the sample figure, followed by a rapid looking from one choice to another, before the final choice was made.

ODDITY RESPONDING

Matching is, of course, only one of the two possible strategies involving a response to the stimulus relationship which may be displayed on a matching task. Rather than responding to the matching stimulus, the subject may respond to the non-matching stimulus. A consistent habit based on this is called *oddity responding* (Young and Harlow, 1943). Looking at oddity responding in terms of the S–R chain model there is no reason to expect it to be any easier to establish than matching (Skinner, 1950, p. 213). But, Wodinsky and Bitterman (1953) and Ginsberg (1957) both report that in fact oddity responding is much easier to establish.

The explanation for this is quite easy to see, but not too easy to describe. It seems that in learning an oddity problem there is no real need to differentiate the sample and the choices, as there is in matching. The subject may merely learn to respond directly to the odd part of the stimulus complex. Oddity responding, therefore, appears to lend itself particularly well to the *Gestalt* approach, mentioned above as a possible method of matching. But, whereas matching requires a *differentiation* of the large homogeneous part of the stimulus field into that-to-be-responded-to and that-not-to-be-responded-to, oddity responding merely involves a response directly to the smaller part of the field. This implies that requiring an orienting response to the sample as part of the oddity habit may actually hinder its acquisition, since it will tend to discourage the subject from taking up this *Gestalt*-type approach to the task.

A MODEL OF MATCHING AND DISCRIMINATION PERFORMANCE

In the preceding twelve chapters a review has been made of the literature on discrimination learning and performance with the object of isolating the sequence of operations which have been observed or inferred to play an essential role in such behaviour.

What follows is a description of the sequence of events that would appear to occur in the performance of a well-practised subject on a single item of a two-choice matching-to-sample task. In no sense does it claim to be the last word. It is a model which has grown naturally out of the writer's researches and his observations during experiments, and there is no reason to think that it should not continue to develop with further research. It does point towards a more complete description of the discrimination process than has yet been offered. It is to be hoped that it will lead to a greater understanding of discrimination behaviour, and particularly lead to fresh avenues of experimental research.

ASSUMPTIONS

First, a few assumptions are necessary.

1. All three stimuli are assumed to be separated from one another by a distance great enough to prevent any more than one of them being received during a single fixation or orienting response. Therefore, to receive each stimulus the subject must make a discrete and distinct orienting response to each of them. Just what the inter-stimulus distance has to be to guarantee this condition is a question for empirical investigation. An alternative method of ensuring one orienting R for each S is suggested by the investigation of Kendler *et al.* (1961), discussed in Chapter 12.

2. We shall assume that the instrumental choice response is to be made to a locus spatially contiguous with the choice stimulus. A

device such as that used by Hively (1962a, b), in which a response is required directly to windows displaying the stimulus figures, would ensure this. (See, for example, the apparatus shown in Fig. 17.2.)

3. We shall assume that the subject whose performance is under analysis has learned to match in the most efficient and economical manner. Probably the best orienting strategy in matching is that in which the sample is looked at first and then one of the two choices. Provided that the subject is set to respond to the relationship of "sameness" between the sample and the choice stimulus, and provided that he perceives the relevant aspects of the stimuli, only one choice stimulus needs to be oriented. If the stimulus oriented is the same as the sample, then the subject will respond to that window. But if it is different, then he will respond to the other window. In the latter case, if a response to a site involves orienting it then, strictly speaking, both choices will be oriented. But the second stimulus need not be analysed unless the subject decides to check to make sure that it is the matching stimulus. Such checking will be logically superfluous in a task in which one of the choice stimuli always matches the sample.

4. It will be assumed that this strategy always involves the subject in orienting the same choice window, say, the one on the left.

MODEL OF MAIN SEQUENCE OF EVENTS IN MATCHING

Figure 14.1a shows diagrammatically the display panel as it appears to the subject. (See also Fig. 5.1.)

TW	Top window
BWL	Bottom window on left
BWR	Bottom window on right
Sa	Sample stimulus presented in TW
C1	Choice stimulus presented in BWL
C2	Choice stimulus presented in BWR

Figure 14.1b shows a diagrammatic representation of the sequence of events that are assumed to take place during the sort of matching performance just described. This model takes the two orienting responses, ro(TW) and ro(BWL), as given. The events leading up to these responses will be shown in Fig. 14.2. The events are assumed to occur in time from left to right. The boxes refer to *operations*, and the lines between the boxes to *information* passing as output from one

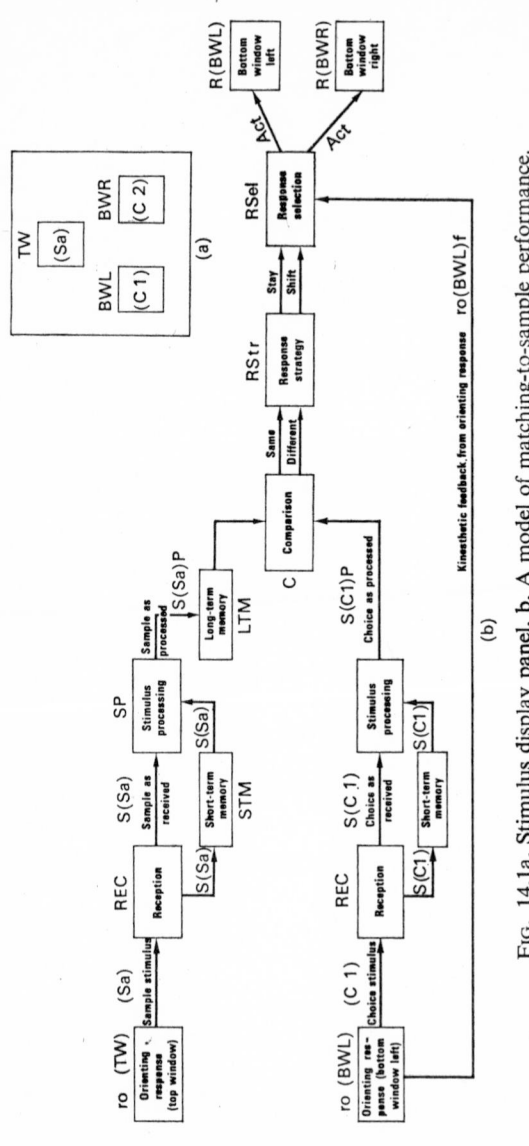

Fig. 14.1a. Stimulus display panel. b. A model of matching-to-sample performance.

operation to another operation as input. The arrows indicate the direction of influence. The following abbreviations are used in the description of the model.

ro(TW)	Orienting response to TW
ro(BWL)	Orienting response to BWL
Sa	Sample stimulus
Cl	Choice stimulus in BWL
REC	Reception unit (retina)
S(Sa)	Sa as received
S(Cl)	Cl as received
SP	Stimulus processing unit
STM	Short-term memory unit
S(Sa)P	Sa as processed
S(Cl)P	Cl as processed
LTM	Long-term memory unit
C	Comparison unit
Same	Output from C
Different	Output from C
RStr	Response strategy unit
Stay	Output from RStr
Shift	Output from RStr
ro(BWL)f	Feedback from ro(BWL)
RSel	Response selection unit
Act	Activation of responses by RSel
R(BWL)	Overt response to BWL
R(BWR)	Overt response to BWR

The *first orienting response* is made to the top window of the display panel—ro(TW). This response corresponds to Spence's receptor-orienting activity and to Wyckoff's observing response. It serves to expose the organism's receptors to the appropriate stimulus —in this case—Sa. Later, we shall consider the sequence of events leading up to this response (see Fig. 14.2). This is the orienting response which, we have seen, Weinstein and Ferster (Chapter 13) were at pains to establish. For the present we shall assume that the subject whose performance is under analysis has learned to make this response.

In the model, the *sample stimulus as received*—S(Sa)—is transmitted to the *stimulus processing operation* (SP). This corresponds to the

perceptual analysis unit in the basic model outlined in Chapter 1. As we have seen, its function is partly *selective* and partly *organizational*; but these operations are difficult to separate in practice. In most of the models we have looked at selection and organization are dealt with as a single operation. This is partly the result of the concentration on explaining learning in relatively simple discrimination situations. When complex stimuli are employed, or when the discrimination itself is difficult, then organizational factors come to the fore, and the distinction is more clear-cut. The remaining chapters of this book will be chiefly concerned with the organizational processes involved in the discrimination of differently orientated forms. Here we shall concentrate upon the selective part of the operation.

The post-reception selective operation (SP) corresponds to the dimension-orienting response of Goodwin and Lawrence (Chapter 3), the attention mechanisms of Zeaman and House (Chapter 4) and White (Chapter 5), the intensification of sensation process of Zaporozhets (Chapter 6), the sampling response of Polidora and Fletcher (Chapter 7) and the stimulus analysis process of Sutherland and Mackintosh (Chapter 8). The mediating response models of Lawrence (Chapter 8) and the Kendlers (Chapter 12) are a little more difficult to fit into our stimulus processing unit.

Recent papers by Mackintosh (1965c) and Kendler and Kendler (1966) have drawn a sharp distinction between the *selective attention* models and the *mediating response* formula. As was shown in Chapter 12, the Kendlers proposed a two-stage discrimination model of the form S–r–s–R, in which the observables (S and R) were mediated by an implicit response (r) and an implicit cue (s). Mackintosh (1965c) argued that this type of model was too vague about the nature of the mechanisms involved and proposed instead the selection model which has been described in Chapter 8. According to Kendler and Kendler (1966) the Mackintosh model can be described either as $S_1-R_1 \rightarrow S_2-R_2$, or as S–s–R. In the first, . . . "The subject orients (R_1) his receptors to a certain portion of the environment (S_1) and, as a result, his receptors are presumably exposed to a component (s_2) of the previous stimulus pattern (S_1)." [*Op. cit.*, pp. 283–4.] In the other, . . . "the physically defined stimulus pattern (S) confronting the organism is filtered and organized to produce an effective stimulus (s) which is directly connected to the response". [*Op. cit.*, p. 284.]

One of the criticisms of the Mackintosh model made by Kendler and Kendler is that it fails to distinguish sharply between these two mechanisms. As we have seen (Chapter 8), this is largely true, for the orienting response is passed over. *The present model* makes up this deficiency by postulating both orienting and selective operations. In the Kendlers' symbolism this would be represented as $S_1-R_1 \rightarrow S_2-s_2-R_2$. Thus, an aspect of the environment (S_1) elicits an orienting response (R_1) which exposes the receptors to a component stimulus (S_2). From this is selected and organized an effective stimulus (s_2). Where the present model differs from the above formulation is that the effective stimulus is not assumed to be associated directly with the final response (R_2).

From this discussion it appears that the present model is closer to the selective attention formulations than it is to the Kendlers' mediating response theory. But the two are not necessarily opposed. For example, in a Hebbian framework, one may visualize the physical stimulus eliciting a mediating process which is supported by other ongoing attentional processes and transformed to some extent by the way the nervous system is programmed. In this conception internalized speech, muscular, and other activities do not, strictly speaking, mediate between S and R, but only *support, guide and help to organize* the basic impulse produced by the physical stimulus. To what extent they can achieve this is clearly related to the developmental level of the organism.

To return to the model in Fig. 14.1 it will be noticed that a *short-term memory* unit (STM) as well as a *long-term memory* unit (LTM) has been included. The distinction made by Broadbent (1958) between these processes is maintained. The STM stores only "raw", unprocessed, data, and only for a relatively short length of time. The LTM stores only processed information and for a longer length of time. Processing is assumed to have the same effect of lengthening the operational life of information as rehearsal (Brown, 1955). (See also Spiker, 1956, and Chapter 9.)

As shown in Fig. 14.1, the SP and the STM units simultaneously receive the stimulus input. This means that in the event of the processing going wrong after the original physical source has been cut off, the raw stimulus is not lost and may be reprocessed from the STM.

From the SP unit the *sample stimulus as processed*, S(Sa)P, passes into the LTM unit for storage. This storage is needed to maintain the

S(Sa)P after the original source, the physical stimulus displayed in the TW, has been cut off by the switch in the orienting response from TW to BWL.

The *second orienting response* is assumed to be made to the bottom window on the left—ro(BWL). This ensures that the choice stimulus (C1) displayed in BWL is received by the subject. The *stimulus as received*, S(C1), provides the input for the SP unit.

The next two units correspond to the *judgement* operation in the basic model of discrimination outlined in Chapter 1. They have no strict counterpart in any of the other models previously discussed. In the main, these latter formulations were concerned to propose mechanisms for the reception and analysis of the sensory input; the product of the analysis, the "effective stimulus", was assumed to be directly connected to the final, instrumental, response. In the present model this link is mediated by a judgemental process involving at least two separate operations. The first of these *compares* the effective stimuli for similarity and for differences. The other is concerned with the *strategy* adopted by the organism in the task, and underlies the hypothesis behaviour which characterizes many discrimination performances.

To return to the description of the model shown in Fig. 14.1, we can see that both the choice stimulus as processed, S(C1)P, and the sample stimulus as processed, S(Sa)P, which has been temporarily stored in the long-term memory unit, pass simultaneously into the *comparison unit*, (C). It is assumed in the model that the C unit must receive its inputs to be compared at the same time. It has two outputs which have been labelled "same" and "different". Its judgement is, of course, dependent upon the effectiveness of the preceding analysis. If the choice stimulus C1 does match Sa in the relevant aspect analysed by the SP unit, then the output "same" will be produced by the C unit. If the two stimuli are not identical in this respect, then the output "different" will be generated.

The output from the Comparison Unit provides the input for the *response strategy unit* (RStr). In the task under analysis, the outputs from RStr indicate whether the final response is to be made to the same locus as the orienting response ("stay") or elsewhere ("shift"). From this it is clear that there are two possible hypotheses based upon the comparison of the sample and choice stimuli. In one case, the strategies would be same → stay and different → shift, which would give us matching to sample. In the other, the strategies would

be same → shift and different → stay, which would produce oddity responding. In order to explain discrimination learning, one would need to make the extra assumption that the choice of strategies by the RStr unit was sensitive to the differential reinforcing effects of the outcomes of the final response.

In order to account for hypotheses based upon the *positions* occupied by the stimuli rather than upon the discriminative features of the stimuli, it is necessary to assume that the outputs of the RStr unit also indicate whether the instrumental response is to be made to the same position as the preceding response ("same"), or to another locus ("different"). Then, *position habits*, such as perseveration and alternation, could be represented as the effects of set within the RStr unit. Such position habits would appear to be accompanied by the blocking of the relevant sensory input, either by inappropriate orienting, or by selective attention. Under these conditions the RStr unit presumably functions autonomously.

To explain the *outcome position hypotheses* we may assume that the RStr unit receives information about outcomes. Thus, in the win–stay, lose–shift hypothesis the unit would respond to a successful outcome with "stay" (i.e. stay with the same position as responded to on the preceding item) and to an unsuccessful one with "shift". For a discussion of hypothesis behaviour and its role in discrimination performance the reader is referred to the Appendix of this book.

It may be noted in passing that the response strategy unit is a likely candidate for the judgemental operation that we have seen from Chapter 1 is influenced by expectations and motives; and it may be responsible for the motor selectivity aspect of the process of set (Hebb, 1966, p. 95).

The output from the RStr unit provides the input for the *response selection unit* (RSel). This is the unit that actually selects the overt responses. A decision has to be made by this unit on the basis of two inputs. On the one hand, it receives an instruction from the RStr unit, either to respond to the same window as oriented, or to shift to the other one. But, in order to carry out this instruction, the RSel unit must have information concerning the window oriented. This it receives in the form of *feedback* (kinesthetic)—ro(BWL)f—from the orienting response. If the instruction is "Stay" then the overt response is activated (Act) to the same window as oriented—R(BWL). If the instruction is "Shift" then the response activated will be to the window other than the one oriented—R(BWR).

MODEL OF EVENTS LEADING TO THE ORIENTING RESPONSES

Figures 14.2a and 14.2b show in diagrammatic form the hypothesized sequence of events leading up to the two orienting responses which, it will be remembered, the model presented in Fig. 14.1 took as given.

Figure 14.2a shows the events leading up to ro(TW), which is the first response shown in Fig. 14.1. The following abbreviations are used in addition to those used in the description of Fig. 14.1.

EXP	Exposure of the task situation to the subject
ts	Task situation
S(ts)	Task situation as received
S(tts)P	This task situation as processed
S(pts)P	Previous task situations as processed
TW	Output from RStr
Search	Output from RStr
ro(Search)	Searching, orienting behaviour
Pe	Position of subject's eyes on exposure to ts
Pef	Feedback from Pe

An item begins with the *exposure* (EXP) of the *task situation* (ts) to the subject. We must assume that the performance under analysis is that of a well-trained subject on the first item of a new training session. This exposure is equivalent to the "Ready Signal" in the Kendler model presented in Chapter 12. In fact, if our model is to describe the performance on items within a training session, unless we re-expose the task situation on every item, then we must replace the EXP operation with some sort of ready signal. This exposure of the task situation, or ready signal, will, through learning, come to evoke the appropriate orienting response to the top window. Figure 14.2a tries to show the events mediating this association.

A distinctive feature of the first link in this chain is that *no orienting response* is required to ensure the reception of the ts by the subject. Exposure, *per se*, is sufficient to guarantee reception. Just what this ts is that comes to evoke the appropriate orienting response is not clear. Its exact constituents will vary from one task to another. Only one thing is certain, and that is that the controlling aspects of ts must remain *relatively unchanged* from one item to the next. They are what Lawrence (1963) referred to as ". . . the contextual or unchanging aspects of the task situation . . ." (p. 191), which, he believed, became

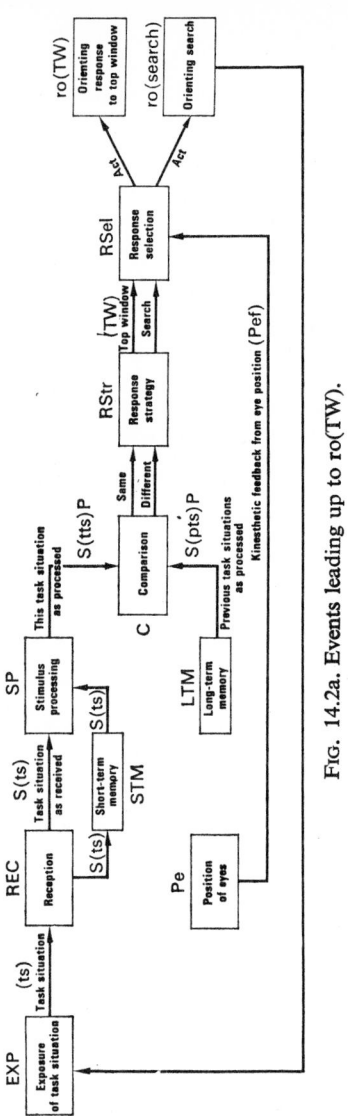

FIG. 14.2a. Events leading up to ro(TW).

directly associated through learning with the appropriate coding response. But, in his model, the overt orienting response appears to be an initial part of the coding response. These operations are not distinguished as they are here (see Chapter 8).

It is assumed that the ts is received (REC), transmitted to the SP unit in the form of S(ts), and processed in the same way as the sample and choice stimuli in Fig. 14.1. The S(ts) as processed passes to the C unit simultaneously with another S(ts) as processed, which has been held in LTM from previous items. The C unit is assumed to compare the two inputs to check, as it were, that *this* task situation as processed, S(tts)P, is the same as *previous* task situations as processed, S(pts)P. This is one way of meeting Lawrence's condition that in order that the same orienting response be evoked on every item, all items must have something in common, some unchanging characteristic which comes to be associated with that response.

The outputs from the C unit, in effect, inform the RStr unit as to whether this task situation is, in fact, the same as the previous task situations, or whether it is different. RStr is assumed to have two outputs. One is the instruction to look at the top window (TW), and the other to look around for the invariant ts ("search"). Through learning the RStr unit comes to respond to the input "same" with "TW" and to the input "different" with "search".

In this case, the RSel unit serves to select the orienting activity to be engaged in. As before it has to make its decision upon the instructions from RStr and the feedback information about the position of the eyes (Pef.) It will either activate (Act) an orienting response to the TW (ro.TW), or a general searching activity (ro. Search).

Figure 14.2b shows the possible sequence of events leading up to the second orienting response—ro(BWL)—shown in Fig. 14.1. The following abbreviations are used in addition to those used in the description of Figs. 14.1 and 14.2a.

S(tSa)P	This sample stimulus as processed
S(pSa)P	Previous sample stimuli as processed
ro(TW)f	Feedback from ro(TW)
ro(BWR)	Orienting response to BWR

From ro(TW) to the output of S(Sa)P from SP the events are as described in Fig. 14.1. But here the output from SP is assumed to pass directly into C, arriving there at the same time as another output

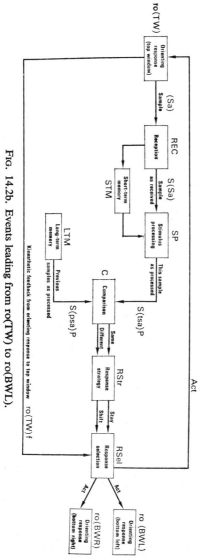

FIG. 14.2b. Events leading from ro(TW) to ro(BWL).

from LTM which has been held over from previous training. The C operation is slightly different here. It is assumed to compare the two inputs to check that *this* sample stimulus (tSa) has been processed so as to yield a similar output to the processing of *previous* sample stimuli (pSa). This operation is not quite the same as that involved in comparing S(tts)P and S(pts)P in the model shown in Fig. 14.2a. For there, there was a direct comparison of a specific stimulus situation as processed with a "generalized" stimulus situation as processed. But here, the comparison is to see whether or not the S(tSa)P fits into the class of S(Sa)P, which is not really a generalization, but a class of all the sorts of outputs produced by the SP unit when faced with S(Sa).

The C unit is again assumed to have two outputs which indicate whether the processing of tSa is of the same type as pSa ("same") or whether it is of a different type ("different"). The problem is to make some sort of distinction between an *appropriate* orienting response, which results in an appropriate analysis of the sample, and an *inappropriate* orienting response, which results in an inappropriate analysis of the sample. If the S(tSa)P is all right then the choices may be oriented. But we want to make sure that ro(TW) stays until we are certain that the sample has been received and processed properly. Otherwise, the sample will have to be re-oriented, which is uneconomical, but which presumably frequently happens in practice. This is indicated by the occasional glances given to the sample after the choices have been oriented (Weinstein, 1945).

The RStr unit has two possible outputs. If the information from C is "different" then the learned strategy will be "stay". This means that the S(tSa)P is not satisfactory and ro(TW) must be maintained. If the input is "same" this gives the go-ahead to RSel to "shift" and to orient one of the lower windows. As before, the RSel unit will make its decision on the basis of the feedback from ro(TW). Though there is a selection from two bottom window orienting responses, we have assumed that the subject has learned to orient BWL.

TEMPORAL RELATIONSHIPS OF THE EVENTS IN MATCHING

Figure 14.3 shows to good advantage the temporal relationships of the events in the chain shown in Figs. 14.1 and 14.2. The figures in the column headed "Time" refer to successive units of time measured

from a point *n* when the task situation is exposed to the subject. In the other columns are shown the relative times of occurrence of the inputs to the various units in the model. The arrows indicate the length of time an event persists. Where there are no arrows the event is assumed to last only 1 unit of time. The holding time of STM of 2 units is arbitrary and is not related to the analysis. We see that

Time	ro	REC	STM	SP	LTM	C	RStr	RSe1	R
						S(pts)P S(pSa)P			
n	Pe	ts							
n+1			S(ts)	S(ts)					
n+2						S(pts)P S(tts)P			
n+3							Same		
n+4								Pef TW	
n+5	TW	Sa							
n+6			S(Sa)	S(Sa)					
n+7					S(Sa)P	S(pSa)P S(tSa)P			
n+8							Same		
n+9								ro(TW)f Shift	
n+10	BWL	C1							
n+11			S(C1)	S(C1)					
n+12						S(Sa)P S(C1)P			
n+13							Same		
n+14								ro(BWL)f Stay	
n+15									BWL

Fig. 14.3. Temporal relationships of events in matching model.

prior to the beginning of the item two pieces of information are held in LTM, which are assumed to persist into and through the item under analysis. Each of the operations, including the transmission of the output to the next unit, is assumed to occupy one unit of time.

Let us now briefly run through the whole sequence of events. At time *n* the task situation (ts) is exposed and simultaneously received (REC) by the subject whose eyes are in a certain position (Pe). The

task situation as received, S(ts), is simultaneously transmitted to the short-term memory unit (STM) and the stimulus processing unit (SP) by time $n + 1$. *This* task situation as processed, S(tts)P, passes into the comparison unit (C) at time $n + 2$, together with the information about the *previous* task situations as processed, S(pts)P, which has been held over in the long-term memory unit (LTM) from previous training. We assume that the output from the C unit is "same", and this provides the input for the response strategy unit (RStr) at time $n + 3$. At time $n + 4$ the response selection unit (RSel) receives two inputs simultaneously, one from RStr to orient the top window (TW), and the other feedback information from the present position of the eyes (Pef).

On the basis of this information RSel activates the orienting-response-to-the-top-window motor unit, ro(TW), which occurs at time $n + 5$, and results in the simultaneous reception of the sample stimulus (Sa). The sample stimulus as received, S(Sa), arrives both at STM and at SP at time $n + 6$. The sample stimulus as processed, S(Sa)P, passes into LTM at $n + 7$. At the same time *this* sample stimulus as processed, S(tSa)P, is transmitted to C simultaneously with information about how *previous* sample stimuli have been processed, S(pSa)P, which has been held over in LTM from previous training. While S(Sa)P is held in LTM, RStr receives "same" as input from C at $n + 8$. At $n + 9$ RSel receives two inputs. From RStr it receives the instruction "shift", and simultaneously it receives feedback information, ro (TW)f, about the present orienting response.

On the basis of this information RSel activates the orienting response to the bottom window on the left, ro(BWL), which occurs at $n + 10$, and results in the simultaneous reception of the choice stimulus displayed in this window (C1). At $n + 11$ the choice stimulus as received, S(C1), arrives both at STM and SP. The choice stimulus as processed, S(C1)P, passes into C at $n + 12$, together with S(Sa)P, which has been held in LTM since $n + 7$. Assuming that C1 matches Sa, the output from the C unit will be "same". This will be received by RStr at $n + 13$. At $n + 14$ RSel receives two inputs. From RStr it receives the instruction "stay" (respond to the same window as that being oriented), and at the same time it receives feedback information, ro(BWL)f about the present orienting response. On the basis of this information RSel activates the overt response to the bottom-window-on-the-left motor unit, R(BWL), which occurs at $n + 15$.

A MODEL OF APPROACH–AVOIDANCE DISCRIMIN-
ATION PERFORMANCE

Let us now see how well the sort of model developed to describe matching-to-sample performance will describe the performance on an approach–avoidance discrimination task. There are two main types of this discrimination task, depending on whether the two discriminative stimuli (Sd's) are presented successively or simultaneously.

1. *Successive Discrimination Performance*

In the successive task one Sd is presented on each trial, and usually a certain time is allowed for the response to occur before the next Sd is presented. The subject's task is to respond only when the positive Sd (Sd+) is present, and not to respond to the negative Sd (Sd−). Only R's to Sd+ are reinforced. There are only two Sd's used. These will be referred to here as Sd1 and Sd2. They are presented in random order from one trial to the next.

Figure 14.4 shows a diagrammatic representation of the possible sequence of operations involved in the performance on a single item of the successive discrimination task. The general scheme of things is much as shown in Figs. 14.1 and 14.2.

We have assumed that no orienting response is required to ensure that the subject receives the Sd presented. As in Spence's (1936) experiments it is assumed that the subject placed in the task situation cannot help receive the Sd. This assumption is not critical for the present account, for if necessary we could easily arrange for the Sd to be exposed by an appropriate orienting response according to the scheme shown in Fig. 14.2a.

So, Fig. 14.4 shows that Sd1 is exposed (EXP) and simultaneously received (REC) by the subject. According to the continuity account of discrimination learning (Chapter 2) there is no need to postulate any mediating event between the reception of the Sd and the final R. But, we have seen that this view is not adequate to explain many of the features of discrimination learning. Though Spence's (1940) receptor-orienting acts could account for the selectivity involved in learning when the relevant and irrelevant cues were spatially separated, it could not explain the selection that occurred when they were *contiguous*. Looking does not entail seeing. Therefore, as we have seen, most of

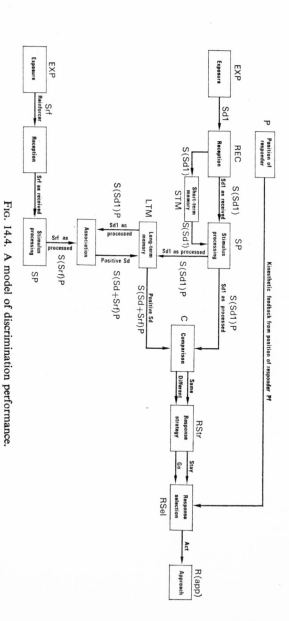

FIG. 14.4. A model of discrimination performance.

the subsequent theories found it necessary to include some sort of implicit, post-reception, perceptual activity. This is represented in the present model by the SP unit.

The Sd1 as received, S(Sd1), passes into the SP unit and the Sd as processed, S(Sd1)P, passes into the C unit at the same time as information from LTM about which is the Sd+. This information indicates which Sd, when responded to in the past, has resulted in reinforcement S(Sd + Srf)P.

Let us consider briefly how this Sd + Srf association may be formed. For the sake of argument assume that Sd1 is Sd+. So, an approach response to it, R(app), will result in the exposure (EXP) of the reinforcing conditions (Srf), which, we assume, is enough to ensure their reception (REC) by the subject. (In practice some sort of orienting response might be needed to guarantee the reception of Srf.) The S(Srf) is processed in SP and the results, S(Srf)P, pass to an association unit (A). This unit also receives S(Sd1)P from LTM which it associates with S(Srf)P to produce S(Sd + Srf)P, which passes to the LTM unit for storage. The S(Sd1)P is assumed to be held in LTM so as to ensure that it arrives at unit A at the same time as S(Srf)P for association.

The C unit compares S(Sd1)P with S(Sd + Srf)P and informs the RStr unit as to whether they are the same or different. If they are the same, which we have assumed they are, RStr will instruct the RSel unit to "go". If, on the other hand, the C unit decided that the Sd processed is not the same as the Sd that has been associated with reinforcement in the past, then the RStr unit will instruct RSel to "stay". If the instruction is "go", then the RSel unit, in conjunction with the feedback information (Pf) about the present position (P) of the subject, will activate (Act) the approach-response motor unit. If the instruction is "stay", then it will activate nothing.

The development of this model of discrimination performance has indicated an omission in the model of matching shown in Figs. 14.1 and 14.2. This is that no provision was made for the effects of differential reinforcement. A chain similar to the one shown in Fig. 14.4 would have to be incorporated. Since the response required in the matching task is to a stimulus relation the effect of the feedback from reinforcement would probably be on the RStr unit. For it is the RStr unit that would subserve a switch from matching to oddity responding.

2. *Simultaneous Discrimination Performance*

In the simultaneous task the two Sd's are presented together on every trial, and the subject is required to make a response to Sd+. Only R's to Sd+ are reinforced. The position of Sd+ is varied from one trial to the next.

The model describing the performance on the simultaneous task will have much in common with that describing the successive discrimination performance. The main difference is that an orienting response will be needed to expose each of the Sd's. But once acquired this orienting behaviour should be very useful in activating first one Sd chain and then the other in quick succession, thus greatly reducing the burden on the memory unit. This should be particularly valuable in cases where the discrimination required was a fine one. For the inevitable distortion of "noise" introduced by the storage system would be at a minimum, thus reducing the risk of a confusion in the C unit between the inputs from the two Sd's as processed. The expectation here is that the more difficult the discrimination the greater will be the efficiency of the simultaneous procedure compared with the successive procedure.

We would also expect the learning curve on the successive task to suggest *continuous* learning more so than on the simultaneous task. For in the latter there is a much greater opportunity for the subject to utilize heuristic orienting skills to facilitate performance. On the other hand, in the successive task there is more pressure put on the storage systems, which, we might assume, tend to operate much more in line with the continuity principle.

In developing the present models we have assumed a *spatial contiguity* between the position of the stimulus and the locus of the response. In Chapter 7 we saw how separating S and R could have disturbing effects on the discrimination performance. In terms of the present model this disturbance is the result of a conflict between S and R positions as receivers of orienting responses. If special emphasis is given to the response part of the task, for example, through motor pretraining or instructions to respond rather than to discriminate (see discussion of Hively's instructions in Chapter 10), then we might expect task strategies based upon the motor part of the task (such as position habits) rather than upon the characteristics of the Sd's. Therefore, in situations where S and R are spatially discontiguous we might expect that unless special attention is paid to establishing

the appropriate orienting activity, then the subject will probably not learn to discriminate; for the necessary chain of events has lost its first element. The double-responding technique (Chapter 7) is one way of ensuring that the appropriate orienting response is made. Such an operation would need to be included in the present model if we are to account for the S–R spatial discontiguity effect.

To account for position habits in situations where S and R are contiguous, we would have to assume that the selection of the position cues occurs at the SP unit. It seems more likely that a separate chain of behaviour is activated which results in position-guided responding, of the sort suggested by Kendler and Kendler (1962).

DIFFERENTIAL CONTROL OVER POSTULATED OPERATIONS IN MATCHING MODEL

So far in this chapter our primary concern has been to develop a model of matching and discrimination performance. Let us now see how this model can help us to control matching in young children.

The model implies that in order for a matching or a discrimination task to be acquired a number of operations have to be made and properly synchronized. We have seen that *differential reinforcement of the final response* is not by itself an efficient way of establishing matching (Chapter 13). This form of training tends to emphasize the motor aspects of the task which will, under certain conditions, lead to position-guided hypotheses. As Skinner (1953) has emphasized, in reinforcing the goal response, we are ignoring the essential continuity of behaviour; and the necessary orienting-preparatory activity will receive little reinforcement.

One way of exercising some differential control over these operations with human subjects would be by means of *verbal communication*. We have seen from Chapter 11 in particular that there may be some difficulty associated with the establishment of a complete plan of the activity required merely by means of pre-task instructions using very young children. However, as has been demonstrated, one way round this problem is to break the instructions down into a number of simple and categorical imperatives to be synchronized with the appropriate event in the task. The actual form and sequence

of these instructions will be very largely guided by the model of matching developed in this present chapter.

Let us briefly run through the instructions that were suggested to control the different operations. To evoke the appropriate orienting response we may prompt the child to look at the sample and both the choices before responding. We may also be able to exercise some control over the processing operation by encouraging the child to look very carefully at the stimulus patterns and possibly by drawing his attention to the relevant features (e.g. the orientation). Some control may be exercised over the memory unit, particularly in a delayed-matching task (Ferster, 1960), or in a successive discrimination task, by instructing the child to make sure that he remembers the stimuli. With respect to the comparison operation we may instruct the child to look at both the stimuli and to compare them to see whether they are the same or different. The response strategy operation may be prompted by instructing the child always to choose the stimulus which is the same as the sample and to ignore the other one. The response selection unit is perhaps the most difficult to influence verbally, and in most tasks a demonstration plus a little practice is usually all that is required to set it up.

As we have seen in a number of the preceding chapters, the orienting operation can be efficiently controlled either by *attracting it* with a novel or intense stimulus (Berlyne, 1960) or, better still, by *guiding it* by means of an overt pointing response, which can then be gradually faded.

A number of possible techniques of controlling the processing operation have been suggested, and these will be elaborated in later chapters. These come under the general heading of "perceptual training" techniques. Whether in fact they can be said to promote *perceptual learning* is a point that will be taken up later. Here we may note that the conventional distinction, between so-called "true" learning and the temporary raising of the level of performance on experimental tasks, is not an absolute one. The problem is that the contingencies present in the experimental situation are not present in the outside world with the inevitable result that the level of performance established in the experiment is not maintained when the subject goes back into the actual world. Clearly, the only permanent changes that can be made, at least in subjects who do not spend their whole life in an experimentally controlled environment, are those which are produced and maintained by the contingencies of the

natural environment. But the experimentally controlled changes are no less "real" because they are not permanent. What an experimentalist is interested in is not so much how subjects do in fact behave in the world as it is, but how they would behave were the world very different from what it is.

CHAPTER 15

THE PERCEPTUAL PROCESS

IN THE remaining chapters of this book we shall be mainly concerned to look into the perceptual process that is involved in making a visual discrimination. So far, we have tended to treat perception, in the guise of the stimulus processing unit, as a "black box". We have noted the input and indicated the likely output in a successful discrimination. We have also noted that the operation seems to have two parts which function very much in unison: attention and organization. Now we shall attempt to throw some light upon the actual mechanism involved, with reference to a particular type of discrimination. We shall be studying what is involved in the rather puzzling and, for many organisms, very difficult discrimination—*the discrimination of differently orientated forms.* It is puzzling because it is a discriminatory skill which seems to lag behind the development of visual shape perception in general. It is, however, a skill of some importance, particularly for humans, since it is absolutely necessary for adequate performance on certain socially essential tasks, such as, reading and writing. Hence, the choice of this skill for special attention was not arbitrary; and our findings should not merely be of academic interest, though it is to be hoped that our investigation will reveal and confirm certain features of visual perception in general, and of shape perception in particular.

As in our analysis of the discrimination process in the preceding chapters, the present investigation will be guided, in the main, by *three questions.* First, what is involved in the successful discrimination of figures differing only in the spatial orientation of a common form? Second, what is the cause of failures to make this type of discrimination? What is the organism doing wrong or failing to do which leads to this error? Third, what can be done in terms of training to improve this discrimination?

DEFINITION OF ORIENTATION

Let us now attempt to define orientation in this context.

Two two-dimensional figures that are identical in form will differ from each other in *spatial orientation* if one can be produced from the other, either by *rotating* the latter about an axis at right-angles to the frontal plane, or by *reversing* it through the third dimension.

The distinction made by Bingham (1914) between form and shape is maintained in this definition. The *form* of a figure is defined in terms of the internal spatial relationships of its parts. The *shape* of a figure is defined in terms of the relationship of the figure with its context. Therefore, though the form of a figure survives changes in the orientation and size of the figure its shape does not. Though a square and a triangle differ in form and shape, an upright and an inverted triangle differ only in shape.

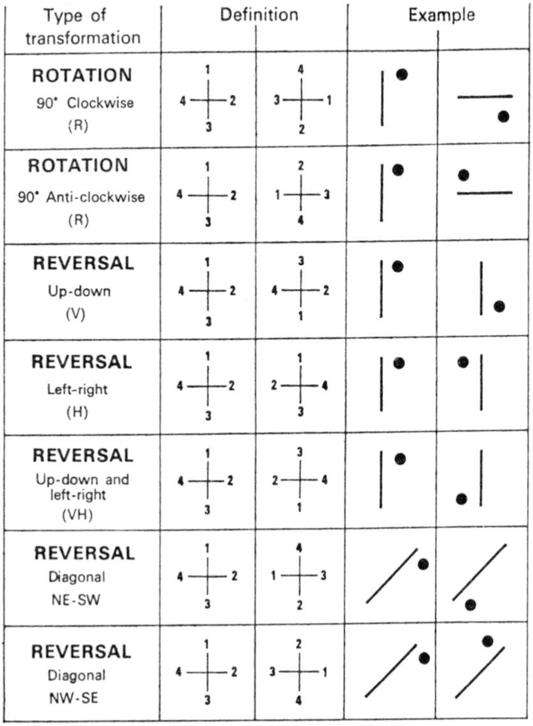

Type of transformation	Definition		Example	
ROTATION 90° Clockwise (R)	1 / 4 —|— 2 / 3	4 / 3 —|— 1 / 2		
ROTATION 90° Anti-clockwise (R)	1 / 4 —|— 2 / 3	2 / 1 —|— 3 / 4		
REVERSAL Up-down (V)	1 / 4 —|— 2 / 3	3 / 4 —|— 2 / 1		
REVERSAL Left-right (H)	1 / 4 —|— 2 / 3	1 / 2 —|— 4 / 3		
REVERSAL Up-down and left-right (VH)	1 / 4 —|— 2 / 3	3 / 2 —|— 4 / 1		
REVERSAL Diagonal NE-SW	1 / 4 —|— 2 / 3	4 / 1 —|— 3 / 2		
REVERSAL Diagonal NW-SE	1 / 4 —|— 2 / 3	2 / 3 —|— 1 / 4		

Fig. 15.1. Definition of orientation.

Sutherland (1961a, p. 32) defines orientation solely in terms of rotation. The present definition extends its denotation to reversals.

Figure 15.1 shows the main types of orientational differences between forms defined in terms of transformations in axes. Under "Example" are shown the standard and appropriate transformation of some of the stimulus figures that were used in the author's experiments discussed in Chapter 5.

The orientation of a figure can be changed either by a rotational or a reversal transformation. A rotation may be either clockwise or anti-clockwise. Only 90° rotations are shown in the figure, though the rotation of a figure may be of any degree.

There are four main types of reversal:

1. *Up–down inversion.* In this there is a shift along the vertical axis (V).

2. *Left–right reversal.* Here there is a shift along the horizontal axis (H).

3. *Up–down inversion and left–right reversal.* Here there is a shift along both vertical and horizontal axes (VH). Such a transformation is the same as a 180° rotation.

4. *Diagonal reversal.* Here the shift may be either along the NE.–SW. diagonal or along the NW.–SE. diagonal.

The letters in brackets will be used to refer to each type of transformation in the following chapters. The letter R will stand for any rotation irrespective of direction.

CHAPTER 16

PERCEPTION OF ORIENTATION BY CHILDREN

In this chapter the principle findings with respect to the perception of the orientation of visual forms by young children will be reviewed. What, first, are the established *facts* with respect to this skill? Vernon (1957) summarizing the evidence writes:

> On one characteristic of the child's perception there seems to be general agreement: that he does not observe, or only observes and remembers with difficulty, the orientation of shapes. . . . [p. 16.]

ERRORS OF REVERSAL IN READING

A major source of evidence for this conclusion is the sort of mistakes a young child makes when he is learning to read; for in reading the child is faced, probably for the first time, with the problem of responding differentially to line figures which differ only in their orientation. These line figures are predominantly the *lower-case letters* of the alphabet.

The following table shows those pairs of lower-case letters, the members of which are similar, if not identical, in form; the main difference between them being in the orientation of the form. The table also shows the type of transformation required to produce one of the pair from the other in terms of the classification system outlined in the preceding chapter.

Lower-case letters	b p	d q	b d	p q	b q	d p	n u	m w	s z	c u
Transformation	V	V	H	H	VH	VH	V/VH	V/VH	H	R

An analysis of the errors made by children when they are learning to read reveals that the letters in these pairs are frequently confused

with each other. For example, the word *bad* in the text may be read as *dad* or *dab* or *dap*, the word *sam* as *saw* and *house* as *honse*. Such errors have attracted a good deal of attention over the years as indicating a possible factor in the aetiology of dyslexia (e.g. Orton, 1925, 1929, 1937). The ideas relating to this will be discussed in Chapter 18.

According to Monroe (1928) and Schonell (1942) errors caused by the confusion of reversible letters (*errors of reversal*) tend to persist in the reading of normal children up to the age of 9 or 10 years, and much later in backward readers. Such reversal errors are most frequent in the absolute beginner (5-year-old) and gradually fall off with increasing age. Monroe (1928) found that about 12 per cent of all the reading errors made by the 6-year-old were due to reversals. Daniels and Diack (1956) and Malmqvist (1958) make this considerably less, and consequently are somewhat surprised at the attention errors of reversal have received. These differences in opinion may be attributable to differences in the technique of error analysis. Concerning the incidence of reversal errors in reading Johnson (1957) reported that 60 per cent of children entering primary school at 6 years of age were making such errors.

As has already been mentioned, there is a *problem of analysis*. The aim is to assess the extent to which the failure of a young child to discriminate between different orientations of the same visual form manifests itself in errors made in reading. But, of course, reading involves a lot more than differentiating forms in different orientations. Though visual perception is one of the skills demanded by reading it is not the only one. Reading also involves making and differentiating sounds, associating sounds and vocal responses with textual material, responding sequentially to letters, words and sentences and translating all this into appropriate thoughts, feelings, actions, etc. Any one, or any combination, of these operations may go wrong and produce an error. Thus, the mistake of reading *bone* for *done* may be due to the problem of discriminating a *b* from a *d*; but it may also be due to a failure to differentiate the vocal responses that lead to the *b* and *d* sounds, or even a failure to discriminate between these two sounds.

The only reliable way to discover just why a child makes a certain error in reading is to test the child on all the operations required by a correct performance on this bit of text, and see which of them he fails on. A pointer to how such an analysis may be achieved is suggested by the recent study of Kass (1963) in which she uses the

Illinois Test of Psycholinguistic Abilities (McCarthy and Kirk, 1961, 1963) to identify the deficient operations in severe dyslexics (i.e. whether decoding, association or encoding).

We are concerned with what the ITPA calls the *visual decoding* operation, or, in other words, visual perception. Clearly, the most direct way to find out whether a child in reading is having any problem discriminating between the reversible letters is to test him directly on these letters to see whether he can discriminate them. The problem is how do we test him?

TESTING A CHILD'S PERCEPTUAL CAPACITY

In testing any perceptual skill it is inevitable that the final performance will be contaminated to some extent by task variables. Reading, clearly, is not a very good way of testing a child's powers of visual discrimination, for, as we have seen, there are a great many other *non-visual skills* involved in reading which will influence the final performance. Many of these non-visual skills can be easily eliminated in a testing procedure in which one letter at a time is presented to the child, who is then required to name the letter or to make the appropriate vocal sound that the letter stands for. However, the following quotation from Vernon (1957) suggests that this too will not be a very good test.

> If the child is given time to perceive the letters carefully he can differentiate them with fair accuracy by the age of 6–7 years. The real difficulty lies in remembering which of the reversible letter shapes corresponds to which sound; and this difficulty persists up to 7–8 years, even in normal readers. [p. 27.]

According to this, therefore, there is a definite instability about the reversible letter—vocal response association up to the age of 8 years. Hence, any errors in our naming test might be attributable to this faulty connection, rather than to any inability actually to discriminate the letter shapes. Similarly, it is often reported (e.g. Hebb, 1949, p. 118) that though a young child certainly "knows" his two hands are different, that one is his left and the other his right, he is very uncertain as to which is which. The problem is an associational or conceptual one, and not perceptual.

We must, it seems, look for an alternative to the naming test. It is obvious that to assess the decoding operations that we are interested in, we must stabilize and be certain of the encoding operation, the

results of which are what we observe. As is clear from the model developed in Chapter 14, there is no direct route from the stimulus processing unit to the final response. It may be meaningful, logically speaking, to say that a child is able to discriminate two differently oriented figures and yet is not able to indicate by an observable activity that he can do this; but, operationally, it is not meaningful.

The fact that a large variety of techniques has been used to assess the discriminative capacities of children (Gibson and Olum, 1960) contributes to the great variety of opinions about these capacities. By far the most popular technique has been *matching-to-sample*. But, as will be clear from a casual glance at the various postulated operations involved in matching shown in Figs. 14.1 and 14.2, this is certainly not a technique which we can be sure will be free from all non-perceptual influences.

MATCHING REVERSIBLE LETTERS

Smith (1928) administered a matching task to 120 6-year-old children using the lower-case letters as samples and choices. Her findings are shown in Fig. 16.1. This figure shows the percentage of incorrect choices made by the children on each sample letter. We see that the reversible letters *b*, *d*, *p* and *q* produced more errors than any other letter. Unfortunately, Smith did not report which letters were in fact incorrectly chosen as matches, though we would suspect that the reversibles were confused with one another.

Hill (1936) reported that the discrimination of isolated letters in matching was very accurate with the exception of the reversibles. But the first step towards an analysis of reversal errors was made by Davidson (1931, 1934, 1935). She found that whereas errors of inversion (V and VH types) were eliminated around MA 6, reversal errors (H types) tended to persist up to MA $7\frac{1}{2}$ on matching tasks. The greater difficulty of H-type discriminations with letters was confirmed by Frank (1935), Wilson and Fleming (1938) and Vernon (1957). The latter reports the she has found that H-type errors occur in 12 per cent of children aged 7–8 years (p. 27).

These findings were confirmed in an experiment conducted by the author into the ability of young normal non-readers and older backward readers in matching the lower-case letters of the alphabet. By far the largest number of errors were caused by the confusion of the letters *b* and *d*, and the letters *p* and *q*. These it will be recalled

are what we term H-type or left–right reversals. Other types of orientation errors occurred no more frequently than certain errors of detail (e.g. *i* and *l*, *i* and *j*, and *h* and *n*). The fact that the distribution of

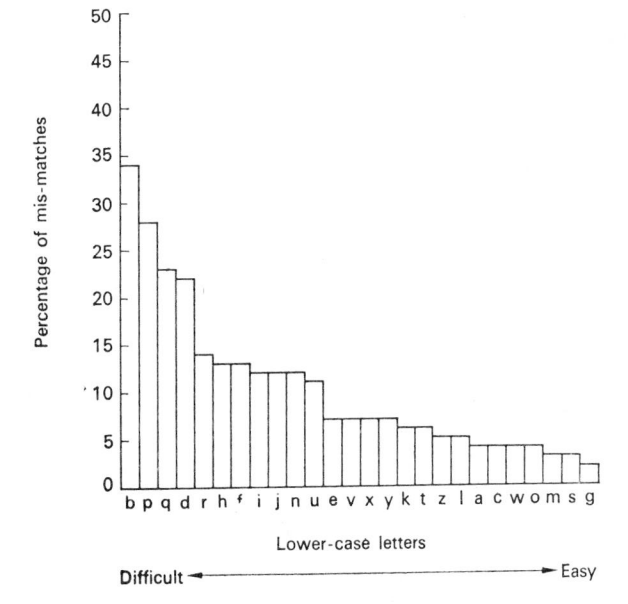

FIG. 16.1. Relative difficulty of matching lower-case letters (based on Smith, 1928).

errors among the various categories of confusion was similar for both groups of children suggests that defective development of visual discrimination skills is a factor retarding progress in reading (Fellows, 1965).

EFFECT OF INSTRUCTION ON REVERSIBLE LETTER DISCRIMINATION

Following this experiment a few preliminary and informal attempts were made to assess the sensitivity of the discrimination of the reversible letters to instruction in the younger children. For example, some children were asked to name each letter as it appeared. If the child hesitated he was prompted, and if he made a mistake he was corrected. This sort of *labelling* pretraining has been advocated by

Spiker (1956, 1963) as having transfer value for the subsequent acquisition of other non-verbal responses to the stimuli. But as was emphasized in Chapter 4, the value of this method depends upon the ability of the individual to attach the labels in the first place. Despite a fairly long training session little progress was made in getting the children in this experiment to name the reversible letters correctly. Jeffrey (1958a) also reports difficulty in training young children to to attach differential verbal labels to differently orientated figures (see Chapter 17).

Another technique tried was to draw the child's attention to the *differentiating features* of the letters. Following Monroe and Backus (1937) the child was first asked to point to the "hump" and to the "tail" of the letters *b*, *d*, *p* and *q*. Since all the letters had humps and tails the next problem was get the child to respond differently to each letter. To do this he was instructed to point in the same direction, first, as the hump, and, then, as the tail. This was not easy to establish and the children made many errors. As an alternative the child was asked to say which way the hump and the tail were pointing in sample letters. But this usually produced responses, such as, "that way" or "this way", which had no discriminatory value. Attempts to get the child to respond with "up" or "down" and "left" or "right" were also unsuccessful.

In a third method the child was given a wooden stylus and instructed to trace over the letters. This derives from the *kinesthetic tracing technique* advocated as a remedial measure in reading by Fernald (1943). The problem was to fit this perceptual skill, which served to differentiate the letters, into a longer chain of responses as are involved in reading or matching. Some success came from the procedure in which the child was asked to trace the sample letter first and then trace the choices until he found the one which matched. In terms of the model presented in Chapter 14 we might describe our activity here as an attempt to alert the comparison unit to the task of detecting similarities and differences in the outputs from the stimulus processing operation, i.e. from the overt tracing behaviour. The question of training perceptual skills for use in other discriminatory tasks will be looked at in more detail in Chapter 20.

The ultimate objective of this work should be to provide the child with some skill by means of which he would be able to differentiate reversible letters and other reversible figures when he meets up with them. Initially, this behaviour will probably have to be overt. But in

time it should become abbreviated and eventually completely internalized. This process might be assisted by some fading technique as discussed in Chapter 10.

This process of internalization might involve merely abbreviation of an overt activity, or it might involve the transfer of skill from hand to eye. In the latter case the finger-pointing activity supports the eye scanning until the latter is firmly established enough to dispense with the former, which will fade away. An example of this is the support moving the finger along a line of print initially gives to the correct left–right eye-scanning movement.

DISCRIMINATION OF OTHER REVERSIBLE FIGURES

To return to the evidence on the child's perception of orientation in general, Rice (1930), using a multiple-choice matching task, found that the orientation of familiar (e.g. spoon) and abstract (e.g. diamond) plane figures arises quite suddenly as a factor in the performance between the ages of 5 and 6 years. Operationally, this means that after this age, most children will either negatively refuse to recognize "sameness" in two figures differing only in orientation, or positively indicate by some word or action that they would be the same if one or the other were re-orientated.

Newson (1955) administered a matching task to 100 5-year-old children on their entry to primary school and discovered a widespread inability to distinguish an abstract figure from its mirror-image (H-type transformation). She noted that this reversal tendency was also present in copying, but to a lesser extent. As with reading, data obtained from copying is affected by many non-visual factors, notably manual dexterity, which would tend to mask the influence of any perceptual problem.

Newson followed up this preliminary investigation with some controlled experiment work. In it she replaced the matching task with an *oddity* task; a wise move, for as we have seen in Chapter 13, oddity responding is a much less complex cognitive task than matching, and therefore should display any perceptual deficiences more clearly. Each child was required to select from a group of 6 line figures one which was different from the others.

To ensure the child understood the concept of "difference", Newson administered a preliminary oddity task in which the figures differed grossly in form. Only those children performing successfully

on this task were transferred to the main task in which the odd figure differed from the others solely in its orientation. This pre-criterion practice not only serves a selective function, but it also established in the child the appropriate task set or strategy which, it is hoped, will be transferred to the criterion task.

In addition to this task pre-training Newson also attempted to exercise some control over the child's stimulus processing and comparison operations by stressing that differences in the orientation of the figures on the main task "counted as different".

Newson found that errors were considerably more frequent when the odd figure was a left–right (*H-type*) reversal than when it was any other type (V or VH or R). This confirms the other findings referred to above with regard to the differentiation of the reversible letters. But Newson added to this information by observing that certain types of figure are more prone to orientational confusions than others. Figure 16.2a shows those forms which Newson found to be the most difficult for young children to discriminate from their mirror-images. They are in order of decreasing difficulty from left to right. She notes that four of these figures (all except the fourth) have the characteristic of *remaining unchanged in spite of a* 180° *rotation*.

This apparently was a more critical feature than symmetry. Figure 16.2b shows two examples of Newson's figures which were either symmetrical about the horizontal axis, about the vertical axis, or about an oblique axis, or asymmetrical. None of these figures caused as much difficulty as the ones shown in Fig. 16.2a.

Other characteristics which Newson found to have a non-significant effect on the discrimination of a form from its orientational transformations were the ratio of length to breadth, meaningfulness, compactness and the number of details that might act as cues.

Gibson *et al.* (1962) conducted a similar study to that of Newson. They used a multiple-choice matching task to assess the ability of 4–8-year-old children to discriminate between various letter-like forms and their orientational and other transformations. The forms employed were constructed on the basis of an analysis of the capital letters of the alphabet.

The twelve standard figures were presented to the child one at a time, and the child asked to select one from the array of thirteen choices (different transformations of the standard form, but including at least one instance of the standard) which was "exactly like" the standard. To establish the appropriate task set each child was given

preliminary training in matching letters. Gibson *et al.* did not report what standard of performance was required on this pre-criterion task.

They found a steady improvement in performance with increasing age. The most significant improvement was in the errors due to the choice of an *orientational* transformation as a match for the standard.

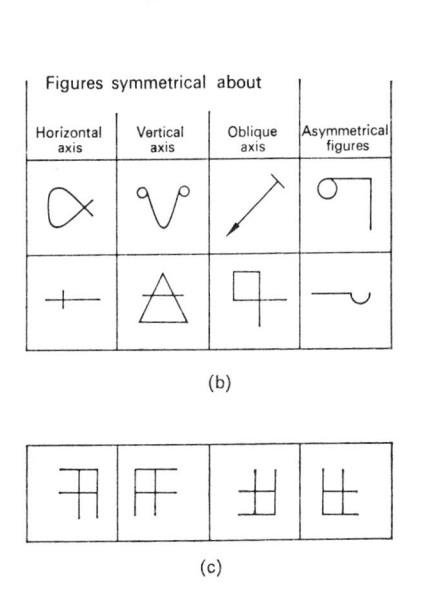

(a)

(b)

(c)

FIG. 16.2a. Most difficult forms to discriminate from their mirror-images (based on Newson, 1955). b. Symmetry of Newson's figures. c. Very difficult forms to discriminate from their mirror-images (based on Krise, 1952).

Such errors fell sharply from 4 to 7 years of age, at which point they were barely significant. It is rather surprising that there appeared to be no significant differences in the rate of errors between the different reversal types.

With regard to the effects of the *absolute* characteristics of a standard form on the ability of the children to pick it out from among

its various transformations, Gibson *et al.* concluded that compared with the effects of transformations they are negligible. Nevertheless, some significant (statistically speaking) effects were detected with regards to the symmetry, the completeness and the proportion of straight to curved lines in the figure. Using Gibson's forms in a two-choice matching task with 5-year-olds the present author found that difficulty in orientation discrimination increased only with the *proportion of curved lines* in the figure (Fellows, 1965).

Also, using the line-spot forms shown in Fig. 15.1, 5-year-olds have been found to make V- and VH-type discriminations significantly easier than H-type.

In addition to the problem of reversals in reading there are two other peculiarities about a child's behaviour which are often said to be manifestations of his inability to perceive differences in the orientation of forms.

MIRROR-WRITING

Firstly, there is mirror-writing. It is a very common observation that children when they are learning to write very often will produce a mirror-image of the appropriate letter or word. That is, this sort of writing will look normal only when viewed through a mirror. The strange thing is that whereas this manner of writing appears to come quite naturally for a young child, it is very difficult for a normal adult to reproduce. The mirror-writing of the child is very likely to be as legible, as correct in detail, as his normal writing. It is as if the child has assimilated the *form* of the letters and words he is writing, but, as yet, is indifferent about their *orientation*.

Preyer (1895) and Stern (1909) were among the earliest to note the frequency of mirror-writing in young children, and their observations have been confirmed by most child researchers ever since. Not only are single letters and words written in reverse but frequently whole sentences (Frank, 1935). Newson (1955) reports that the most common reversals in writing involve the letters *S*, *N* and *e*. The fact that these letters, when reversed, do not produce another letter, indicates that the problem is not merely a matter of confusing one letter with another.

Townsend (1951) reports a similar indifference to the orientation of a figure in the copying behaviour of children. But the tendency to re-orientate figures fell markedly between MA $6\frac{1}{2}$ and MA $7\frac{1}{2}$.

RECOGNITION OF INVERTED PICTURES AND FIGURES

The second peculiarity about a child's behaviour which has often been interpreted in terms of his failure to perceive the difference between differently orientated forms is his apparent indifference to the orientation of a book or a picture he may be looking at. His pleasure and recognition of what he is looking at seem little affected if it is upside-down (Stern, 1926). (However, from observations of his own children the present author feels that this is definitely not the case, even with children as young as 2 years.)

Koffka, in his book *The Growth of Mind* (1924), argues: ". . . to a child form is much more independent of its absolute spatial position than it is to us adults." [p. 313.] Thus, while the ability of an adult to identify a realistic figure which has a definite right-way-up is markedly reduced if it is presented to him in an unusual orientation (Gibson and Robinson, 1935), it is thought that the child is relatively little affected by such a change (Vernon, 1954).

This opinion has also been recently challenged by Ghent (1960). Presenting mono-oriented realistic pictures (e.g. of a boat, a clown, a house, a wagon) tachistoscopically, in each of four orientations to 3- and 4-year-olds, she found that significantly more figures were correctly recognized if they were presented the right-way-up than if they were presented in any other position. However, older children, aged 5–7 years, did behave as expected, recognizing the pictures equally well in any orientation.

But Ghent (1961) is careful to point out that her findings do not necessarily conflict with the work which showed that matching in children is affected by the need to make orientation discriminations. For matching and recognition (naming in Ghent's experiment) involve very different cognitive processes which are sure to interact with the perceptual operations to yield different final performances. The child's failure on the matching tasks Ghent argues may be due to ". . . an inability to make the complex comparison of the relations required for the judgement." [1961, p. 187.] This re-emphasizes the point already made that any discrimination performance involves a variety of different operations, the failure in any one of which may lead to errors in the final observed performance. Therefore, information about perceptual-discriminatory capacities cannot be divorced from the method which yielded it.

That children are sensitive to the orientation of forms is suggested by a further experiment by Ghent (1961) in which she found that 4- and 5-year-olds exhibited consistent preferences for the orientation of non-realistic forms. That is, they unanimously regarded certain figures as being "right" (right-way-up) or "wrong" (upside-down). Ghent's ideas about the explanation of these preferences will be considered in Chapter 20.

Here we may note that all Ghent's work is concerned with the effects of inversion and rotation, whereas, as we have seen, the child's biggest problem involves the discrimination of *reversed* figures (i.e. H-type transformations).

That inversion and reversal transformations do differentially affect a child's recognition is shown by Newhall (1937). He found that a child's *awareness* of these two types of orientation changes was different. If, in a recognition task, a picture, or a figure which the subject had chosen were handed back to the child upside-down, he would tend to invert it and replace it in the choice array the right way up. But, were the picture or figure handed back reversed, the child would rarely replace it in its original orientation.

CHAPTER 17

LEARNING AND THE PERCEPTION
OF ORIENTATION

IN THIS and the following three chapters we shall be considering some of the views that have been expressed as to the *nature of the operation* involved in the perception of the orientation of a form and some of the *variables which affect it.* The objective is to discover just why it is that a young child has trouble in making discriminations based upon orientation, or just what it is that he is doing wrong or failing to do as compared with an older child or an adult. On the more practical side, we shall be on the look-out for changes which can be made in the experimental situation which will enable us to exercise some degree of control over the perceptual operations involved in the discrimination of differently orientated forms. In terms of our model (Chapter 14) we shall be looking for ways to *externalize* the stimulus processing operation so that we can make sure that distinctively different inputs are received by the comparison unit from each of the differently orientated figures.

In the present chapter we shall be considering some views and experimental findings with respect to the sensitivity of a child's perception of orientation to learning or training conditions.

ENVIRONMENTAL LEARNING

The view is very frequently expressed that it is not at all surprising that a child overlooks the orientation of forms, for one of the things he has to learn in early childhood is that objects *retain their identity through changes in the position in space* (Vernon, 1957, p. 16; Gibson *et al.* 1962). This is unquestionably true. A chair is a chair and a spoon a spoon no matter which way round one looks at it. So, it is important for a child to learn that the identity of an object survives changes in its orientation. *But,* it is also important for him to learn that though a chair upside-down is a chair it cannot be sat upon; and that a spoon

which is held upside-down will be no use for eating with. So, a child must learn not only that the identity of an object survives changes in its orientation, but also that such changes are often *operationally significant*. The fact that a child usually does learn both these things clearly indicates that he is not indifferent or insensitive to orientation; for the orientation of an object is an important variable controlling his behaviour.

It may be argued, in defence of the view just attacked, that though the up–down dimension is operationally important the *left–right dimension* is not. Which way the handle of a spoon is pointing makes little difference to the child who has yet to develop lateral preference. However, there are a few examples where a left–right orientation discrimination is required. Putting on shoes involves this sort of discrimination. And the fact that such skills are but slowly acquired does suggest that there is something peculiar about the left–right dimension which makes it intrinsically more difficult to respond to than other dimensions. But, since the opportunity for practice in these different dimensions is unequal this view cannot be established merely by naturalistic observations. What is needed is a controlled experiment in which both skills are given equal amounts of training.

The fact that the child receives more practice in his everyday life in discriminating objects differing in the up–down dimension (V) than differing in the left–right dimension (H) might provide an explanation of why letters and forms differing on the horizontal dimension (H-type) are more difficult to discriminate than those differing on the vertical dimension (V- or VH-type). But, as we shall see, there are other factors contributing to this difference.

DISTINCTIVE FEATURES THEORY

Gibson *et al.* (1962) proposed a distinctive features theory of discrimination. They argued that just as phonemes have distinctive features by means of which we are able to identify and discriminate them (Jakobsen and Halle, 1956), so graphemes also have such features; and the extent to which we are able to discriminate two graphemes will be a function of the *number of different distinctive features* each possesses. The present author found that this theory provided a very reasonable account of the differences in the discriminability of certain lower-case letters (Fellows, 1965), but that it failed to give an adequate explanation of the relative indiscriminability

of the reversible letters. Gibson, however, attempts to explain reversal and other *transformational* confusions in terms of this distinctive features hypothesis. But, as Brown (1963) has pointed out, distinctive features refer only to *absolute* characteristics of figures, such as their symmetry or their completeness. Orientational transformations, on the other hand, involve the relationship between two figures. No figure can be said to be reversed or rotated except by reference to a standard.

However, a defence can be made out for a distinctive features approach to orientational differences. It is not exactly true that the difference between two figures differing solely in orientation cannot be described without reference to both of them. For, as we have seen in the discussion of experiments in Chapter 16, the reversible lower-case letters can be described and differentiated in terms of the positions or the directions in which the "humps" and "tails" are pointing. These, then, can be described as the distinctive features of the reversible letters. They differ from the features describing differences in form in that they refer to the *spatial context* of the figure, and thus assume that the figure is in a definite spatial framework.

The *practical implication* of the distinctive features theory is that it suggests a way in which a child may be trained to discriminate figures. As has been demonstrated (Chapter 16), putting this suggestion into practice is not too easy and demands a considerable degree of control over task contingencies. Gibson is not too optimistic about the value of such training; but it would be wise to suspend judgement until it has been properly tried. The work of Monroe and Backus (1937) definitely suggests that training children to pay attention to the "humps" and "tails" of reversible letters will facilitate their subsequent discrimination.

HEURISTIC SKILLS

A remedial teacher at a local Special School visited by the author advocated the following technique as helping his boys to distinguish *b*'s and *d*'s. He taught the boy that whenever he came across a *b* or a *d* in the text, and he was uncertain about which it was, he should think of a bed. The boy knew that the word *bed* began with the sound *b* and ended with the sound *d*. He also knew what a bed looked like. Now it so happens that the shape of the printed word *bed* resembles the shape of an actual bed, with the *b* representing the headboard and

the pillow and *d* the tailboard. So all the boy had to do to identify a *b* or *d* shape he came across in the text was to imagine a bed, to fit the shape either to the head or the tail and, depending on the result of this, connect the letter up to the beginning or the end sound of the spoken word *bed*.

Of course, it is one thing to train a subject to adopt a *heuristic* discriminatory technique like this, but quite another to get him to make the discrimination *without* this aid. This teacher did not have any special way of achieving this, thinking it best to leave it to the child. There are two dangers in this attitude. Firstly, the child might become *overdependent* on this aid and not be able to do without it. Or, secondly, and in practice far more likely, the child might *abandon it prematurely*, before he is able to do without it. In practice, the first possibility is unlikely, since there appears to be some sort of built-in mechanism which leads to the *spontaneous internalization* of overt heuristic techniques (Piaget and Inhelder, 1956)—a mechanism which appears to work according to Zipf's (1949) principle of least effort. However, such internalization does not always occur. In such cases, some sort of control to ensure the maintenance of the aid and its gradual internalization by means of a fading procedure would be of great value. The problem, of course, is to set up such control. But the fact that something is practically difficult, if not impossible, should not prevent us from asking what if it were the case.

It is clear from casual introspection that a number of our discriminatory skills are based upon internalized, originally overt, heuristic behaviour. An example from the writer's own experience. When I was a young boy, I found a little game extremely useful for identifying my left and right hands. The technique was to engage my two hands in a miniature wrestling match. The one that won, the stronger one, I knew was my right hand. I distinctly remember continuing to engage in this game mentally, as an aid to identification of my hands, long after I had ceased to do it overtly. This is what Miller *et al.* (1960) would call having a plan for hand identification.

KINESTHETIC TRACING TECHNIQUE

Another training technique which has been reported to have been very successful in improving a child's reading and writing and visual perception in general is the kinesthetic-tracing technique which is chiefly associated with the work of Fernald (1943). This simply

involves the child in tracing over the letters or figures to be identified or discriminated. Again, there is the problem of subsequent internalization, or the withdrawal of heuristic support.

The facilitation produced by the tracing method, as the use of the word "kinesthetic" implies, is usually explained in terms of the association of the kinesthetic feedback from the tracing movements with the visual figure, as a stimulus input. This association is said to enhance the *distinctiveness* of the stimuli (Miller, 1948; Dollard and Miller, 1950 (see Chapter 9)). There is another explanation which is suggested by the work on cross-modal transfer from haptic to visual perception (Piaget and Inhelder, 1956; Piaget, 1961; Rudel, 1963) and S–R spatial contiguity (Chapter 7). If it is the case that a child fixates where he points, then tracing a figure with the finger will carry along with it a scanning of its contours by the eyes. After a little practice we would expect some stimulus generalization to occur. Operationally this means that the mere exposure of the figure will tend to produce some scanning of its contours, even in the *absence* of the overt tracing movements. If we see this as an instance of the acquisition of stimulus control over the scanning, then we should, in principle, be able to apply the fading paradigms (Chapter 10) in facilitating the transfer.

EXPERIMENTAL STUDIES OF ORIENTATION LEARNING

As with any performance that shows a steady improvement with age there has been a strong tendency to pronounce the discrimination of orientation as being a function of age or of some maturational mechanism (e.g. Davidson, 1934). Thus, Vernon (1957) concludes that a child's inability to remember the orientation of forms is the "... result of lack of maturation" (p. 27). No doubt there is a lot of truth in this, but it is not very helpful. For the use of a term such as "maturation" implies that the behaviour has been adequately accounted for and that it is a waste of time to look for any environmental variables that may influence it.

Fortunately, such categorical statements have failed to discourage a number of investigators from looking into the possibility of exerting some experimental control over a child's discrimination of orientation with the primary objective of seeing whether anything can be done to improve it. Three such studies will now be discussed, all of which

clearly suggest that orientation perception in children is a skill which is sensitive to the manipulation of task variables and training.

1. *Newson's Directional Training*

Taking them in chronological order we begin with Newson (1955) whose work has already been referred to in Chapter 16. It will be remembered that she reported that young 5-year-olds found it extremely difficult consistently to pick an odd figure from an array of six, if this figure was a mirror-image or *H-type* reversal of the others in the array. She decided to see what the effects of giving the children some special tuition would be.

Newson's main teaching programme involved directional training. The chief objective of this was to arouse in the child a *consciousness of direction* and an efficient left–right discrimination, without necessarily using the words "left" and "right". First, the child was asked to point in the direction in which things in pictures were moving, facing or pointing (e.g. a girl riding a scooter, a policeman pointing, a flag flying). To emphasize the distinction between the child's hands distinctive marks were placed on them. Next, the child was instructed to fit some cut-out figures into a form board. These were so constructed that they would only fit in one orientation. This obviously drew the child's attention to the need to make left–right reversal discriminations, and provided him with some practice on them with immediate feedback. The third game involved placing wire figures on the top of identical drawings so that they fitted. As a transition to the final criterion oddity task the child was allowed to use the wire figures as an aid to identifying the oddly orientated figure. Finally, this aid was removed and the child was back on the oddity task.

This training was spread over 5 days, each child receiving, on average, a total of 20 minutes' training. Newson found that this training programme considerably facilitated the performance of a group of children on the criterion oddity task, as compared with a group of children who received equivalent practice solely on this task. She found that children of 4–$4\frac{1}{2}$ years were performing considerably better after training than 5-year-olds, who had received no training. The effect of training was, however, more significant in a group of 5-year-olds.

Newson concluded from these findings that the existence of an inability to discriminate between different orientations of the same

form was entirely due to the child's *lack of opportunity to practice the necessary constituent skills.* As to what these skills are she writes, "Awareness of directional differences is a prerequisite for mirror-image discrimination" (*op. cit.*, p. 150).

There is one point that needs to be made about Newson's conclusion. What, in fact, she succeeded in doing was to raise the level of performance of children on a fairly specific oddity task involving mirror-image discriminations. What is not known is how permanent and generalizable is the skill thus acquired. What would be very interesting would be to know whether in fact the training given by Newson really did get rid of the child's tendency to confuse reversals, and whether this training had the effect of improving their reading, writing and any other skills dependent upon the efficient discrimination of orientation. But, as has already been emphasized in Chapter 14, the fact that learning in experimental situations is often not permanent and generalizable to other situations does not destroy its significance.

2. *Jeffrey's Perceptual Response*

The second study to be described also shows how a young child's standard of performance on a task requiring the discrimination between differently oriented forms can be raised by means of a training programme. Jeffrey (1958a) reported that 11 out of 14 children aged 3:11 to 4:9 could not learn to respond differentially to two differently oriented stick-figures merely by means of trial and error practice. The two stick-figures, of the sort shown in Fig. 17.1, differed from each other in that one had its left arm raised and the other its right arm. The two figures were presented successively to the child, in a random sequence, and the child was required to respond to the one by calling it "Jack" and the other by calling it "Jill".

Jeffrey found that verbally instructing the child to notice the differences between the figures had no effect on the performance; i.e. the stimulus processing operation involved in the perception of the orientation of figures could not be controlled through verbal instruction. This is probably what we would have expected from the age shift theory of verbal mediation (Chapter 11).

The first step, therefore, in the training programme was to discover some sort of response by means of which the children could differentiate the figures. Jeffrey decided to try two button-pressing responses

to buttons which were located in direct line with the raised arm of each figure. Figure 17.1 shows the set-up as it appeared to the subject. The stimulus card was placed onto the display panel in the position shown. In the example shown the child would be required to press the right-hand button, towards which the stick-figure's arm is pointing. When the other stick-figure was presented a response to the left-hand button would be required.

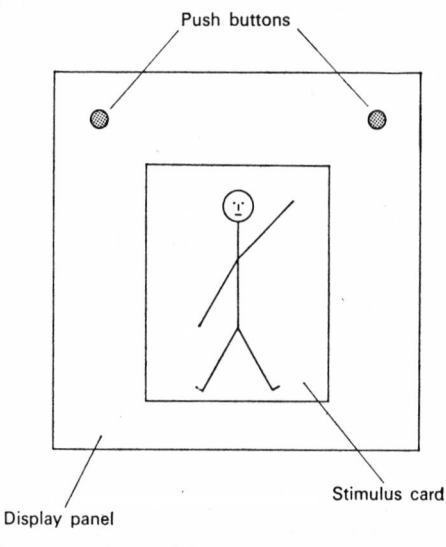

FIG. 17.1. Apparatus for training a perceptual response (based on Jeffrey, 1958a).

Jeffrey found that all fourteen subjects administered with this button-pressing task quickly reached a criterion of ten consecutive correct responses, under differential feedback conditions (music through earphones). He also found that on transfer to the criterion naming task only one child failed to learn to attach the appropriate labels.

Jeffrey's study very clearly demonstrates not only that *differential responses can be made by young children to differently orientated figures*, but also that *practice in making such responses facilitates the acquisition of other discriminatory responses (verbal labels), which previously could not be made*. Obviously, something has been learned in the button-pressing task which transferred to the labelling task. In terms of our model (Chapter 14), this something can be seen as a

stimulus processing operation which serves to generate distinctively different outputs from the differently orientated figures.

The question remains, how did this learning take place? One way of looking at it would be to see the button-pressing R's as overt manifestations of a basic perceptual activity. This would mean that on transfer to the labelling task the child did not completely discard the button-pressing behaviour, but retained an *abbreviated* or *internalized* version of it, which he engaged in when faced with a stick-figure. This activity may have acted so as to make the figures more distinctively different than they would appear merely by looking at them, probably by the addition of distinctive kinesthetic feedback stimulation (Chapter 9).

This interpretation receives some support from Jeffrey's observation that many of the children attempted to retain the button-pressing response, or, at least, a fractional part of it, as an integral part of the criterion task naming skill. He writes,

> In one case, a child who had been told twice to discontinue the button pressing started lifting the appropriate shoulder for each stimulus before applying the labels. Other children would look at the appropriate button before supplying the name of the figure. [1958a, p. 274.]

The Perceptual Response in Matching

Some steps have been taken by the present author with 5-year-old children to insert this type of perceptual response into the chain of responses required by a matching-to-sample task (Fellows, 1965).

Figure 17.2 shows the basic matching apparatus as used in other experiments (see Chapters 5 and 10) together with a new response panel. This panel has four response buttons in the same positions relative to a vertical line as the spots in the four stimulus figures.

The child's first task was to learn to press the appropriate button for each stimulus, i.e. the button matching the position of the spot in the figure. The next problem, which has yet to be successfully overcome, involved *inserting this stimulus analysis response into the matching chain at the right point and without disturbing the continuity of the behaviour.*

Following the model developed in Chapter 14 an attempt was made to establish the following sequence of observable events:

1. Ready signal (EXP of ts).
2. Child presses on the top window (ro. TW).
3. Presentation of sample stimulus (Sa).

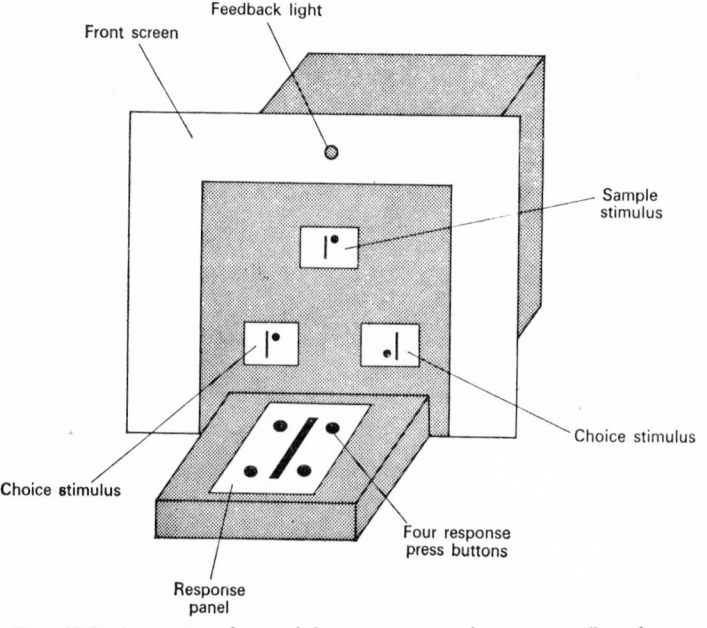

Fig. 17.2. Apparatus for training a perceptual response (based on Fellows, 1965).

4. Child responds to perceptual response panel (SP → S(Sa)P).
5. Presentation of choice stimulus in left-hand window (C1).
6. Child responds to perceptual response panel (SP → S(C1)P).
7. Presentation of choice stimulus in right-hand window (C2).
8. Child makes final choice by pressing on one of the lower windows (R).
9. Feedback stimulus (Srf).

The letters in brackets refer to the corresponding events in the model of matching shown in Figs. 14.1 and 14.2. Strictly speaking, an orienting response must occur to each of the lower windows in order to expose the stimuli C1 and C2. No attempt, however, was made to establish an overt orienting response at this point for it would inevitably tend to interfere with the final choice response. It was also found expedient to cut out the overt sample-orienting response; hence the ready signal led directly onto the presentation of the sample.

As already indicated, work is continuing on the problem of integrating the perceptual response into the chain. The first impressions are that the response would be more effective if it were actually made

to the stimulus rather than to a separate panel. This S–R discontiguity is one major problem (see also Chapter 7). Another is the fact that the overt responses tend to interfere with one another. This is one reason that makes vocal behaviour such a good mediator (see Chapter 11).

3. *Bijou's Stimulus Training Programme*

The third study to be discussed is a little different from the previous two in that the training is given along the *stimulus dimension* instead of along the response dimension. In that the manipulations are made in the discrimination required rather than in the differentiating R, the procedure used in this study has more in common with the transfer of a discrimination along a continuum paradigm than with a stimulus predifferentiation technique (see Chapter 9).

As in the previous two studies, this investigation by Bijou (1962) arose out of a general dissatisfaction with the conventional interpretation of mirror-image discrimination in children in terms of maturation. He sees his investigation as the application of programmed instruction to the study of the development of non-verbal concepts involving rotated geometrical forms with left–right orientational differences.

Figure 17.3 shows the ten stimulus forms employed by Bijou. The

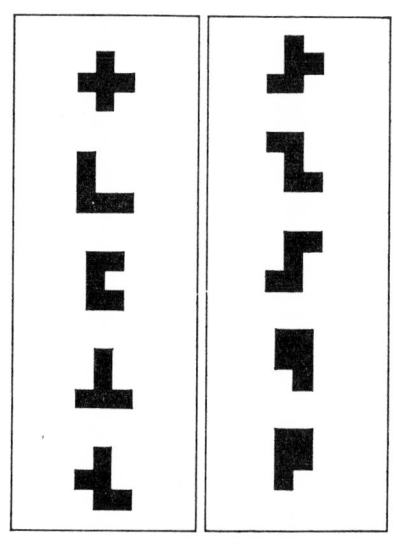

FIG. 17.3. Stimulus figures (based on Bijou, 1962).

task was a multiple-choice matching-to-sample procedure. The 270-item stimulus programme was divided into three sets.

The *Elementary Set* (24 items) was designed chiefly ". . . to ease the youngster into operating the apparatus . . ." and ". . . to instruct the child to engage in the attending behaviour necessary for making the matching response" (*op. cit.*, p. 8).

Figure 17.4a shows a few items from the Elementary Set. The set began with easily distinguishable forms in a three-choice matching task. These easy forms were progressively eliminated from one item to the next and the criterion forms introduced. Item 10 was the last frame in which an easy form was present. The discrimination required throughout this Elementary Set was of form. But as can be seen from Fig. 17.4a the task was made progressively more difficult by the rotation of the correct match, until, by item 24, the sample and the matching choice differed by a 90° rotation. But we must be clear that this does not involve the discrimination of orientation; rather it involves the recognition of a form irrespective of its orientation, that is, responding to the form of a figure not to its orientation.

The *Intermediate Set* (40 items) provided more training in the skill of picking out the correct form irrespective of orientational discrepancies between the sample and the matching choice of up to 180°. The middle and final items of this set are shown in Fig. 17.4b (items 20 and 40).

The *Advanced Set* (206 items) was designed ". . . to train in discriminating between mirror-images and non-mirror-images of three forms, presented in upright positions and then with rotations in the vertical plane". This was achieved by means of the sort of transfer of a discrimination along a continuum or the fading-in of stimulus differences procedure discussed in Chapters 9 and 10. The mirror-image of the sample form was progressively introduced from one item to the next as an incorrect choice. Prior to this all choices differed in form; now they were beginning to get more and more alike in form and differing solely in orientation.

The way this *fade-in of the mirror-image* was achieved is illustrated in items 1–1 to 1–35 shown in Fig. 17.4c. We see that a form, originally quite different from the sample, was progressively transformed so that it became more and more like the form of the sample, but its mirror-image (i.e. H-type reversal). For example, the F-shaped form shown in item 1–1 of Fig. 17.4c was gradually changed until by item 1–29 it was very nearly the mirror-image of the sample. The final

step is shown in item 1–35 where the F-form has now become the H-type reversal of the sample.

There is one feature of this progression which differentiates it from the transfer of a discrimination along a continuum procedure. It is not quite accurate to say that the mirror-image discrimination was faded-in by moving it along an orientation dimension; for what in fact happened was that the form of the figures was progressively

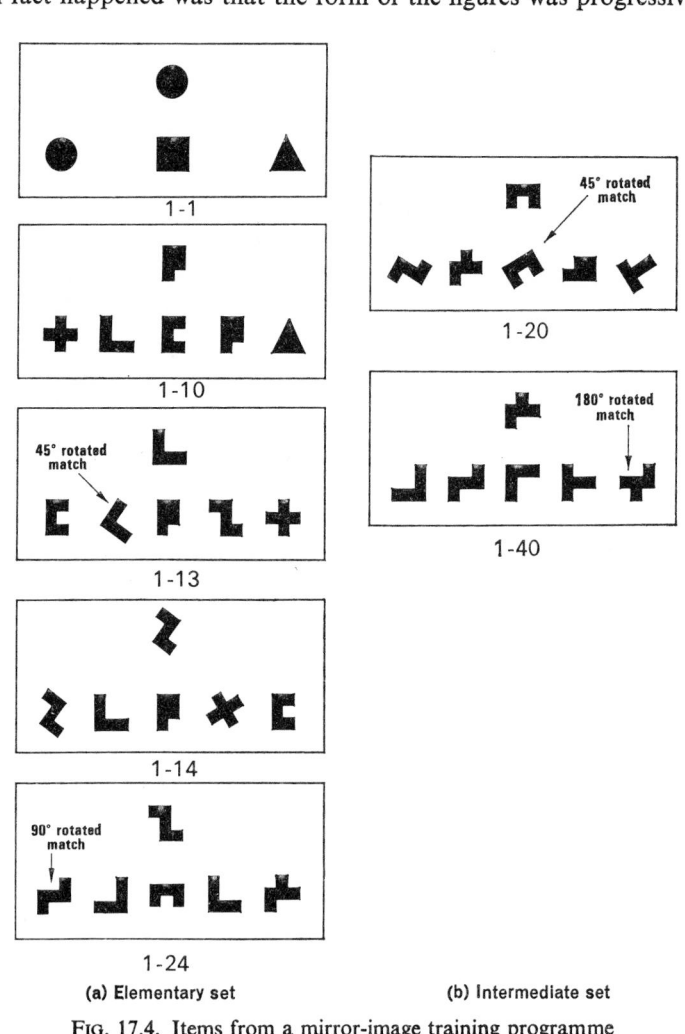

(a) Elementary set   (b) Intermediate set

FIG. 17.4. Items from a mirror-image training programme (based on Bijou, 1962).

changed and not their orientation. However, it is not easy to see how else the mirror-image could have been faded-in. One cannot make a mirror-image out of a form by rotating it in the frontal plane. One could possibly have rotated it through a third dimension, but this would appear on a two-dimensional surface to be merely a change in form.

The fading-in of the mirror-image was followed by other changes

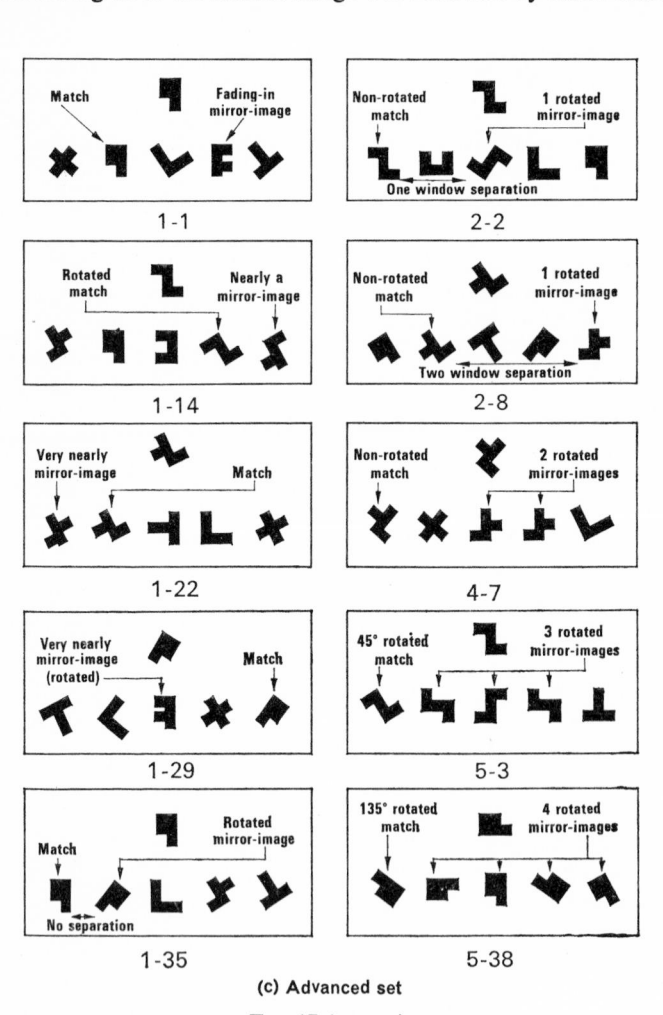

(c) Advanced set

Fig. 17.4 (cont.).

in the programme, such as increasing the orientational discrepancy of the sample and match, separating the locations of the match and the mirror-image and increasing the number of incorrect mirror-image choices. These changes are illustrated in the items 2–2 to 5–38 in Fig. 17.4c.

The objective of this stimulus programme was to enable a young child to pass from the easy discriminations involved on the first few items of the Elementary Set (Fig. 17.4a, Item 1) to the highly complex orientational discriminations demanded by the final items on the Advanced Set (Fig. 17.4c, Item 5–38) without the matching behaviour breaking down. Two groups of children were employed as subjects: a young normal group (N = 90, CA = 3:3 to 6:11), and an older retarded group (N = 89, CA = 6:4 to 16:11, MA = 3:10 to 8:10). In the vast majority of cases the programme succeeded in its objective, and in only a few cases in both groups did the overall error rate rise much above 5 to 10 per cent. Subsequent work by Heid (1964) suggested that the effectiveness of the programme could be much improved by making certain changes in the general instructions to the subject, the nature of the response required and the feedback contingencies.

In an attempt to assess the effectiveness of the training programme in *improving all-round orientation perception*, Bijou administered pre- and post-training discrimination tests to the children employing different sorts of figures to those used in the programme. He found a significant improvement in the performances of both groups on both the post-training tests. This finding to some extent satisfies the question of the generality of the skills acquired on experimental tasks which has been raised above in connection with Newson's and Jeffrey's findings.

One final comment about Bijou's study. He makes considerable use of the *method of individual analysis*. This is a controversial though potentially very valuable source of information. The techniques of analysis are, as yet, crude. The Skinnerean cumulative record approach is not entirely satisfactory, particularly when restricted to the rate of response measure. In the Appendix of this book an attempt is made to extend the individual analysis approach by measuring the cumulative growth of "hypotheses" in a performance.

The findings of these three studies have been generally confirmed in two more recent investigations. Hendrickson and Muehl (1962) found that training 5- and 6-year-olds to attend to the directional

differences between the letters *b* and *d* significantly improved their ability to name these letters, as compared with children who did not receive this training. Jones *et al.* (1966) report a study in which 4- and 5-year-old children were successfully trained to discriminate between the reversible letters by means of a programme of carefully graded discrimination problems. In this programme a large variety of cueing techniques were employed in order to draw the child's attention to the directional characteristics of pictures, figures, letters and words.

In summary, it may be said that the research reviewed in this chapter clearly indicates that orientation discrimination in children is not solely a function of maturation; it is in fact a skill quite sensitive to training. This finding emphasizes the caution that must be used in employing the concept of readiness for prescribing age levels for the acquisition of perceptual-motor skills. As Hendrickson and Muehl conclude,

> Age norms derived from tests built to assess a given skill level provide no certain evidence as to what age the skill might first be taught and learned provided the learning conditions were effectively arranged. [*Op. cit.*, pp. 240–1.]

CHAPTER 18

LATERALITY AND THE PERCEPTION OF ORIENTATION

IN THE present chapter we shall consider what is perhaps the most widely held belief about the cause of a child's deficiency in the discrimination of differently orientated forms. This is, that it is in some way connected with the child's *undeveloped lateral dominance* and his *inability to discriminate right from left*.

MACH'S THEORY OF CEREBRAL ASYMMETRY

An early presentation of this idea was by Ernst Mach in *The Analysis of Sensations* (1914). In discussing the nature of spatial perception Mach writes,

> It is *a priori* extremely probable that the sensations of space are connected in some way with the motor apparatus of the eye. [*Op. cit.*, p. 110.]

He argues that as a result of the symmetry of the visual apparatus with respect to the median plane of the head

> ... the symmetrical movements of looking will be connected with like, or approximately like, space sensations. [p. 110.]

This idea reminds one very much of the internalization of overt haptic activity theory of perception (cf. Chapter 20). The following example of Mach's helps to illustrate his argument.

> If, ... because my right hand happens to be engaged, I grasp a micrometer screw or a key with my left hand, I am certain (unless I reflect beforehand) to turn it in the wrong direction—that is, I always perform the movement which is symmetrical to the usual movement, confusing the two because of the similarity of the sensations. [p. 111.]

This experience is not easy to duplicate. The main problem is to exclude reflection or knowledge about the correct way the key should be turned. Nevertheless, there does appear to be a tendency to behave in the way Mach suggests.

Mach extends this argument to eye movements. Thus symmetrical figures are said to result in *symmetrical eye movements*, which in turn will produce very similar subjectively experienced sensations.

The assumption that symmetrical figures produce symmetrical eye movements cannot be accepted without qualification since figures may be perceived tachistopically without any overt eye movement.

We are, Mach argues, able to discriminate symmetrical figures (by which he means left–right or H-type reversals) only as a result of the *development of a slight bodily asymmetry*, especially in the brain, which produces lateral dominance. A young child confuses reversible letters and has difficulty in identifying his left and right hands because this asymmetry has yet to develop. This asymmetry is said to work by means of the resulting *modification of sensations* arising from symmetrical movements. Thus symmetrical movements, whether bodily or eye, do produce different sensations in individuals having a developed lateral dominance.

With regard to *training* Mach advocates writing and copying as useful activities in the improvement of perception. In this way, as we have already argued, connections are probably established between the space sensations of the eye and the kinesthetic feedback from hand movements, thus making a more distinctive complex of stimulation from the figure observed. But Mach notes,

> ... the confusion of right and left still occurs ... with regard to figures which have no motor, but only a purely optical (e.g., ornamental) interest. [*Op. cit.*, p. 111.]

This means that when discriminations are difficult looking, or visual scanning, may need supplementing with manual exploration (see Chapter 20). This idea is very clearly a forerunner of Hebb's (1949) approach to perception.

ORTON'S THEORY OF STREPHOSYMBOLIA

Orton (1925, 1929, 1937) proposed a similar theory of orientation perception to that of Mach. Both theories emphasized the role of lateral dominance. But whereas Mach gave a mainly behavioural account of the relationship between laterality and orientation, Orton attempted to express the relationship in neurological terms.

Orton's main concern was to explain the incidence of *reading backwardness* in children of otherwise normal intellectual capacity, a

syndrome variously referred to as "congenital word blindness" (Hinchelwood, 1917), "dyslexia" (Wallin, 1921) or "developmental dyslexia" (Critchley, 1964). The relative specificity of this disability has attracted the interest of a large number of neurologists, hoping to discover, by clinical observation, a single underlying cause (e.g. Hermann, 1960; Franklin, 1962; Critchley, 1964). However, mounting psychological evidence seems to indicate that there are as many causes of reading backwardness as there are backward readers (Vernon, 1957; Meredith, 1962, 1963; Kass, 1963).

For Orton the clue to the neurological disorder underlying reading backwardness was the frequent occurrence of reversals. He distinguished two sorts of reversal errors: (1) *kinetic reversals*, in which the order of letters in a word or the order of words in a sentence is reversed; and (2) *static reversals*, which involve confusing a single letter with its mirror-image. In the present survey we have considered only static reversals, since we are primarily interested in the discrimination of orientation and not in the process involved in the temporal confusion of sequential images. However, it is possible to interpret a kinetic as a static reversal if we regard the whole word or phrase as a unit of perception, or a Gestalt. Orton himself seems to interpret it in this way.

The tendency towards reversals in reading Orton termed "*strephosymbolia*" which literally means "twisted symbols". So, for Orton, strephosymbolia is a cause, and maybe the cause, of reading backwardness. Here, we shall be specifically concerned with outlining Orton's account of how a certain neurological process causes the child to confuse different orientations of the same visual form. His argument goes as follows.

The patterns of excitation that are aroused in the two cortical hemispheres by a single figure are identical except that they are *mirror-images* of each other. He writes,

> The brain contains right and left visual areas which are exactly alike except for their opposite orientation, and we think, therefore, that the existence in the non-dominant hemisphere of engrams of different orientation from those in the dominant hemisphere cannot be lightly dismissed as the probable source of static and kinetic reversals and of the spontaneous ability in mirror reading and mirror writing. [1937, p. 155.]

So, according to this theory, the discrimination of orientation problem arises in the following way. Since a single form arouses two patterns of excitation (engrams) which are mirror-images, so we

should expect the mirror-image of this form to arouse the same two patterns though this time in the opposite hemispheres.

If this is the case, how then do we manage to discriminate a figure from its mirror-image at all? Orton's answer to this is the same as Mach's—through the development of *lateral dominance*. His explanation of how it works, however, is different.

Mach, it will be recalled, hypothesized that the stimulation resulting from the symmetrical movements of the eyes would be modified by laterality. Orton, on the other hand, argued that lateral dominance enabled one cortical hemisphere to *suppress* the engrams of the other. This meant that a single form would arouse only a single pattern of excitation in the cortex of an individual in whom lateral dominance had developed; and the mirror-image of this form would arouse a different pattern (i.e. the mirror-image of the former).

So, it is Orton's theory that mirror-image discrimination is difficult when there is a similarity between the engrams in the two hemispheres, and that this happens when there is incomplete dominance. With the development of laterality the excitations in the non-dominant hemisphere are elided leaving a relatively simple shape discrimination to be made within the dominant hemisphere. We must assume here, of course, that the physiological discrimination of cortical patterns is based upon shape and not form (see Chapter 15 for this distinction), and so is not confused by engrams which are mirror-images.

EVALUATION OF ORTON'S THEORY

Orton's strephosymbolia theory of *reading backwardness* is not currently in favour, either with neurologists (Critchley, 1964) or with psychologists (Vernon, 1957). It is denied, for example, that reversals really are a problem in reading (Daniels and Diack, 1956). It is also denied that there is any connection between progress in reading and lateralization (Hillman, 1956; Belmont and Birch, 1963; Coleman and Deutsch, 1964), though this view is disputed (Hildreth, 1949; Harris, 1957.)

But here we are less concerned with Orton's views on reading backwardness than with his explanation of *reversals*. One finding that seems to be damaging to this part of Orton's theory, made by Monroe (1939) and confirmed by Beck (1960), is that children of *mixed laterality* (left-handedness and right-eyedness, or *vice versa*) do not exhibit any greater tendency to make reversal errors than those with

unilaterality. This clearly denies that the establishment of lateral dominance has any effect on reversals. We may be able to defend Orton here by arguing that by dominance he means *occipital or perceptual* dominance and not limb or motor dominance (though in fact Orton himself apparently did not mean this). But this weakens the operational power of the theory by cutting it off from one of its empirical supports.

Is there any way of assessing perceptual dominance as opposed to motor dominance? One possible method is the Jasper and Raney (1937) test which utilizes the phi-phenomenon. McFie (1952) successfully used this test to demonstrate the relative lack of occipital dominance in retarded readers. To the knowledge of the writer there is no reported investigation using this technique to assess the relationship postulated by Orton's theory between occipital dominance and reversal confusions. Zangwill (1960), who has also used the phi-technique in connection with retarded readers, expresses considerable optimism that ". . . the technique may prove of real value in the study of problems of dominance" (p. 24).

A second criticism of Orton's theory comes from a study of the *effects of severing the corpus callosum* in humans to relieve epilepsy by Smith (1945). Smith reported that there was little disturbance in handedness, footedness or eyedness as a result of this operation and concluded that the corpus callosum plays little part in laterality and that one hemisphere does not dominate over or inhibit the other directly by means of impulses passing through it. But, as it stands, this negative finding is not critical for Orton's theory. What would have been very damaging would have been the finding that orientation perception was also not upset by the operation. However, the fact that Smith did not report any change augurs badly for Orton. In order to defend his theory now we would have to argue that the integrity of the corpus callosum is essential only for the development of occipital dominance; once established, other mechanisms, independent of the commissures, take over and maintain it.

The recent development of the *split-brain* experimental technique (Sperry, 1961, 1964; Mountcastle, 1962) clearly makes many of these qualifications to Orton's theory immediately testable. For example, it may be possible to compare the development of orientation perception in a normal monkey with that in a split-brain preparation. Much of the groundwork, in terms of efficient and well-controlled discrimination learning techniques, has been already done. The fact

that the rhesus monkey has been shown to have much the same reversal discrimination problems as man (Riopelle *et al.*, 1964) would, it seems, make it a very suitable animal for such research.

Sperry (1964) contrasts two sorts of learning or *memory systems* that may be used by an organism. Engrams may be laid down in both hemispheres simultaneously, or they may be laid down in one only, but the information thus stored being available to the other hemisphere by way of the corpus callosum. Sectioning the commissures after learning is one way of determining which system a particular organism uses. It seems possible that the single-engram system is a sign of lateral dominance. Thus, while *man* uses the single-engram system, the *lower animals*, such as the cat, use the double-engram system, with *monkeys* somewhere in between, sometimes using one and sometimes the other system. This distribution seems to correspond to the relative extent of lateral dominance in these three species: man with most laterality and cats with least.

So far, this is exactly what Orton's theory would predict. But it would also predict that the ability to make discriminations on the basis of orientation would be a *direct function of the extent of lateralization in a species*. Therefore, we would expect cats to perform less well than monkeys, and all species less well than man. In fact the evidence seems to indicate that exactly the opposite of this is the case. With respect to *rats* Lashley (1938a) concluded "In general there is no clear evidence that the normal animal confuses mirror-image figures" (p. 159).

Also, Sutherland (1963d) was quite surprised at the facility with which *cats* discriminated between differently orientated oblique rectangles, which, he says, ". . . was in marked contrast to my own powers of discrimination in relation to these shapes" (p. 210). However, the evidence is not all in the same direction, for *octopuses* (Sutherland, 1957a, b, 1960a) and *goldfish* (Mackintosh and Sutherland, 1963) appear to have the same sort of problems as man.

Clearly, Orton's theory as it stands is not adequate to meet these various criticisms and to explain all these findings. An alternative theory of Sutherland will be considered in the next chapter. Nevertheless, it seems that Orton's theory has very much greater heuristic value than it has been given credit for, particularly now with the recent advent of the split-brain techniques.

It was suggested to the writer by a person engaged in split-brain work that maybe the orientation discrimination by children would be

easier if they were only allowed to use *one eye*. A similar hypothesis was proposed by Betts (1935) who argued "If we were a one-eyed race our reading difficulties would be few" (p. 575).

Reversals according to this view are attributable to the lack of co-ordination of the eyes and the failure of the brain to fuse the images from them.

This hypothesis was conclusively refuted by Beck (1960) who found that children who reverse letters and words when viewed binocularly do not make significantly more or less reversals when they use only one eye. Beck also showed that children who make monocular reversals do not make more or less reversals with either eye. Thus, *eye dominance* has no effect on orientation discrimination either.

CHAPTER 19

ORIENTATION DISCRIMINATION IN ANIMALS

IN THE present chapter we shall be considering some experimental investigations into the discrimination of differently oriented forms by animals that seem to throw some light onto the nature of the operation required. In particular we shall be considering Sutherland's recent work on this topic and his ideas on how the discrimination might work.

EARLY WORK

The discrimination of orientation was a subject which interested some of the very early experimentalists. For example, Bingham (1913) demonstrated that the discrimination performance of the chicken did not survive the inversion of the positive Sd (an upright triangle). Bingham concluded that in this situation the chicken was discriminating on the basis of the *shape* of the Sd's and not their *form*. Fields (1932) demonstrated with rats that form discrimination could be induced by employing a variety of positive Sd's in the task, all the same in form, but differing in orientation and shape.

There is a small mystery here which it would be as well to clear up. Since Bingham's chickens were discriminating on the basis of shape this would mean that they would discriminate easily between different orientations of the same form. But does this really mean that they are discriminating *orientation*? One way of answering this question was suggested by Lashley (1938a, p. 158). He argued that there appeared to be three stages in the development of the perception of figures. *First*, the organism responds purely on the basis of the distribution of light and shade on the retina (i.e. on the basis of shape). This is the stage Bingham's chickens are at. *Next*, the organism abstracts form and begins to respond on the basis of the relationships and proportions of the figure's constituent parts. This presumably is the stage

the young child is at; he responds to the form of a figure, not to its shape, and so overlooks differences in orientation. *Finally*, in order to respond to the orientation of a form a further abstraction has to be made; this is to ensure that the spatial relationship of a form to its environmental context is noticed. Though behaviourally a performance of an organism at the first stage would be very similar to that of an organism at the third stage, there would be differences. The chief difference would be that whereas the latter organism would, if called upon, be able to discriminate on the basis of form, the former would not.

It is interesting to note that these three stages correspond to what we have referred to as the receptive, attentional and organizational operations involved in the discrimination process (Chapters 1 and 14). This would suggest a developmentally based *hierarchical organization* of mechanisms in perception and discrimination (cf. White, 1964c).

An alternative explanation of Bingham's findings would be that the chickens responded, not to the *whole* figure, but to certain *parts* of it. The tendency of rats to discriminate on the basis of certain aspects of the Sd's has also been reported in rats (Lashley, 1938a; Ehrenfreund, 1948). It might be that the shape perception stage is characterized by such selectivity.

Lashley's (1938a) classic study of the *rat's* capacity for detail vision included a few experiments concerned with the discrimination of differently orientated forms. He found that the *nature of the form* used as an Sd had a greater effect upon a rat's discrimination performance than the difference between them. Thus, whereas triangles and U-shapes are easily discriminated from their orientational transformations, N-, Z- and S-shaped forms are not. Lashley's explanation of this discrepancy is in terms of a distinctive features hypothesis similar to that recently proposed by Gibson *et al.* (1962) (see Chapter 17).

Lashley failed to find any consistent difference between the difficulty of the H-type and the other reversals of the sort that has been reported in the preceding chapters. With U-shapes the H-type reversal was more difficult to learn than the V-type, but Lashley put this down to the rat's tendency to discriminate on the basis of the lower portions of the figures, a tendency which would clearly result in a similar analysis of H-type reversals of this form. He did not find this difference with triangular forms, but did report that **oblique** striations were more difficult to discriminate than horizontal and

vertical striations. After reviewing the literature on this question Sutherland (1961a) concludes,

> ... in all animals tested it has been found that it is more difficult to discriminate between figures which are reversed along the horizontal axis than between figures which are reversed along the vertical axis. [p. 35.]

This conclusion has recently been confirmed with rhesus monkeys by Riopelle *et al.* (1964). Using a wide variety of line figures and twelve animals, they found that "lateral mirror-images", or what we call H-type reversals, were significantly more difficult to discriminate than "vertical mirror-images" (V-type). Non-mirror-image discriminations were found to be of intermediate difficulty.

In order to explain these differences Riopelle observes that in H-type discriminations the *lateral edges* of the figures provide the distinctive differences while the upper and lower edges are similar. In the case of V-type discriminations the situation is reversed. On the basis of this he proposes that there is some *observational habit* which causes the monkey to restrict its attention to the upper and lower edges of the Sd's, a habit which would lead to the better discrimination of V-type than H-type reversals. This is much the same as Lashley's selectivity hypothesis of discrimination.

SUTHERLAND'S STIMULUS ANALYSING MECHANISM

The last decade has witnessed a renewal of interest in the perceptual aspect of discrimination, which underwent a decline following the continuity versus non-continuity controversy of the thirties. Researchers such as Deutsch (1955), Sutherland (1957a) and Dodwell (1957a, b) have all proposed that more attention must be paid to the *manner in which the Sd's are perceived* before any adequate theory of discrimination learning can be constructed. As a result of this work interesting theories about the nature of the *stimulus processing* operation have been proposed. Here we shall consider only the model proposed by Sutherland, partly, because it is currently the most well-documented and empirically testable account of discriminability, and partly, because it deals in particular detail with the perceptual operations involved in the discrimination of differently orientated forms.

Sutherland (1957a, b) reported that octopuses learn to discriminate a vertical and a horizontal rectangle much more easily than two

oblique rectangles at 45° to the vertical and horizontal. To explain this difference Sutherland proposed a *shape analysing mechanism* comprising a two-dimensional array of cells. This mechanism served to count the horizontal extent of a shape at each point on the vertical axis, and the vertical extent of a shape at each point on the horizontal axis. The results of these two operations are called the horizontal and vertical projections, respectively, of the shape analysed.

Figure 19.1a shows the horizontal and vertical projections of a horizontal rectangle imposed upon an array of cells.

Figure 19.1b shows the horizontal and vertical projections of the four orientations of the rectangular form as used by Sutherland

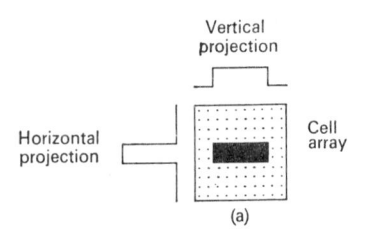

(a)

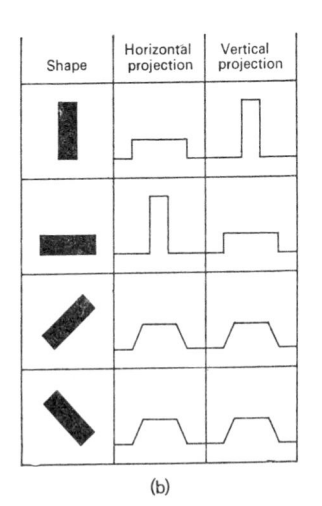

(b)

Fig. 19.1a. Sutherland's shape analysing model (based on Sutherland, 1957). b. Horizontal and vertical projections of differently oriented rectangles.

(1957a, b). To aid comparison both projections are shown in the same orientation.

We see from Fig. 19.1b that whereas the horizontal and the vertical projections give different results from the vertical and horizontal rectangles, they fail to differentiate between the oblique rectangles. So, we would expect that if the octopus uses *either* of these two methods in its stimulus processing it would *fail* to respond differentially to the oblique rectangles, whereas it would *succeed* in discriminating the vertical and horizontal rectangles. This is roughly what Sutherland found. But the fact that the octopuses *could* learn to discriminate the oblique rectangles indicates that this model does not tell the whole story.

It would be also expected from the model that the discrimination between either the vertical or the horizontal rectangle and one of the oblique rectangles would be of *intermediate* difficulty. This is based upon the relative differences between the horizontal and vertical projections of these shapes as shown in Fig. 19.1b. This prediction was confirmed by Sutherland (1958a), again using octopuses.

What we would expect if the organism were to use *both* methods simultaneously is not so clear. Sutherland (1957a) appears to envisage this as producing a composite projection. Thus the vertical rectangle would produce ". . . strong excitations over a narrow band of points on lateral axis, weak excitations over a broad band of points on vertical axis . . ." (*op. cit.*, p. 68). The horizontal rectangle would produce the reverse of this. Again, as when both methods were used separately, this sort of analysis of the oblique rectangles would generate the same output for each: ". . . medium excitation over a medium band of points both on the lateral and vertical axes" (p. 68). Therefore, it appears that the same expectations about discriminability would arise if the organism's perceptual system counted the vertical and the horizontal extents of the shapes simultaneously.

This becomes a little clearer when Sutherland indicates that a *critical test* of whether the octopuses were using a horizontal, or a vertical, or a horizontal and vertical method of analysis, would be the discriminability of the pairs of T-forms shown in Fig. 19.2.

Figure 19.2 shows the horizontal, vertical and composite projections of the four orientations of the T-form. The horizontal counts have been made from the bottom upwards and the vertical counts from left to right.

It is clear from this figure that the three different methods of stimulus analysis will yield different results on a task involving the discrimination of the various combinations of T-shapes. If the method of analysis used by the organism produces a *horizontal* projection of the shape, then T-shapes 1 and 2 should be more easily discriminated than 3 and 4. If the method used produces a *vertical* projection, then T-shapes 3 and 4 should be more easily discriminated than 1 and 2. If the method of analysis used produces a *composite* projection, then T-shapes 1 and 3 and 2 and 4 should be easier to discriminate than 1 and 4 and 2 and 3.

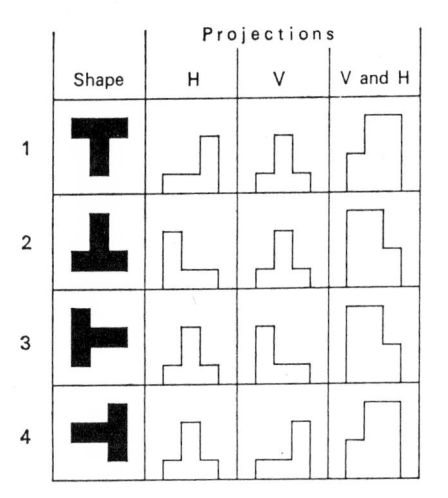

FIG. 19.2. Vertical, horizontal and composite projections of T-shapes (based on Sutherland, 1960a).

Sutherland (1960a) using both T-shapes and U-shapes (about which the predictions would be the same) found that octopuses appeared to have more difficulty in discriminating shapes 3 and 4 than any other combination. In terms of the above model this implies that they used the method of stimulus analysis which served to count the *horizontal* extent of the shape at each point on the vertical axis, thus producing a horizontal projection of the shape.

What are the implications of Sutherland's theory for other findings with respect to orientation discrimination? On the basis of the system outlined in Chapter 15 the pairs of T-shapes shown in Fig. 19.2 may be classified into the following transformation types.

1. H-type reversal: 3–4
2. V- or VH-type reversal: 1–2
3. 90° rotation: 1–3, 1–4, 2–3, 2–4

Since young children also seem to have the greatest difficulty in discriminating H-type reversals, we might argue that their method of shape analysis is apparently the same as that used by the octopus, i.e. horizontal counting. This counting seems to imply that some sort of *implicit scanning* operation is performed on the stimulus input, probably in a similar manner to that suggested by Hebb (1949); and that this scanning takes place in a horizontal fashion, from one side to the other, gradually working up from the bottom of the shape to the top until all of it has been scanned. The output from this scanning operation, according to Sutherland's model of discrimination behaviour (Chapter 8), provides the input for a response mechanism which connects up the outputs from the two Sd's with the appropriate R's. According to our own model, described in Chapter 14, these outputs pass to the comparison unit.

For other work than that on orientation discrimination relating to this stimulus analysis model of shape perception, see Sutherland (1958b, 1959a, b, c, 1960b, c, d, 1961b, 1962, 1963a, b, c, 1964), Sutherland and Carr (1962, 1963), Sutherland *et al.* (1962, 1963c) and Mackintosh and Sutherland (1963).

This original model of stimulus analysis has subsequently been revised in the light of new evidence from the microelectrode studies of the visual cortex of the cat (Hubel and Wiesel, 1959, 1962; Hubel, 1963) and the octopus (Young, 1960, 1962, 1964) and as a result of certain non-confirmatory behavioural data.

RETINAL RECEPTIVE FIELDS OF STRIATE CELLS

Hubel and Wiesel (1959), by stimulating the cat's retina with a spot of light, found that it was possible to map out the *receptive field*, on the retina, of individual striate cells. That is, they were able to discover which points on the retina, when stimulated by light, affected the firing of a single cell in the cat's striate cortex.

Figure 19.3 shows one type of receptive field that they discovered which has an *excitatory* centre strip (marked by +'s) flanked by two *inhibitory* strips (marked by −'s). The *simple* striate cell having this retinal receptive field is fired by light which is projected on the centre

strip, and inhibited by light which is projected onto the two flanking strips. Thus, this type of cell will be maximally fired by a strip of light projected down the centre of its receptive field. A small rotation of this strip of light would cause it to cover some of the inhibitory area as well as the excitatory area with the result that the cell probably would not fire (if the inhibitory stimulation were greater than or equal to the excitatory stimulation).

Now, if this is the mechanism by which an organism's visual system classifies a shape, and Sutherland (1963a) believes that it is, then on the basis of the sort of receptive fields possessed by the cells

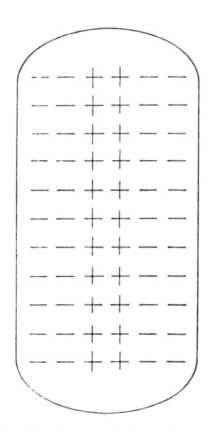

FIG. 19.3. Receptive field of a "simple" striate cell (based on Hubel and Weisel, 1959).

of a particular organism's cortex, we should be able to make some predictions about the relative *discriminability of shapes* for that organism.

For example, Hubel and Wiesel have found that there are a large number of cells in the *cat's* occipital cortex which have the sort of receptive field shown in Fig. 19.3, but, and this is the significant fact, the orientation of the centre excitatory strip is not constant, but varies from one cell to another; and *no one orientation is any more common than any other*. This implies that no matter in what orientation a strip of light is projected onto a cat's retina it will always fire a cell in that cat's cortex; and different orientations will fire different cells. This being the case, and assuming the cat bases its discriminatory behaviour upon the differential firing of these cells, then we might expect it to be able to discriminate equally well between

rectangles (of light) in any orientation. Thus, we might expect that, unlike the octopus, the cat will have no greater difficulty in learning to discriminate *oblique* rectangles than *vertical and horizontal* rectangles.

This prediction has been tested and confirmed by Sutherland (1963d). He found that cats discriminate oblique rectangles and vertical and horizontal rectangles equally well.

Are there any comparable arrangements in the visual system of the *octopus* that might account for its relative inability to discriminate obliques? Young (1960, 1962) found that the dendritic pick-up fields of cells in the optic lobe of the octopus tend to be elliptical in shape, as in the cat. However, in the octopus there are more fields with their excitatory strip in a horizontal orientation with respect to the eye than in a vertical orientation. This may help to explain the feature of Sutherland's original theory in which the horizontal projection of a form was more prominent in determining behaviour than the vertical projection. But, more significant, is that fact that Young found *very few receptive fields in a diagonal orientation*. This is, of course, exactly what we would expect from the performance of the octopus on discrimination tasks.

IMPLICATIONS FOR ORIENTATION DISCRIMINATION IN CHILDREN

What, finally, has this new model of Sutherland's to say about orientation discrimination in *children*? Rudel and Teuber (1963) performed an experiment, on similar lines to the ones with animals, but using children. They found that very few of the children, aged 3–9 years, failed to learn a simultaneous two-choice task involving the discrimination of either vertical and horizontal rectangles or upright and inverted U-shapes. But, as we might expect, many had considerable difficulty in learning when the discrimination required was between oblique rectangles or H-type reversed U-shapes.

These results, particularly with respect to the difficulty in discriminating oblique rectangles, suggest that like the octopus, but unlike the cat, the young child's striate cortex may consist of cells which have, in most cases, receptive fields with the centre excitatory strip either horizontally or vertically oriented with respect to the eye. But, there are one or two important *questions* not answered. For example, why does the child have more difficulty in discriminating

between H-type reversals, such as in Rudel and Teuber's U-shapes or the reversible lower-case letters, than other types? Though Sutherland's original model gave an answer to this question the new model does not. Also, we may ask that since adults and reasonably mature children can discriminate oblique rectangles (though admittedly not without some difficulty), does this mean that cells with diagonally orientated receptive fields take some time to develop or become operational?

The writer's feeling about these issues is that maybe there is some *physiological predisposition* for human beings to confuse different orientations of the same visual form. Though this disposition remains, with increasing maturity man learns various *techniques* which enable him to overcome this tendency, and thus respond differentially to differently orientated forms. The physiological predisposition probably has at least *two* aspects; one concerns lateral or cerebral dominance, the other the orientation of the retinal receptive fields of the striate cells. Our problem, as behavioural scientists, is to discover just what the heuristic techniques are that a child has to learn to enable him to become proficient in orientation discrimination tasks. In doing this we shall also be concerned in finding out how these skills can be established and maintained.

One point that has been repeatedly emphasized in this book (e.g. p. 128) and which is critical for theories of shape analysis is that the difficulty that an organism has in learning to discriminate two shapes does not necessarily give a true index of the similarity of the signals produced in the visual system by these shapes; there are many other determining variables. This point is also made in a recent note by Over (1967), who stresses the *memory factor*. He suggests that poor discrimination may be due to the failure to remember from trial to trial which R goes with which S. He tested this idea by comparing recognition (normal discrimination learning) and detection (same-different) measures of the discrimination of obliques by 4–6-year-olds and found that though many children failed to acquire discriminatory R's to the obliques very few made errors in judging whether the two lines were orientated similarly or differently. This suggests that failure to discriminate obliques by children (and maybe also by animals) arises not from the inability of the shape analyser to generate distinctively different outputs from the lines, but from deficiencies in the system by which the information is stored.

CHAPTER 20

PERCEPTUAL ACTIVITY IN DISCRIMINATION BEHAVIOUR

IN THE preceding chapter it was argued that in order to overcome a physiological predisposition towards treating differently orientated forms as identical the child has to learn certain heuristic techniques. In terms of our Chapter 14 model these techniques, to be successful, must serve to generate distinctively different outputs from the stimulus processing unit for the differently orientated forms. They are "heuristic" in the sense that they are valuable only in the attainment of this end; any technique will do so long as it works. In the present chapter we shall be considering some observations and some speculations about what sort of activity a child indulges in in making a discrimination on the basis of orientation, particularly that activity which appears to facilitate the discrimination of the stimulus figures.

HEAD MOVEMENT

It is a common observation that people tend to incline their heads to one side when "trying to make something out", that is, when faced by a difficult perception such as an abstract painting. It is as if they were trying to discover an *appropriate orientation* for the picture, one that gives it meaning, so that it can be recognized as something. This is the sort of activity which would seem to qualify as a heuristic perceptual technique. That there appears to be a significant conformity in people's judgement about which way is the right-way-up for an abstract picture (Arnheim, 1954) points to the basis of this technique.

Head movement has been observed as being an intrinsic part of a child's behaviour on a discrimination learning task. Gellerman (1933a, b) reported the occurrence of changes in head orientation in the identification of rotated triangles both in 2-year-old children and in chimpanzees. Hunton (1955) noticed a similar tendency in the identification of rotated realistic figures by children.

Though head movement is rarely one of the behavioural phenomena that an experimenter records, its *theoretical importance* certainly

makes it worth observing, or preferably controlling. In terms of the revised Sutherland–Hubel model of shape analysis (Chapter 19) head rotation may serve to make indiscriminable shapes, such as oblique rectangles, discriminable by transferring their retinal projections to available receptive fields. So, by an appropriate head movement, an oblique rectangle could be changed into a vertical or horizontal rectangle with respect to the eye, and so fall into the receptive fields of those striate cells which normally only respond to vertical or horizontal rectangles. In the same way a difficult H-type reversal discrimination could be transformed into an easy V-type by a 90° rotation of the head.

Of course, the usefulness of head movement as a heuristic perceptual activity in the discrimination of differently orientated forms will depend to a large extent upon the individual's ability to take account of the position of his head in making a final choice. This variable could easily be incorporated into our Chapter 14 model, in the same way as an allowance has been made for feedback information from the position of the eyes on exposure of the task situation (Pe) to reach the response selection unit (Fig. 14.2).

There are clearly great opportunities for useful experimental research into the role of head movements in discrimination and other perceptual behaviour. For head movements are in principle not difficult to observe or control. There are a number of thorny theoretical disputes relating to just this issue (e.g. between Dodwell, 1958 and Deutsch, 1960) which might be clarified by such research. Let us now turn to consideration of more implicit, less easily observable and controllable, activities which also seem to qualify as heuristic perceptual techniques.

HEBB'S SCANNING THEORY

In the Western World, at least, interest in the motor aspects of perception arose chiefly from Hebb's *The Organisation of Behaviour* (1949). Hebb rejected the widely held Gestalt view of perception (Koffka, 1924, 1935; Köhler, 1925, 1929, 1940). According to this view when one perceives a simple figure one perceives it directly as a distinctive unlearned whole. Hebb argued, on the contrary, that

> ... simple perceptions are in fact complex, that they are additive, that they depend partly on motor activity, and that their apparent simplicity is only the end result of a long learning process. [*Op. cit.*, p. 17.]

So, for Hebb, *eye movements* are, like head movements, activities which facilitate perception. By themselves they are not sufficient. For, clearly, a perception is more than an eye movement pattern; it also involves an *image*, an input from the environment. Nor are they necessary for perception; for witness the facility of an adult in identifying simple figures tachistoscopically (presented at a speed that allows only a single fixation). Nevertheless, eye movements do seem to enable very much more complex perceptions to take place than would be possible without them. This is demonstrated in the extremely defective tachistoscopic recognition by adults of all but the most simple forms.

It would be as well at this point to distinguish the eye movements under consideration here from those involuntary eyeball movements called "physiological nystagmus" (Marshall and Talbot, 1942), whose importance in effective image formation has recently been so well demonstrated (Pritchard *et al.*, 1960; Pritchard, 1961). These, unlike the heuristic scanning movements, are physiological and involuntary, and apparently not sensitive to learning (see Chapter 1).

For Hebb, there are two sorts of scanning, one overt and observable, the other implicit, and unobservable without the use of special recording techniques. The *implicit scanning* is conceived of as an internalized or faded version of overt eye movements. When the perception to be made is a complex one the scanning usually takes on an overt form and, as we shall see, may be reinforced by tactual exploratory movements. Only when the perception required is simple, and the perceiver a mature individual, will the implicit scanning activity, which Hebb sees as the motor facilitation of a cell assembly, be sufficient to allow an appropriate analysis of the pattern input received. By "appropriate" is meant the capacity to generate distinctively different outputs from patterns whose differentiation is important for the perceiver; such as, if he is performing on a discrimination learning task.

GHENT'S SCANNING THEORY

Hebb suggested that the efficient perception of a pattern involved a number of fixations on certain *focal* aspects of it, notably, the lines and their intersections (*op. cit.*, pp. 80–91). Ghent (1960) followed up this idea by hypothesizing that the sequential consideration of a figure may take place in a certain *direction* from these focal points.

Ghent found that the tachistoscopic recognition of a realistic figure by young children was markedly affected by its orientation (see Chapter 16). If a picture is presented upside-down it is less easily recognized by the child than if it is presented the right-way-up. Ghent hypothesized that such figures have their focal points at the *top*. Hence, if the figure is presented upside-down its focal point will be at the bottom. Now, if we assume that the child habitually scans a figure in a downwards direction, beginning from the focal point, then we would expect his perception of a figure, having its focal point at the bottom, to be incomplete, and thus, more difficult to recognize than a figure having its focal point at the top. This accords with what Ghent found.

As it stands this argument of Ghent's is circular. If we ask what makes figures difficult to recognize the answer would be because they have their focal points at the bottom. But if we ask which figures have their focal points at the bottom we are referred back to our original query, the answer being, those figures which are difficult to recognize. The problem is to have some other way of detecting the position of a focal point *independent* of the difficulty in recognition observation.

One way of doing this would be to record on film the child's eye movements when he is presented with a figure to recognize. This would certainly be the most direct and most satisfactory way to determine just where the child fixates. But, of course, there are many variables that might interfere with this record and the results are unlikely to be clear-cut. Nevertheless, this should not prevent us trying (see Chapter 5).

However, Ghent prefers to use a more *indirect* method: to ask the opinion of the child about the orientation of abstract figures. She found (Ghent, 1961) that 4- and 5-year-olds were remarkably consistent in their judgement of what was the right-way-up or the wrong-way-up of abstract figures. Six- and seven-year-olds were less consistent.

Figure 20.1a shows those figures which the younger children were fairly unanimous about as being "wrong" or upside-down.

It is not clear from a casual analysis of these figures just what it is about them that makes the children think they are upside-down. There are probably a number of factors affecting a child's judgement. One of these may be the apparent *stability* of a figure in a certain orientation. Thus, figures 1, 2, 3, 4, 5 and 6 would probably seem

more stable the other way round. Figure 7 is probably upside-down because it looks like the letter T and figure 8 because it looks like a lollypop.

Ghent thought that maybe these figures were considered to be upside-down because they have their focal points at the *bottom*. To avoid circularity again we must specify just what features of the figures are focal points. From Hebb we would expect that angles and

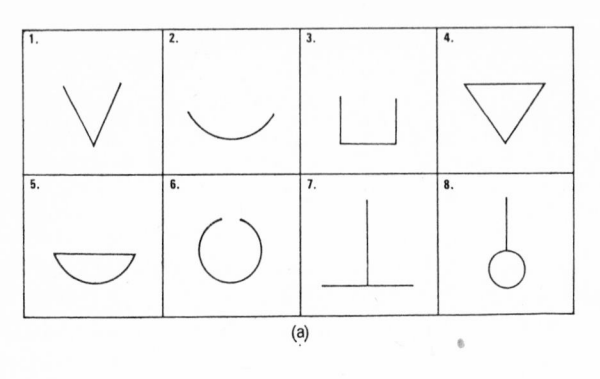

(a)

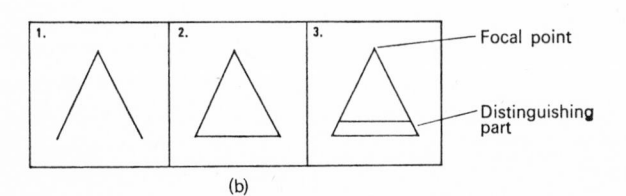

(b)

FIG. 20.1a. Figures considered by children to be upside-down—having their focal point at the bottom (based on Ghent, 1961). b. Figures having their focal point and distinguishing part separated (based on Ghent, 1963).

junctions of lines to be immediate points for fixation. On this sort of analysis we could argue that figures 1, 3, 4, 7 and 8 seem to have their focal point at or near the base. With respect to figures 2, 5 and 6 it seems we must assume that a bend or a curve also acts as a focal point.

In her more recent work Ghent (1963, 1964) has been working on the tachistoscopic recognition of geometrical figures in which the focal point and the distinguishing part are *separated*. Figure 20.1b shows three triangular figures in which the assumed focal point is the

apex and the distinguishing part the base. If the focal point of these figures is the apex, and if children do tend to scan a figure in a downwards direction beginning from the focal point, then we might expect that the recognition of these figures in the orientation shown would be better than if they were inverted. For if these figures were inverted the focal point would be at the bottom and the distinguishing part at the top, which would mean that the distinguishing part would not be scanned or received by the child's perceptual apparatus.

Ghent (1963) has found that 3-year-olds do recognize these figures better in the orientation shown in Fig. 20.1b. But children aged $4\frac{1}{2}$–6 years and adults recognize them better when inverted. She interprets this as showing that whereas the scanning habit of the 3-year-old is to begin at the focal point and move downwards, that of the older child and adult is to begin at the top of the figure regardless of the location of the focal point.

It is interesting to note in connection with Ghent's work that the critical distinguishing features of most letters of the alphabet are located in the top half. This is reflected in the greater difficulty experienced in reading script that has had its top half cut away over that which has lost its lower half (Bartlett, 1951, pp. 60–61). This apparently "natural" evolution of the alphabet may reflect a greater facility in man for perceiving and responding to the upper part of figures.

A recent study by Kerpelman and Pollack (1964) seems to give some support to this idea. They found that in a multiple-choice matching task children aged $3\frac{1}{2}$–$7\frac{1}{2}$ years tend to use features in the lower half of the stimulus figures (irregular pentagons) more than those in the upper half for their discrimination. There is, however, a tendency with increasing age to utilize more and more features in the upper part of the figure. This may be a maturational change, governed by biological variables, or it may be the result of the learning involved in responding to printed text, which demands greater attention to the upper parts of figures.

It will be remembered that in connection with the distinctive features theory of Gibson *et al.* (1962) it was argued that the orientation of a form may possibly be described in terms of certain *absolute* characteristics than that particular shape possesses (Chapter 17). Ghent (1961) proposes a similar view.

> It is generally assumed that the judgement [of orientation] refers to a comparison of the relation between a given form and its framework with

the relation between another instance of the form and its framework. In contrast, it is proposed here that the perception of orientation in the young child is a judgement of whether or not the form is oriented in such a way as to conform with factors that operate in the actual perception of the form. [p. 187.]

Ghent is here denying that to define the orientation of a form it is necessary to refer to some other, standard, orientation, as we have done in Chapter 15. Though this may well be possible, as has been argued in Chapter 17, it does not appear possible to differentiate between orientations of the same form without reference to the spatial context of the form. Thus, even Ghent has to talk in terms of the "top" and the "bottom" of the figure and "downwards" scanning movements. But, these terms do not refer to "absolute" features of the form; rather they refer to the relationship between a certain feature and another feature of the environment extrinsic to the form.

There are *two* contextual determinants of the meanings of the words "top" and "bottom", and "upwards" and "downwards". We may say that a feature of a pattern is at the "top" or the "bottom" with respect to the earth and the force of *gravity*. This seems to be the usual way of defining these terms. The other way, which to an astronaut floating in space is the only way, is to use *one's own body* as a reference point.

What Ghent seems to be asserting is that the young child tends to use this latter method in making judgements about the orientation of things. Testing this Ghent *et al.* (1960) asked children to judge the orientation of realistic and geometrical figures while standing with their heads between their legs. Nine out of ten children consistently judged figures to be upside-down, which were upside-down with respect to their eyes, but which were the right way up with respect to the environment.

That the orientation perception of young children is predominantly *field-dependent* has also been shown by Witkin (1959) using the tilting-room-tilting-chair experiment. He found that their judgement of the upright was determined more by the visual field (the orientation of the room) than their own position in space (the orientation of the chair). With increasing age, up to about 13 years, there is a gradual reduction in this field-dependency.

This dependence of the child on the retinal framework or visual field would also account for his tendency to rotate his head in order to identify misorientated figures. But what is not so clear is that

this dependence is confined to children. Adults also move their heads about in order to get a picture into a meaningful orientation.

There is a problem with using adults, that probably does not arise with children; that of distinguishing between what they *perceive* and what they *know*. Consider the writer's own experience. I look at an object, such as a photograph of someone's face, which has a definite right-way-up. The face is familiar and easy to recognize. I turn it upside-down and it is less familiar. Leaving the photograph upside-down with respect to the environment I change my own orientation by standing on my head. Once again the face is familiar and easy to recognize. Now, if someone were to ask me whether the photograph was upside-down or not, I would reply that it was upside-down. I *know* it is upside-down with respect to the environment, even though it looks the right-way-up to me. Clearly, what I do in making a judgement about orientation is take into account what I know is the correct orientation, and my own orientation. I am able to distinguish between how a thing looks to me and how it actually is. The young child, on the other hand, cannot, or at least does not, make this distinction, and hence his judgement is dependent upon his perception.

One final word about Ghent's theory. It will be recalled that Sutherland's first version of the shape analyser assumed that the octopus, and probably the child, classifies a shape by counting its horizontal extent on each point on the vertical axis (Chapter 19). Such a counting operation seems to imply some sort of implicit scanning of the shape as proposed by Ghent. It may be possible, therefore, to link up Sutherland's analysing model with Ghent's scanning hypothesis, to the mutual benefit of both. Sutherland's model would gain from some attention to overt perceptual activity, and Ghent's by the consideration of left–right as well as up–down reversals.

PIAGET'S THEORY OF INTERNALIZATION OF PERCEPTUAL ACTIVITY

Besides Hebb, the other main source of ideas in the Western World about the role of motor activity in perception is the work of Piaget and his collaborators (Piaget, 1947, 1961; Piaget and Inhelder, 1956), though, as yet, they have not had the impact on experimental research that Hebb's work has. Their ideas are, however, very similar to those of Hebb as the following quotation illustrates.

> Every movement may be regarded as a transformation of the perceptual field as a group of relationships determined by movements. . . . Hence we find visual perception itself made up of a system of relationships determined by probable movements of the eyes. . . . [Piaget and Inhelder, 1956, pp. 15–16.]

According to Piaget efficient perception develops through *stages*. At first, the appropriate observing activity is disorganized and uncontrolled, but gradually control is established and the heuristic exploratory activity becomes internalized. At this point complicated perceptual images can be stored and operated upon implicitly. For Piaget these operations are not the result of the interaction between the cohesive and restraining field forces innately laid down in the nervous system, as the Gestalt theory would have us believe (Koffka, 1935, pp. 138–9; Köhler,· 1940); rather they are the product of a lengthy period of learning, through the constant interaction between the individual and the environment.

Piaget emphasizes, as did Hebb, the relationship of tactual or *haptic* perception and visual perception. The expression "haptic perception" was coined by Revèsz (1950) and used by Langdon and Lunzer as an English equivalent for Piaget and Inhelder's (1956) term "stereognostique". Haptic perception, then, refers to the perception of an object by touch.

According to Piaget and Inhelder,

> The shape is abstracted from an object by virtue of the actions which the subject performs on it; such as following its contour step by step, surrounding it, traversing it, separating it and so on . . . . [*Op. cit.*, p. 17.]

In this way the child is said to establish a representative *schema* which is a kind of referent common to vision and touch. It is very similar to Zaporozhets' (1957, 1961) *image* (Chapter 6).

Piaget and Inhelder continue,

> Thus the whole trend of events appears to suggest that the power to imagine the shapes visually, when they are perceived through the sense of touch alone, is an expression of the sensori-motor schema involved in their perception. [*Op. cit.*, p. 41.]

This *cross-model* transfer from touch to vision, if substantiated, should provide a valuable heuristic technique in perception. It probably forms the basis of the widely acknowledged kinesthetic-tracing technipue (Chapters 16, 17). Also it is a common observation that a child faced with a complex object to perceive will spontaneously supplement looking, with some sort of manual exploration (Zinchenko and Lomov, 1960 (see below)).

Experimental studies of cross-modal transfer, however, have, as yet, failed to confirm Piaget's ideas. Rudel (1963) concludes,

> Our results so far cast doubt on any theory which demands the early associative use of touch for organising the shape or size of the visually perceived world. Even at the age of 3 years, children do not seem to utilize touch to tell them much about the shape of things. Their visual efficiency along this dimension is far superior. [p. 13.]

This conclusion is not only damaging to Piaget's ideas but it also goes directly against the widely held theory about the relative dominance of the modalities in young children. White (1964) and Hermelin and O'Connor (1964), for example, argue that initially interoceptive and visceral sensations are dominant in behaviour, and that this dominance is gradually superceded first by tactile and kinesthetic and then by telereceptors. It will be remembered that White uses this theory to account for the dominance of position-guided responding in children (Chapter 5). Clearly, more well-controlled, experimental research is required on these issues.

RUSSIAN WORK ON PERCEPTUAL ACTIVITY

The recent interest in contemporary Soviet psychology (see Chapter 6) has revealed an approach to perception which has much in common with that of Hebb and Piaget. The *general theory* predominant in Russia according to Pick (1963) is that perception is a joint function of the sensory input and the feedback from the motor activity involved in ensuring the reception of this input: the looking at, the listening to, the feeling of the objects in the external world.

Such a theory is particularly appropriate for describing the process of *haptic* perception. We encounter an object and we explore it with our fingers. The image or schema we build up will be the product of the sensations arising from the tactile receptors and kinesthetic feedback from our exploratory movements. In *visual* perception, as we have seen, the exploratory movements include overt eye movements and implicit scanning activity. Again the perception will be a function of the input and the feedback from these movements. But visual perception also involves, according to our model, *a change* in the nature of the stimulus input. The input is operated upon and altered by the scanning or perceptual processing activity. Perception is not merely a matter of adding feedback stimulation to stimulus input; for what activity we indulge in determines what we will receive

as input. This is not to deny that some facilitation does take place through such addition; all it says is that this is not the whole story (see Chapter 9).

The study of Zinchenko and Lomov (1960) will serve to illustrate the Russian approach. They argue that the perception of a form by a child is the end product of a long chain of behaviour concerned with the exploration of the stimulus. Thus, 3-year-olds could visually discriminate figures only after having learned to follow the contours with a finger. Older children were able to do without this heuristic activity. This finding needs further confirmation.

Ruzskaia (1958) also reports that the discrimination of a triangle and a rectangle was most effectively trained by instructing the child to follow the contours of the figures with his fingers and his eyes while counting the sides. Instructions merely to attend to the upper, distinguishing, parts of the figures were less effective.

With regard to the function of such tracing movements Zinchenko and Lomov report that in the absence of such activity eye movements of 3- and 4-year-olds are irregular, saccadic and generally within the figure. This implies that the finger movements served as *a guide* to the eye movements in the appropriate scanning of the figure. With increasing practice and maturity the child is progressively able to do without such guides, and is able to bring his eye movements under the control of the appropriate aspects of the stimulus shape, so as to guarantee an efficient perception of it.

In practice, the situation is complicated by the fact that though tracing is an efficient heuristic technique in visual perception, it too has to be trained. Zinchenko and Lomov report that before the age of 6 or 7 years finger tracing is slow and clumsy, and does not keep to the contours. However, it is relatively easily trained; partly, no doubt on account of the fact that it involves behaviour which the experimenter finds it easy to exercise control over, unlike eye movements; and partly, maybe due to the intrinsic ease at a low maturity level to establish visual–manual associations.

Zinchenko and Lomov also observed, in a three-choice matching task in which the sample was projected onto a screen, that the very young children would tend to trace out spontaneously the contours of the sample form with their fingers in the air. These children would succeed on the task only so long as they were allowed to perform the same operations on the choices in front of them.

CHAPTER 21

SUMMARY

IN THIS book we have been studying discrimination. This was *defined* as the process by means of which an organism responds to differences between stimuli (Chapter 1). This process was assumed to begin with the exposure of the discriminative stimuli in the presence of the organism and end with the organism making a discriminatory response. We have been concerned to discover *what happens* in between these two events.

In this enterprise we have been guided in the main by the following three questions:

1. What is involved in the successful performance on a discrimination task?
2. In the event of an unsuccessful performance what went wrong?
3. What can be done to improve performance in the latter case?

These questions were asked in particular of the performance of *a young child on a matching to sample task involving the discrimination of differently orientated forms*. This skill was chosen for examination since it seemed likely that it would illustrate many of the operations in the discrimination process. Also, there was some chance that our study would throw light on general aspects of cognitive and perceptual development in children. On the practical side, the analysis of orientation discrimination revealed ways in which children might be helped to acquire this skill which is so vital for efficient reading.

Let us now see to what extent these questions have been answered in this book.

With regard to the *first* question an examination was made of existing experimental and theoretical work relating to the process and the learning of discriminations, on the basis of which a "paper and pencil" *model* was developed to show the functional and temporal relationships of the various operations (Chapter 14). Starting with the exposure of the discriminative stimuli, or the task situation, in the

presence of the organism the model proposed that an *orienting response* has to be made in order to expose the relevant stimuli to the receptors of the organism (Spence, Chapter 2; Wyckoff, Chapter 3; Kurtz and Zeaman and House, Chapter 4; Polidora and Fletcher, Chapter 7; Kendler, Chapter 12). The sequence of operations assumed to lead up to this response are shown in Fig. 14.2. The orienting response is elicited by the invariant features of the task situation (Lawrence, Chapter 8).

The stimulus as received then passes to a *stimulus processing* unit, whose function it is to generate distinctively different outputs from the discriminative stimuli (Goodwin and Lawrence, Chapter 3; Zeaman and House, Chapter 4; Polidora and Fletcher, Chapter 7; Sutherland and Mackintosh and Lawrence, Chapter 8; Kendler, Chapter 12). The exact nature of this operation will, of course, depend upon the type of stimuli and the differences between them. Some suggestions as to how this processing might work on two-dimensional visual forms differing in orientation were discussed in Chapters 17 to 20.

There were two different sorts of account of this perceptual operation. One, which we might call the *motor* theory, emphasizes the role of active exploration of the stimuli by hand and by eye (Fernald, Chapter 17; Hebb, Ghent, Piaget and the Russians, Chapter 20). The discrimination of orientation probably involves the association of the stimuli with kinesthetic, directional and laterality cues thus making them more distinctively different (Newson, Jeffrey, Chapter 17; Mach, Orton, Chapter 18).

The other account, which we might call the *perceptual* theory, emphasizes the purely perceptual features of the discrimination, and gives a better description of the actual process involved. Sutherland's early theory proposed that the discrimination was made on the basis of the neural counting of the vertical and the horizontal extents of figures. A later version emphasized the differential firing of cortical striate cells as a result of the projection of differently orientated forms on the retina. (Chapter 19). The distinctive features theory (Chapter 17) would also probably fall under this heading.

In all the theories considered the outputs from the stimulus processing operation are assumed to become directly attached to the final, overt, discriminatory responses. In order to account for the response factors in discrimination the model presented in Chapter 14 proposed three intervening operations. The *comparison* unit was assumed to

receive the stimuli as processed and to inform the *response strategy* unit as to whether they are the same or different. It is then left to the strategy unit to decide what action to take and to instruct the *response selection* unit to carry it out.

With regard to our *second* question the research literature was examined to discover, first, how a young child performs on a matching task involving the discrimination of orientation. This, together with the author's own findings, indicated clearly that the child's performance is not reliable. The main task then was to find out what factors contributed to the poor performance.

Two main types of deficiency were isolated, which corresponded to the major of the discrimination process already made. On the *cognitive* side, there were defects in the mediation of the task behaviour, which were closely associated with the development of language (Chapter 11). Also, there was an inability to build up an image or plan of the activity required, either through the use of language, or by the internalization of orienting behaviour (Chapter 6). A further factor hindering the execution of an efficient discrimination was a child's tendency to respond initially on the basis of information from his near receptors (White, Chapter 5). This apparently represents a primitive method of responding, which is manifested in position habits. Response strategies or "hypotheses" (Appendix) are assumed to be hierarchically arranged, and regressions in hypotheses can be observed as resulting from changes in the difficulty of the perceptual discriminations (Chapter 5).

The evidence reviewed suggests that there is an *age limit* to these cognitive deficiencies. This is put somewhere around $4\frac{1}{2}$–5 years of age. (White, Chapter 5; Luria, Kendler, Chapter 11). The quality of discrimination, and particularly matching, performance changes at about this age. The author's own research lends some support to this conclusion (Chapters 5, 10 and 11). Before this age the child tends to tackle complex discrimination problems in a concrete, non-mediated, way, and his performance is characterized by short latency responses and typical trial and error learning. The author feels, however, that considerable caution should be exercised in drawing any definite conclusions about this age shift. Undoubtably a shift does occur, but whether it is related to chronological age in any simple way is less easy to decide. There are so many variables influencing the performance that much better controlled experiments must be conducted before any definite conclusions can be made.

The Zeaman–House attention deficiency theory of retardate discrimination learning (Chapter 4) also suggests the influence of general maturational variables. But as the work of Skinner (1961b), Bijou and Baer (1961, 1963), Fowler (1962) and Staats and Staats (1963) illustrates we should be wary of proposing maturation or age as an independent variable.

The second main factor in a child's poor performance on discrimination tasks is a *perceptual* deficiency. With respect to the discrimination of orientation the young child shares with many species of animal a biological predisposition to treat differently orientated forms as equivalent. This might be a function of two factors. First, there is the incomplete development of lateral or cerebral dominance in the young child (Chapter 18). And second, there is the method of shape analysis employed by the perceptual system and maybe the lack of striate cells having differently orientated retinal receptive fields (Chapter 19). This second explanation is, of course, speculative; there being no direct evidence from children.

It appears that man learns certain perceptual skills that enable him to overcome this predisposition. We have seen how a young child can be trained to acquire these skills and thus improve his orientation discrimination (Chapter 17).

This takes us on to our *third* question: What can be done to improve a child's discrimination performance? On the *cognitive* side we have seen how verbal instruction can be successfully used with a pre-mediatory child provided it is broken down into simple, categorical imperatives and synchronized with the corresponding event in the task (Chapter 11). Zaporozhets (Chapter 6) showed how control of the child's orienting behaviour would improve performance. An indirect way of establishing the appropriate skills is illustrated in Hively's stimulus training programme (Chapter 10). The work on the S–R spatial discontiguity effect (Chapter 7) suggests we put the loci of the stimuli and of the responses close together in space. For example, asking the child to press on a window displaying the stimulus is an efficient way of ensuring that the stimulus is oriented (see apparatus in Fig. 17.2).

Compared with the covert comparison and strategy operations the overt orienting response is relatively easy to control. White's technique of varying the positions in which the discriminitive stimuli are displayed (Chapter 5) is one indirect method of curbing position habits. Others involve the gradual programming of the discrimination

according to the principles discussed in Chapters 9 and 10. By making transitions from easy to difficult discriminations very gradual the tendency towards regression in task hypotheses is controlled.

Ways of improving the *stimulus processing* operation were discussed in Chapters 17 and 20. Again there was an emphasis on control by means of perceptual orienting activity. The kinesthetic tracing technique is emphasized by Ghent, Piaget and the Russian workers (Chapter 20) as a means of controlling visual scanning. Newson's work shows how a little directional training can improve a child's discrimination of reversible line figures (Chapter 17). The value of Jeffrey's perceptual response training was confirmed by the author. A completely different approach to the problem was found in Bijou's efforts to establish orientation discrimination (Chapter 17). In this an attempt was made to maintain discrimination performance while mirror-image forms were gradually faded-in.

This work suggests that contrary to the opinions of Davidson (1931, 1934, 1935) and Vernon (1957) the child's discrimination of orientation is sensitive to training. This should have important practical implications particularly in the remedial treatment of backward readers who, we have seen (Chapter 16), have very similar discrimination problems as the young child.

THE METHOD OF HYPOTHESIS ANALYSIS

"HYPOTHESES" IN DISCRIMINATION PERFORMANCE

In the 1920's, mainly as a result of Thorndike's (1913) work on the learning of cats in puzzle-boxes, it was widely held that an organism, suitably motivated, and placed in a situation requiring a certain response or sequence of responses to produce a reward, behaved initially in a completely *random* manner.

Lashley (1929) challenged this idea. He argued that ". . . one does not realise the meaning of random behaviour until he has compared a normal animal with one having extensive cortical destruction" (p. 138). Such a comparison highlights a kind of *order and system* in the behaviour of the normal animal which is absent in abnormal animal. The normal animal's pre-solution behaviour is far from random. It is characterized by what Lashley called "attempted solutions". The animal, as it were, tries one method of responding after another until the correct one, that which yields 100 per cent reinforcement, is hit upon, at which point the unfortunate animal is usually removed from the task or given something else to learn.

This *systematic pre-solution behaviour* is, of course, only observable in those situations which allow it. It is not surprising that Thorndike, using the puzzle-box and the latency of the final solution response as the behavioural measure, failed to observe it. The two-choice discrimination learning experiment is, on the other hand, an ideal situation for observing such systematic habits.

But, in addition to the right sort of situation for this type of pre-solution behaviour to occur, we also require the right method of *performance examination* for it to be observed. For a start, we need an analysis of individual performances, for the group mean tells us little about what the individuals comprising the group are doing. But an individual learning curve, in which correct responses or errors are plotted against trials, also conceals many features of the subject's actual performance. For example, the learning curve obtained by

Zeaman and House (1963), referred to in Chapter 4, had an initial flat portion followed by a rapid acceleration to criterion performance. But this measure only samples one dimension of the subject's behaviour. During the flat portion of the curve the subject is undoubtedly responding in a *chance* manner with respect to the positive and negative values of the discriminative stimuli. But what would this part of the performance look like if assessed in some other way? Clearly, in addition to the individual analysis approach, we require some comprehensive method of assessing a subject's performance when it appears to be random with respect to certain criteria of assessment. This is where the method of *hypothesis analysis* comes in.

Lashley (1929) noted that, prior to attaining solution, rats on the jumping stand discrimination apparatus would typically respond on the basis of the positions of the stimulus figures, to alteration and to cues from the experimenter's movements. But he stresses, "There is no present way to record such behaviour objectively, and I can present the description only as an impression from the training of several hundred animals in these problems." [*Op. cit.*, p. 136.]

Krechevsky's (1932c) work was the first attempt to construct a method by which this systematic pre-solution behaviour could be objectively recorded. In accordance with Tolman's (1932) theory of learning, Krechevsky called these systematic attempts at solution "*hypotheses*". Though he is very careful to insist this word is merely ". . . a convenient tag for such behaviour" (*op. cit.*, p. 529); that it has, in itself, no explanatory power; that it simply describes the sort of behaviour that occurs in a two-choice discrimination problem, prior to solution; nevertheless, one cannot escape its mentalistic implications. This is clear from Krechevsky's tabulation of the main characteristics of an hypothesis:

(1) behaviour which is systematic;
(2) behaviour which is purposive (displaying an "if-then" character);
(3) behaviour which involves some degree of abstraction; and finally,
(4) behaviour which does not depend entirely upon the immediate environment for its initiation and performance. [*Op. cit.*, p. 529.]

Though this may be a very accurate description of what we intuitively know hypothesis behaviour to be like, the problem remains to indicate just what observable features about the performance these characteristics refer to. These speculations are valuable in so far that they direct our attention towards the need for more precise and detailed description of what actually happens in a discrimination

performance. But in themselves they are, operationally speaking, of limited value.

HYPOTHESIS ANALYSIS

Krechevsky's (1932c) method of representing the hypothesis behaviour of a rat in a two-choice discrimination task was as follows. The following measures were taken of each performance: (1) the number of errors made; (2) the number of turns to the right; (3) the number of turns to the left; (4) the number of alternating responses; and (5) the number of perseverative responses. From each of these measures a different performance curve was plotted for each rat.

An *example* of Krechevsky's analysis is shown in Fig. A.1. Here we see the performance of a rat on the second part of a reversal learning task. The rat has been trained up to criterion on a brightness discrimination task. The figure shows what happens to the perform-ance when instead of being rewarded for responding to the lighter S

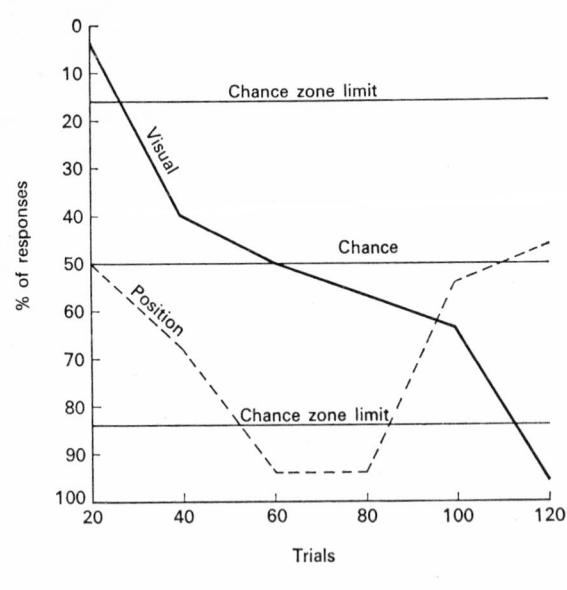

FIG. A.1. Progress of position and visual habits in a rat on a two-choice visual discrimination task (from Krechevsky (1932c)).

the rat is now rewarded for responding to the darker S. The graph shows the percentage of R's made to the dark S and the percentage of R's to the S on the right, irrespective of whether it is dark or light, on each consecutive block of twenty trials.

We see that over the first twenty trials, following the reversal of S values, the percentage of R's made to the dark S is very small, well below the chance zone limit (50 per cent $\pm$ 3SD); while an equal number of R's are made to the left and to the right. Clearly, the light-going habit acquired in the initial discrimination learning is still operating.

Over the next twenty trials the position changes. Now only about 60 per cent of the R's are being made to the light S while nearly 70 per cent are being made to the right. Clearly, what is happening here is that the rat is gradually transferring from the non-reinforced light-going hypothesis to the 50 per cent reinforced right-going position habit. This is confirmed over the next forty trials during which time over 90 per cent of the responses are made to the right, while the number of light-going and dark-going R's are about equal. Finally, the position habit is broken, the number of right and left R's becoming equal; and the correct 100 per cent rewarded dark-going habit fully adopted.

The next major advance in the analysis of incorrect methods of responding on discrimination tasks was Harlow's (1950) explanation of the acquisition of a learning set by monkeys in terms of the elimination of *error factors*. According to Harlow's recent formulation of this theory (Harlow, 1959), learning is seen as a *uniprocess* as opposed to the more widely accepted view of it as a duoprocess. That is, learning consists entirely of the inhibition of error-producing tendencies. There is no positive or strengthening part to learning.

Harlow identified four main error factors. These were stimulus perseveration, differential cue, response shift and position habits. Clearly, what Harlow calls "error factors" derive from similar observations about a discrimination performance that prompted Lashley to postulate "attempted solutions" and Krechevsky "hypotheses". This is very obvious from Harlow's (1959) definition of error factors as ". . . reaction tendencies leading to ordered, but inappropriate, responses to the problems presented" (p. 513).

Harlow's error factor analysis was taken a step further by Levine (1959). He was dissatisfied with the piecemeal approach to the

analysis of discrimination performance and consequently set out a logically derived list of all the possible behaviour sequences involving the discriminatory stimuli and their positions. He reintroduced the term "hypothesis" (H) to describe these sequences, but expurgated it of all its aetiological connotations. Each H was operationally defined in terms of a specific sequence of R's. Levine listed nine H's which could be identified in a three-trials-per-problem learning set task. Many of these had previously been identified by Krechevsky and Harlow in other types of task though one or two are relatively specific to the particular task used by Levine.

This first analysis by Levine was not perfect. Bowman (1963) and Levinson and Reese (1963) modified it slightly so that it would be more logical and less specific.

In his revision, Levine (1963) draws a useful distinction between two types of H. A *Prediction H* is manifested in behaviour which is contingent upon outcomes. A *Response-set H* is manifested in behaviour which is independent of outcomes.

Levine's revised list of hypotheses are defined in Table A.1. The analysis is in its present form most suitable for a two-trials-per-problem, two choice, discrimination learning set task. The first column shows the response made to the first item, which by the nature of the learning set procedure must be chance. "S1" is the stimulus and "P1" the position responded to on this item. The second column shows the outcome of the R to item 1. "$+$" is a positive and "$-$" a negative outcome. The third column shows the R made to the second item. This is the R under analysis. "S2" refers to the stimulus not responded to on item 1 and "P2" to the position not responded to on item 1.

As well as Levine's description of each H, Bowman's (1963) and a more conventional description are given.

HYPOTHESIS ANALYSIS OF MATCHING

The hypothesis analysis shown in Table A.1 may be slightly modified for use in the examination of matching performances. As we have seen (Chapter 13), matching is like the discrimination learning set procedure in that a number of different discrimination problems make up the task. This contrasts with the classical discrimination learning tasks in which there was only a single problem to be learned, that is, only two S's to be discriminated. But, whereas the learning set

task requires at least *two* trials per problem, the first to discover the S+ and the second to respond to it, the matching task requires only *one* trial per problem.

TABLE A.1. HYPOTHESES IN TWO-CHOICE TASK

Item 1	Out-come	Item 2	Bowman	Levine	Conventional
S1	+	S1	Win–stay S	Prediction: correct	Correct
S1	−	S2	Lose–shift S	S same on both trials	behaviour
S1	+	S2	Win–shift S	Prediction: correct	Incorrect
S1	−	S1	Lose–stay S	S will alternate	behaviour
P1	+	P1	Win–stay P	Prediction: one P is	Win–stay,
P1	−	P2	Lose–shift P	correct	lose–shift
P1	+	P2	Win–shift P	Prediction: correct	Win–shift,
P1	−	P1	Lose–stay P	position alternates	lose–stay
S1	+	S1	Win–stay S	R set to R to the	Stimulus
S1	−	S1	Lose–stay S	same S	perseveration
S1	+	S2	Win–shift S	R set to R to	Stimulus
S1	−	S2	Lose–shift S	alternate S	alternation
P1	+	P1	Win–stay P	R set to R to the	Position
P1	−	P1	Lose–stay P	same position	perseveration
P1	+	P2	Win–shift P	R set to R to	Position
P1	−	P2	Lose–shift P	alternate position	alternation

There does not appear to have been any published report of an H analysis of matching. Moon and Harlow (1955), however, analysed oddity responding and identified all the error factors that Harlow (1950) had found operative in the discrimination learning set.

Table A.2 shows the hypotheses that may be used in the description of the matching performances. The first column shows the response made on the item preceding the response under analysis. Since matching is a one-item-per-problem procedure this item 1 can be anywhere in the task. As before, P1 is the position responded to on the first item and P2 the position not responded to. The second column shows the outcomes of the first response, and the third

column the response under analysis. Rm indicates a response to the matching stimulus and Ro a response to the non-matching or odd, stimulus.

TABLE A.2. HYPOTHESES IN MATCHING

Item 1	Outcome	Item 2	Description	Label
		Rm	Matching	M
		Ro	Oddity responding	O
P1	+	P1	Win–stay	W
P1	−	P2	Lose–shift	
P1	+	P2	Lose–stay	L
P1	−	P1	Win–shift	
P1		P1	Position perseveration	P
P1		P2	Position alternation	A

Using this analysis each response in the matching performance can be described by *three* H's. The response will be either to the *matching* stimulus, in which case the hypothesis is M, or to the *non-matching* stimulus, in which case the hypothesis is O. Secondly the response will be made either to the *same* position as the preceding R, in which case the hypothesis will be P, or to the *other* position, in which case the hypothesis will be A. Thirdly, the hypothesis will be W if the preceding R had a *positive* outcome and the R under analysis were made to the *same* position, or if the preceding R had a *negative* outcome and the R under analysis were made to the *other* position. And the hypothesis will be L if the preceding R had a *negative* outcome and the R under analysis were made to the *same* position, or if the preceding R had a *positive* outcome and the R under analysis were made to the *other* position.

The next problem is how we are going to use these three sets of hypotheses to describe the performance of a subject. Firstly, here are two quantitative methods that might be used.

1. *Hypothesis Preference*

The H preference score is calculated by adding up the number of times a particular H occurs in the whole performance. Such a score should provide us with some information about the relative predominance of each H over the performance. Thus, a high M preference score will indicate that the matching hypothesis was strong. A high A score will indicate that the simple alternation hypothesis was dominant. The preference scores also enable us to compare the performance of one subject with that of another.

The preference score on its own, however, does not tell us much about the performance. Particularly, it says nothing about the extent to which a number of consecutive instances of an H occurred. For this we need a habit score.

2. *Hypothesis Habit*

The hypothesis habit score is designed to indicate the extent to which *runs* of a particular H occurred in the performance. There are two possible ways of calculating H habit scores.

(*a*) *Cumulative method.* In this, instead of counting up H's in units of one, they are counted cumulatively. Thus, if the R to item 1 is an A response, then this counts 1 towards the A habit score. If the next R is also an A response, then this counts 2, if the next one also then this counts 3, and so on. Of course, if there is a break in a run then the counting goes back to the beginning.

(*b*) *Limits method.* In this a certain limit or base of consecutive H's is set from which the calculation begins. For example, a base of 5 may be used. This means that only runs of over 5 consecutive H's will count towards the H habit score. So, if there were a run of 6 A responses this would count as 1 towards the A habit score. A run of 7 would count 2, a run of 8, 3, and so on.

The H habit score also has its limits. Though it tells us about the extent to which an H has dominated periods of responding in the performance, it does not tell us how many periods there were and how they were related to one another. In lieu of more sophisticated quantitative methods to assess these characteristics it might be valuable to examine them qualitatively. For example, a method of visual presentation such as used by Krechevsky might be employed.

In order to illustrate these methods let us look in some detail

at the matching performances of two 5-year-old children selected from the author's experiments. Both these examples illustrate *regression in task strategies* which was discussed in Chapter 5.

Table A.3 shows a quantitative analysis of the performances into hypothesis preference and hypothesis habit scores.

TABLE A.3. QUANTITATIVE ANALYSIS OF TWO MATCHING PERFORMANCES

	Easy		Difficult Task							
	T E		M	O	X	P1 P2 A			W	L
Subject 1	19 0	Pref.	34	13	1	−4 0		+4	+4	−4
		Hab.	23	1	0	0 0		1	2	0
Subject 2	30 6	Pref.	21	27	0	−2 0		+2	+23	−23
		Hab.	0	3	0	0 0		0	21	0

In the analysis of the easy discrimination task T refers to the number of trials needed by the subject to attain the required standard for transfer to the difficult task (19 correct from 20 consecutive choices), and E to the number of errors made. In the difficult task the symbols are as in Table A.2 except for X which refers to simultaneous responses to both choice stimuli. The H preference scores (Pref.) have been corrected by subtracting from them the score that would have been expected from a perfect matching performance. This was necessary because of a *bias* towards the A and L hypotheses in the sequences used to determine the relative positions of the matching and the non-matching choice stimuli.

The H habit scores (Hab.) were calculated by the limits method using a base of 5.

This analysis gives us a reasonably clear picture of the overall performance. The significant features are the M habit score of Subject 1, and the high W habit score of Subject 2. So, whereas matching was the predominant hypothesis in the performance of Subject 1, Subject 2's performance was dominated by a strong win–stay, lose–shift hypothesis. These scores are most useful for determining group means when we wish to compare the results of different experimental treatments. For detailed individual analyses the *graphical representations* shown in Figs. A.2 and A.3 are of most value. These figures show the cumulative growth of matching (M) versus oddity (O) responses,

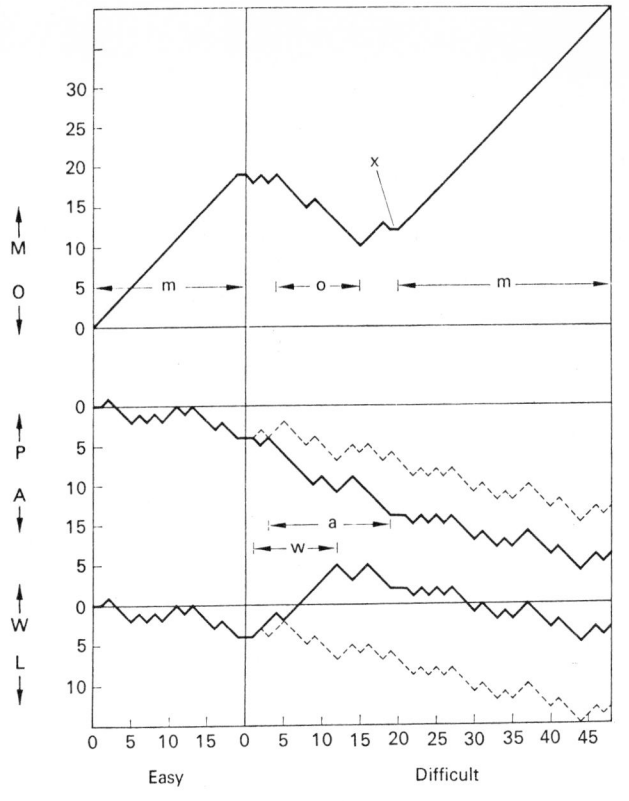

FIG. A.2. Subject 1.

position perseveration (P) versus position alternation (A) responses, and win–stay lose–shift (W) versus lose–stay win–shift (L) responses throughout the two tasks. The dotted lines indicate the curves that would result from perfect matching, i.e. they indicate the bias of the sequences used towards the reinforcement of the A and the L hypotheses. These were Gellerman (1933c) sequences, which require revision (Fellows, 1967).

The graph of Subject 1 shows very clearly the *breakdown in matching* following the transition to the difficult discrimination task. It also shows the reestablishment of matching on the difficult task from item 20 onwards. There are three possible interpretations of what happens in between. First, the upper section of the graph suggests that the effect of the difficult discriminations and the making

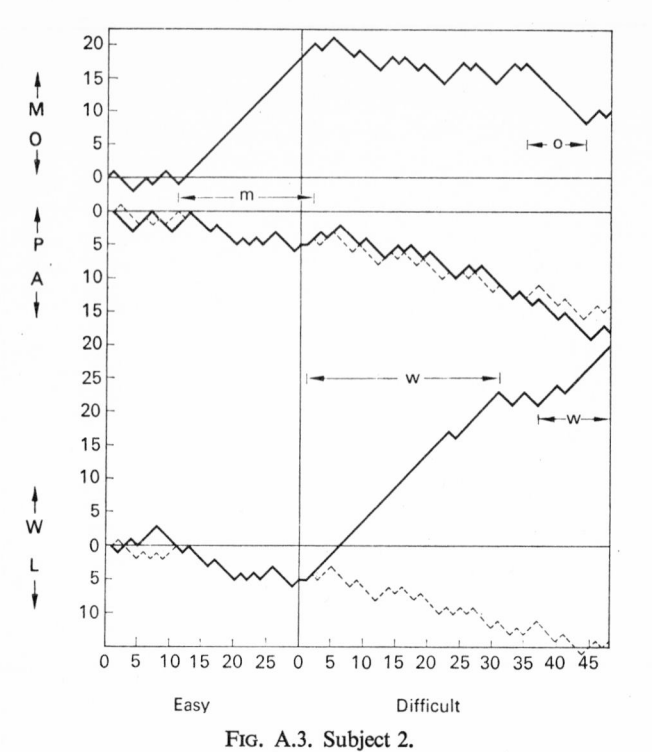

FIG. A.3. Subject 2.

of errors was to switch the child over from matching to oddity responding which continued with one to break item 15. In terms of the model presented in Chapter 14 this switch would only involve the response strategy operation; the appropriate orienting response would remain. This is the favoured interpretation since the other two both entail a different orienting response. From a slightly different viewpoint one might argue that the switch to the cognitively simpler oddity hypothesis relieved the pressure on the cognitive operations so as to allow the perceptual operations to get to grips with the new discriminations. Once this latter had been achieved the system might be prepared to shoulder the whole burden of matching plus the difficult discriminations. See Chapter 5 for further discussion of this in terms of the regression hypothesis.

The other two interpretations of the initial behaviour on the new task are suggested by the lower two sections of Fig. A.2. It can be seen that there is a tendency towards alternation over the first 20

items and a stronger tendency towards the win–stay lose–shift hypothesis over the first 12 items. As indicated already, these interpretations are not favoured by theoretical considerations. In addition, whereas in all the author's observations only one instance of matching taking over from a position habit was seen, there were at least four other examples of the switch from matching to oddity and back to matching.

REFERENCES

ALBERTS, E. and EHRENFREUND, D. (1951) Transposition in children as a function of age, *J. exp. Psychol.* **41**, 30–38.

ARNHEIM, R. (1954) *Art and Visual Perception: A Psychology of the Creative Eye*, Berkeley, Univ. of California Press.

ARNOULT, M. D. (1953) Transfer of predifferentiation training in simple and multiple shape discrimination, *J. exp. Psychol.* **45**, 401–9.

ARNOULT, M. D. (1957) Stimulus predifferentiation: some generalisations and hypotheses, *Psychol. Bull.* **54**, 339–50.

ATKINSON, R. C. (1958) A Markov model for discrimination learning, *Psychometrika* **34**, 309–22.

ATKINSON, R. C. (1959) A theory of stimulus discrimination learning, in K. J. Arrow, S. Karlin and P. Suppes (eds.), *Mathematical Methods in the Social Sciences*, Stanford, Stanford Univ. Press.

ATKINSON, R. C. (1961) The observing response in discrimination learning, *J. exp. Psychol.* **62**, 253–62.

ATKINSON, R. C. (1963) Mathematical models in research with children, in J. C. Wright and J. Kagan (eds.), *Basic Cognitive Processes in Children*, Soc., Res. Child Develpm., **28**, No. 2, 145–64.

BAER, D. M. (1961) The effect of withdrawal of positive reinforcement on an extinguishing response in young children, *Child Develpm.*, **32**, 67–74.

BAKER, R. A. and OSGOOD, S. W. (1954) Discrimination transfer along a pitch continuum, *J. exp. Psychol.* **48**, 241–6.

BARTLETT, F. (1951) *The Mind at Work and Play*, London, Allen and Unwin.

BECK, H. S. (1960) The relationship of symbol reversals to monocular and binocular vision, *Peabody J. Educ.* **38**, 137–42.

BEKHTEREV, V. M. (1933) *General Principles of Human Reflexology*, New York, International Publishers.

BELMONT, L. and BIRCH, H. G. (1963) Lateral dominance and right–left awareness in normal children, *Child Develpm.* **34**, 257–70.

BERLYNE, D. E. (1960) *Conflict, Arousal and Curiosity*, McGraw-Hill.

BERLYNE, D. E. (1963a) Soviet research on intellectual processes in children, in J. C. Wright and J. Kagan (eds.), *Basic Cognitive Processes in Children*, Soc. Res. Child Develpm., **28**, No. 2, 165–83.

BERLYNE, D. E. (1963b) Psychology in the U.S.S.R., *Canad. Psychol.* **4**, 1–13.

BERRYMAN, R., CUMMING, W. W. and NEVIN, J. A. (1963) Acquisition of delayed matching in the pigeon, *J. exp. Anal. Behav.* **6**, 101–8.

BETTS, E. A. (1935). Binocular coordination in reading, in C. E. Skinner (ed.), *Readings in Psychology*, New York, Farrar & Rinehart.

BIJOU, S. W. (1955) A systematic approach to an experimental analysis of young children, *Child Develpm.* **26**, 161–8.

BIJOU, S. W. (1957) Methodology for an experimental analysis of child behaviour, *Psychol. Rep.* **3**, 243–50.

BIJOU, S. W. (1958a) A child study laboratory on wheels, *Child Develpm.* **29**, 425–7.

BIJOU, S. W. (1958b) A standard candy for research with children, *J. exp. Anal. Behav.* **1**, 314.

BIJOU, S. W. (1958c) Operant extinction after fixed interval schedules with young children, *J. exp. Anal. Behav.* **1**, 25–29.

BIJOU, S. W. (1961) Discrimination performance as a baseline for individual analysis of young children, *Child Develpm.* **32**, 163.

BIJOU, S. W. (1962) Systematic instruction in the attainment of right–left form concepts in young and retarded children, unpubl. rep.

BIJOU, S. W. and BAER, D. M. (1960) The laboratory—experimental study of child behaviour, in P. H. Mussen (ed.), *Handbook of Research Methods in Child Development*, New York, Wiley, chap. 4.

BIJOU, S. W. and BAER, D. M. (1961) *Child Development: A Systematic and Empirical Theory*, New York, Appleton–Centry–Crofts.

BIJOU, S. W. and BAER, D. M. (1963) Some methodological contributions from a functional analysis of child development, in L. P. Lipsitt and C. C. Spiker (eds.), *Advances in Child Development and Behaviour*, Vol. 1, New York, Academic Press, pp. 197–231.

BIJOU, S. W. and ORLANDO, R. (1961) Rapid development of multiple schedule performance with retarded children, *J. exp. Anal. Behav.* **4**, 7–16.

BIJOU, S. W. and STURGES, P. T. (1959) Positive reinforcers for experimental studies with children, *Child Develpm.* **30**, 151–70.

BINGHAM, H. C. (1913) Size and form perception in *Gallus domesticus*, *J. Animal Behav.* **3**, 65–113.

BINGHAM, H. C. (1914) A definition of form, *J. Animal Behav.* **4**, 136–41.

BIRCH, H. G. (1962) Dyslexia and the maturation of the visual function, in J. Morey (ed.), *Reading Disability*, Baltimore, Johns Hopkins Press.

BIRCH, H. G. and LEFFORD, A. (1963) *Intersensory Development in Children*, Monogr. Soc. Res. Child Develpm., No. 89.

BOWMAN, R. E. (1963) Discrimination learning set performance under intermittent and secondary reinforcement, *J. comp. physiol. Psychol.* **56**, 429–34.

BROADBENT, D. E. (1958) *Perception and Communication*, Pergamon.

BROWN, J. (1955) Immediate Memory, doctoral thesis, Univ. of Cambridge. See also *Quart. J. exp. Psychol.* **10**, 12–21.

BROWN, R. W. (1963) Discussion of E. J. Gibson's paper, Development of perception, in J. C. Wright and J. Kagan (eds.), *Basic Cognitive Processes in Children*, Monogr. Soc. Res. Child Develpm., **28**, No. 2, pp. 29–32.

BROZEK, J. (1964) Recent developments in Soviet psychology, *Ann. Rev. Psychol.* **15**, 493–594.

BRUNER, J. S. and GOODMAN, C. C. (1947) Value and need as organising factors in perception, *J. abnorm. soc. Psychol.* **42**, 33–44.

BRUNER, J. S. and MINTURN, A. L. (1955) Perceptual identification and perceptual organisation, *J. gen. Psychol.* **53**, 21–28.

BUSH, R. R. and MOSTELLER, F. (1955) *Stochastic Models for Learning*, New York, Wiley.

CANTOR, G. N. (1955) The effects of three types of pretraining on discrimination learning in children, *J. exp. Psychol.* **49**, 339–42.

CANTOR, J. H. (1955) Amount of pretraining as a factor in stimulus predifferentiation and performance set, *J. exp. Psychol.* **50**, 180–4.

CAPALDI, E. J. and STEVENSON, H. W. (1957) Response reversal following different amounts of overtraining, *J. comp. physiol. Psychol.* **50**, 195–8.

CARR, H. A. (1930) Teaching and learning, *J. genet. Psychol.* **37**, 189–219.

CLARKE, A. D. B. and BLAKEMORE, C. B. (1961) Age and perceptual motor transfer in imbeciles, *Brit. J. Psychol.* **52**, 125–32.

CLARKE, A. D. B. and COOKSON, M. (1962) Perceptual motor transfer in imbeciles, *Brit. J. Psychol.* **53**, 321–30.

COLEMAN, R. I. and DEUTSCH, C. P. (1964) Lateral dominance and right–left discrimination: a comparison of normal and retarded readers, *Percept. mot. Skills* **19**, 43–50.

CRITCHLEY, M. (1964) *Developmental Dyslexia*, Heineman.

DANIELS, J. C. and DIACK, H. (1956) *Progress in Reading*, Univ. of Nottingham Institute of Education.

DAVIDSON, H. P. (1931) An experimental study of bright, average and dull children at the four year mental level, *Genet. Psychol. Monogr.* **9**, 119–289.

DAVIDSON, H. P. (1934) A study of reversals in the young child, *J. genet. Psychol.* **45**, 452–65.

DAVIDSON, H. P. (1935) A study of the confusing letters *b*, *d*, *p* and *q*, *J. genet. Psychol.* **47**, 458–68.

DAVIS, R. T., LAMPERT, A. and RUMELHART, D. E. (1964) Perception by monkeys: II. Use of cues at a distance by young and old monkeys, *Psychon. Sci.* **1**, 107–8.

DEUTSCH, J. A. (1955) A theory of shape recognition, *Brit. J. Psychol.* **46**, 30–37.

DEUTSCH, J. A. (1960) *The Structural Basis of Behaviour*, Camb. Univ. Press.

DITCHBURN, R. W. and GINSBORG, B. L. (1952) Vision with a stabilised retinal image, *Nature* **170**, 36–37.

DODWELL, P. C. (1957a) Shape recognition in the octopus and in the rat, *Nature* **179**, 1088.

DODWELL, P. C. (1957b) Shape recognition in rats, *Brit. J. Psychol.* **48**, 221–9.

DODWELL, P. C. (1958) Shape recognition: a reply to Deutsch, *Brit. J. Psychol.* **49**, 158.

DODWELL, P. C. (1961) Coding and learning in shape discrimination, *Psychol. Rev.* **68**, 373–82.

DODWELL, P. C. (1964) A coupled system for coding and learning in shape discrimination, *Psychol. Rev.* **71**, 148–59.

DOLLARD, J. and MILLER, N. E. (1950) *Personality and Psychotherapy*, New York, McGraw-Hill.

EDFELDT, A. W. (1959) *Silent Speech and Silent Reading*, Stockholm, Almquist & Wiskell.

EHRENFREUND, D. (1948) An experimental test of the continuity theory of discrimination learning with pattern vision, *J. comp. physiol. Psychol.* **41**, 408–22.

EVANS, C. R. (1965) Some studies of pattern perception using a stabilised retinal image, *Brit J. Psychol.* **56**.

FELLOWS, B. J. (1965) A theoretical and experimental analysis of visual discrimination performance, unpublished doctoral dissertation, Univ. of Bristol, 1965.

FELLOWS, B. J. (1967) Chance stimulus sequences for discrimination tasks, *Psychol. Bull.* **67**, 87–92.

FERNALD, G. M. (1943) *Remedial Techniques in Basic School Subjects*, New York, McGraw-Hill.

FERSTER, C. B. (1960) Intermittent reinforcement of matching to sample in the pigeon, *J. exp. Anal. Behav.* **3**, 259–72.

FERSTER, C. B. (1964) Arithmetic behaviour in chimpanzees, *Sci. Amer.* **210**, 98–106.

FERSTER, C. B. and SKINNER, B. F. (1957) *Schedules of Reinforcement*, New York, Appleton–Century–Crofts.

FIELDS, P. E. (1928) Form discrimination in the white rat, *J. comp. Psychol.* **8**, 143–58.

FIELDS, P. E. (1929) The white rat's use of visual stimuli in the discrimination of geometric figures, *J. comp. Psychol.* **9**, 107–22.

FIELDS, P. E. (1931) Contributions to visual figure discrimination in the white rat, *J. comp. Psychol.* **11**, 349–67.

FIELDS, P. E. (1932) Studies in concept formation: 1. The development of the concept of triangularity by the white rat, *Comp. Psychol. Monogr.* **9**, No. 2.

FORGUS, R. H. (1966) *Perception*, New York, McGraw-Hill.

FOWLER, W. (1962) Cognitive learning in infancy and early childhood, *Psychol. Bull.* **59**, 116–52.

FRANK, H. (1935) A comparative study of children who are backward in reading and beginners in the infant school, *Brit. J. Psychol.* **5**, 41–57.

FRANKLIN, A. W. (1962) (ed.) *Word Blindness or Specific Developmental Dyslexia*, Pitman Med. Publ. Co.

FROSTIG, M. (1961) *Developmental Test of Visual Perception*, 3rd edition, L. A., Calif. Marianne Frostig School for Educational Therapy.

FROSTIG, M. (1963) Visual perception in the brain injured child *Amer. J. Orthopsychiatry* **33**, 665–71.

FROSTIG, M. and HORNE, D. (1964) *The Frostig Programme for the Development of Visual Perception*, Chicago, Follet.

FROSTIG, M., LEFEVER, D. W. and WHITTLESEY, J. R. B. (1961) A developmental test of visual perception for evaluating normal and neurologically handicapped children, *Percpt. mot. Skills* **12**, 383–94.

FROSTIG, M., LEFEVER, D. W. and WHITTLESEY, J. R. B. (1964) *Developmental Test of Visual Perception*, Palo Alto, Calif. Consulting Psychologists Press.

GAGNE, R. M. and BAKER, K. E. (1950) Stimulus predifferentiation as a factor in the transfer of training, *J. exp. Psychol.* **40**, 439–51.

GALANTER, E. (1962) Contemporary psychophysics, in R. Brown *et al.*, *New Directions in Psychology*, New York, Holt, Rinehart & Winston.

GELLERMAN, L. W. (1933a) Form discrimination in chimpanzees and two year old children: I. Form (triangularity) *per se*, *J. genet. Psychol.* **42**, 3–29.

GELLERMAN, L. W. (1933b) Form discrimination in chimpanzees and two year old children: II. Form versus background, *J. genet. Psychol.* **42**, 29–50.

GELLERMAN, L. W. (1933c) Chance orders of alternating stimuli in visual discrimination experiments, *J. genet. Psychol.* **42**, 207–8.

GEORGE, F. H. (1961) *The Brain as a Computer*, Pergamon, Oxford.

GHENT, L. (1960) Recognition by children of realistic figures presented in various orientations, *Canad. J. Psychol.* **14**, 249–56.

GHENT, L. (1961) Form and its orientation: a child's-eye view, *Amer. J. Psychol.* **74**, 177–90.

GHENT, L. (1963) Personal communication.

GHENT, L. (1964) Age changes in the mode of perceiving geometric forms. Paper read at Eastern Psychol. Assoc., Philadelphia.

GHENT, L., BERNSTEIN, L. and GOLDWEBER, A. M. (1960) Preferences for orientation of form under varying conditions, *Percept. mot. Skills* **11**, 46.

GIBSON, E. J. (1963) Perceptual learning, *Ann. Rev. Psychol.* **14**, 29–56.

GIBSON, E. J., GIBSON, J. J., PICK, A. D. and OSSER, H. (1962) A developmental study of the discrimination of letter-like forms, *J. comp. physiol. Psychol.* **55**, 897–906.

GIBSON, E. J. and OLUM, V. (1960) Experimental methods of studying perception in children, in P. H. Mussen (ed.), *Handbook of Research Methods in Child Development*, New York, Wiley, pp. 311–73.

GIBSON, J. J. and ROBINSON, D. (1935) Orientations in visual perception: recognition of familiar plane forms in different orientations, *Psychol. Monogr.* **46**, No. 210, 39–47.

GILHOUSEN, H. C. (1931) An investigation of "insight" in rats, *Science* **73**, 711–12.

GINSBURG, N. (1957) Matching in pigeons, *J. comp. physiol. Psychol.* **50**, 261–3.

GIRARDEAU, F. L. (1959) The formation of discrimination learning sets in mongoloid and normal children, *J. comp. physiol. Psychol.* **52**, 566–70.

GOODWIN, W. R. and LAWRENCE, D. H. (1955) The functional independence of two discrimination habits associated with a constant stimulus situation, *J. comp. physiol. Psychol.* **48**, 437–43.

GOSS, A. E. and WISCHNER, G. J. (1956) Vicarious trial and error and related behaviour, *Psychol. Bull.* **53**, 35–54.

GRAY, J. A. (1964) (ed.), *Pavlov's Typology*, Pergamon.

GRIM, P. F. and WHITE, S. H. (1964) The relationship between amount of qualitative stimulus change and amount of perceptual disparity response, *J. exp. Psychol.*

GUTHRIE, E. R. (1935) *The Psychology of Learning*, New York, Harper.

GUTHRIE, E. R. (1938) *The Psychology of Human Conflict*, New York, Harper.

HAKE, H. W. and ERIKSEN, C. W. (1955) Effect of number of permissible response categories on learning of a constant number of visual stimuli, *J. exp. Psychol.* **50**, 161–7.

HAMILTON, G. V. (1911) A study of trial and error reaction in animals, *J. Animal Behav.* **1**, 33–36.

HARLOW, H. F. (1949) The formation of learning sets, *Psychol. Rev.* **56**, 51–65.

HARLOW, H. F. (1950) Analysis of discrimination learning by monkeys, *J. exp. Psychol.* **40**, 26–39.

HARLOW, H. F. (1959) Learning set and error factor theory, in S. Koch (ed.), *Psychology: A Study of a Science*, Vol. 2, New York, McGraw-Hill, 492–537.

HARRIS, A. J. (1957) Lateral dominance, directional confusion, and reading disability, *J. Psychol.* **44**, 283–94.

HEBB, D. O. (1949) *The Organisation of Behaviour: A Neuropsychological Theory*, New York, Wiley.

HEBB, D. O. (1966) *A Textbook of Psychology*, 2nd ed., Philadelphia, Saunders.

HEBRON, M. E. (1966) *Motivated Learning*, London, Methuen.

HEID, W. H. (1964) Non-verbal Conceptual Behaviour of Young Children with Programmed Material, Unpubl. doct. dissert., Univ. of Washington.

HELSON, H. (1947) Adaptation level as a frame of reference for prediction of psychophysical data, *Amer. J. Psychol.* **60**, 1–29.

HELSON, H. (1959) Adaption level theory, in S. Koch, *Psychology: the Study of a Science*, Vol. 1, McGraw-Hill, 565–621.

HENDRICKSON, L. N. and MUEHL, S. (1962) The effect of attention and motor response pretraining on learning to discriminate b and d in kindergarten children, *J. educ. Psychol.* **53**, 236–41.

HERMANN, K. (1960) *Reading Disability: A Medical Study of Wordblindness and Related Handicaps*, Springfield, Ill., C. C. Thomas.

HERMELIN, B. and O'CONNOR, N. (1964) Effects of sensory input and sensory dominance on severely disturbed, autistic children and on subnormal controls, *Brit. J. Psychol.* **55**, 201–6.

HERNANDEZ-PEON, R., SCHERRER, H. and JOUVET, M. (1956) Modification of electric activity in cochlear nucleus during "attention" in unanesthetized cats, *Sci.* **123**, 331–2.

HICKS, J. A. and STEWARD, F. D. (1935) The learning of abstract concepts of size, *Child Develpm.* **6**, 120–40.

HILDRETH, G. (1949) The development and training of hand dominance, *J. genet. Psychol.* **75**, 197–275.

HILGARD, E. R. (1951) Methods and procedures in the study of learning, in S. S. Stevens (ed.), *Handbook of Experimental Psychology*, New York, Wiley, pp. 517–67.

HILL, M. B. (1936) A study of the process of word discrimination in individuals beginning to read, *J. educ. Res.* **29**, 487–500.

HILLMAN, H. H. (1956) The effect of laterality upon reading ability, *Durham Res. Rev.*, No. 7, 86–96.

HINCHELWOOD, J. (1917) *Congenital Word Blindness*, London, H. K. Lewis.

HIVELY, W. (1962a) Programming stimuli in matching to sample, *J. exp. Anal. Behav.* **5**, 279–98.

HIVELY, W. (1962b) A Multiple-choice Visual Discrimination Apparatus, Unpub. report.

HOFFMAN, M. L. and HOFFMAN, L. W. (eds.) (1964) *Review of Child Development Research*, Vol. 1, New York, Russell Sage Found.

HOLLAND, J. G. (1962) New directions in teaching-machine research, in J. E. Coulson (ed.), *Programmed Learning and Computer-based Instruction*, New York, Wiley, pp. 46–57.

HOLLAND, J. G. and SKINNER, B. F. (1961) *The Analysis of Behaviour*, New York, McGraw-Hill.

HOLT, E. B. (1931) *Animal Drive and the Learning Process*, New York, Holt.

HOUSE, B. J., ORLANDO, R. and ZEAMAN, D. (1957) Role of positive and negative cues in the discrimination learning of mental defectives, *Percept. mot. Skills.* **7**, 73–79.

HOUSE, B. J. and ZEAMAN, D. (1958) A comparison of discrimination learning in normal and mentally defective children, *Child Develpm.* **29**, 411–16.

HOUSE, B. J. and ZEAMAN, D. (1960a) Transfer of a discrimination from objects to patterns, *J. exp. Psychol.* **59**, 298–302.

HOUSE, B. J. and ZEAMAN, D. (1960b) Visual discrimination learning and intelligence in defectives of low mental age, *Amer. J. ment. Defic.* **65**, 51–58.

HUBEL, D. H. (1963) The visual cortex of the brain, *Sci. Amer.* **208**.

HUBEL, D. H. and WIESEL, T. N. (1959) Receptive fields of single neurons in the cat's striate cortex, *J. Physiol.* **148**, 574–91.

HUBEL, D. H. and WIESEL, T. N. (1962) Receptive fields, binocular interaction and functional architecture in the cat's visual cortex, *J. Physiol.* **160**, 106–54.

HULL, C. L. (1930a) Simple trial and error learning: a study in psychological theory, *Psychol. Rev.* **37**, 241–56.

HULL, C. L. (1930b) Knowledge and purpose as habit mechanisms, *Psychol. Rev.* **37**, 511–25.

HULL, C. L. (1943) *Principles of Behaviour*, New York, Appleton–Century–Crofts.

HULL, C. L. (1951) *Essentials of Behaviour*, New Haven, Yale Univ. Press.

HUNTER, I. M. L. (1952) An experimental investigation of the absolute and relative theories of transpositional behaviour in children, *Brit. J. Psychol.* **43**, 113–128.

HUNTON, V. (1955) The recognition of inverted pictures by children, *J. genet. Psychol.* **86**, 281–8.

ITARD, J. M. G. (1932) *The Wild Boy of Aveyon*, New York, Century.

JACOBSON, E. (1932) The electrophysiology of mental activities, *Amer. J. Physiol.* **44**, 677–94.

JAKOBSON, R. and HALLE, M. (1956) *Fundamentals of Language*, The Hague, Netherlands, Moulton.

JAMES, W. (1890) *The Principles of Psychology*, New York, Holt. (Republished 1950 by Dover.)

JASPER, H. M. and RANEY, E. T. (1937) The phi test of lateral dominance, *Amer. J. Psychol.* **49**, 450–57.

JEFFREY, W. E. (1958a) Variables in early discrimination learning: I. Motor responses in the training of a left–right discrimination, *Child Develpm.* **29**, 269–75.

JEFFREY, W. E. (1958b) Variables in early discrimination learning: II. Mode of response and stimulus difference in the discrimination of tonal frequencies, *Child Develpm.* **29**, 531–8.

JEFFREY, W. E. and COHEN, L. B. (1964) Effect of spatial separation of stimulus, response and reward on selective learning in children, *J. exp. Psychol.* **67**, 577–80.

JENKINS, W. O. (1943) A spatial factor in chimpanzee learning, *J. comp. physiol. Psychol.* **35**, 81–84.

JOHNSON, M. S. (1957) Factors related to disability in reading, *J. exp. Educ.* **26**, 10.

JONES, C. H., LEITH, G. O. M. and GULLIFORD, R. (1966) *Programming and Aspect of Reading Readiness*, Research Report, National Centre for Programmed Learning, Univ. of Birmingham.

KAGAN, J., MOSS, H. A. and SIGEL, I. E. (1963) Psychological significance of styles of conceptualization, in J. C. Wright and J. Kagan (eds.), *Basic Cognitive Processes in Children*, Monogr. Soc. Res. Child Develpm. **28**, No. 2, 73–124.

KASS, C. E. (1963) Some psychological correlates of severe reading disability (dyslexia), in *Selected Studies on the Illinois Test of Psycholinguistic Abilities*. Madison, Wisconsin, Photo Press Inc., pp. 87–96.

KATZ, D. (1953) *Animals and Men*, Penguin.

KELLEHER, R. T. (1956) Discrimination learning as a function of reversal and non-reversal shifts, *J. exp. Psychol.* **51**, 379–84.

KENDLER, H. H., GLUCKSBERG, S. and KESTON, R. (1961) Perception and mediation in concept learning, *J. exp. Psychol.* **61**, 186–91.

KENDLER, H. H. and KENDLER, T. S. (1956) Inferential behaviour in preschool children, *J. exp. Psychol.* **51**, 311–14.

KENDLER, H. H. and KENDLER, T. S. (1961a) Effect of verbalisation on reversal shifts in children, *Sci.* **134**, 1619–20.

KENDLER, H. H. and KENDLER, T. S. (1962a) Vertical and horizontal processes in problem solving, *Psychol. Rev.* **69**, 1–16.

KENDLER, H. H. and KENDLER, T. S. (1966) Selective attention versus mediation: Some comments on Mackintosh's analysis of two-stage models of discrimination learning, *Psychol. Bull.* **66**, 282–8.

KENDLER, T. S. and KENDLER, H. H. (1959) Reversal and non-reversal shifts in kindergarten children, *J. exp. Psychol.* **58**, 56–60.

KENDLER, T. S. and KENDLER, H. H. (1961b) Inferential behaviour in children: II. The influence of order of presentation, *J. exp. Psychol.* **61**, 442–8.

KENDLER, T. S. and KENDLER, H. H. (1962b) Inferential behaviour in children as a function of age and subgoal constancy, *J. exp. Psychol.* **64**, 460–66.

KENDLER, T. S., KENDLER, H. H. and WELLS, D. (1960) Reversal and non-reversal shifts in nursery school children, *J. comp. physiol. Psychol.* **53**, 83–88.

KERPELMAN, L. C. and POLLACK, R. H. (1964) Developmental changes in location of form discrimination cues, *Percept. mot. Skills* **19**, 375–82.

KLÜVER, H. (1933) *Behaviour Mechanisms in Monkeys*, Chicago, Univ. of Chicago Press.

KOFFKA, K. (1924) *The Growth of the Mind*, London, Kegan Paul, Trench, Trubner & Co.

KOFFKA, K. (1935) *Principles of Gestalt Psychology*, New York, Harcourt, Brace.

KÖHLER, W. (1925) *The Mentality of Apes*, Penguin.

KÖHLER, W. (1929) *Gestalt Psychology*, New York, Liveright.

KÖHLER, W. (1940) *Dynamics in Psychology*, New York, Liveright.

KRECHEVSKY, I. (1932a) "Hypotheses" versus "chance" in the pre-solution period in sensory discrimination learning. *Univer. Calif. Publ. Psychol.* **6**, 27–44.

KRECHEVSKY, I. (1932b) The genesis of "hypotheses" in rats, *Univer. Calif. Publ. Psychol.* **6**, 45–64.

KRECHEVSKY, I. (1932c) "Hypotheses" in rats, *Psychol. Rev.* **39**, 516–32.

KRECHEVSKY, I. (1932d) Antagonistic visual discrimination habits in the white rat, *J. comp. Psychol.* **14**, 253–77.

KRECHEVSKY, I. (1933a) The docile nature of "hypotheses", *J. comp. Psychol.* **15**, 429–41.

KRECHEVSKY, I. (1933b) Heriditary nature of "hypotheses", *J. comp. Psychol.* **16**, 99–116.

KRECHEVSKY, I. (1935) Brain mechanisms and hypotheses, *J. comp. Psychol.* **19**, 425–62.

KRECHEVSKY, I. (1938) A study of the continuity of the problem solving process, *Psychol. Rev.* **45**, 107–33.

KRISE, E. M. (1952) An experimental investigation of theories of reversals in reading, *J. educ. Psychol.* **43**, 405–22.

KUENNE, M. K. (1946) Experimental investigation of the relation of language to transposition behaviour in young children, *J. exp. Psychol.* **36**, 471–90.

KURTZ, K. H. (1955) Discrimination of complex stimuli: the relationship of training and test stimuli in the transfer of a discrimination, *J. exp. Psychol.* **50**, 283–92.

LASHLEY, K. S. (1929) *Brain Mechanisms and Intelligence*, Univ. of Chicago Press.

LASHLEY, K. S. (1930) The mechanism of vision: I. A method for rapid analysis of pattern vision in the rat, *J. genet. Psychol.* **37**, 453–60.

LASHLEY, K. S. (1938a) The mechanism of vision: XV. Preliminary studies of the rat's capacity for detail vision, *J. Gen. Psychol.* **18**, 123–93.

LASHLEY, K. S. (1938b) Conditional reactions in the rat, *J. Psychol.* **6**, 311–24. Also in F. A. Beach *et al.* (eds.), *The Neuropsychology of Lashley*, McGraw-Hill, 1960, pp. 361–71.

LASHLEY, K. S. (1949) Persistent problems in the evolution of mind, *Quart. Rev. Biol.* **24**, 28–42.

LAWRENCE, D. H. (1949) Acquired distinctiveness of cues. I. Transfer between discriminations on the basis of familiarity with the stimulus, *J. exp. Psychol.* **39**, 770–84.

LAWRENCE, D. H. (1950) Acquired distinctiveness of cues: II. Selective association in a constant stimulus situation, *J. exp. Psychol.* **40**, 175–88.

LAWRENCE, D. H. (1952) The transfer of a discrimination along a continuum, *J. comp. physiol. Psychol.* **45**, 511–16.

LAWRENCE, D. H. (1963) The nature of a stimulus: some relationships between learning and perception, in S. Koch (ed.), *Psychology: A Study of a Science*, Vol. 5, 179–212.

LAWRENCE, D. H. and MASON, W. A. (1955) Systematic behaviour during discrimination reversal and change of dimension, *J. comp. physiol. Psychol.* **48**, 1–7.

LEVINE, M. (1959) A model of hypothesis behaviour in discrimination learning set, *Psychol. Rev.* **66**, 353–66.

LEVINE, M. (1963) Mediating processes in humans at the outset of discrimination learning, *Psychol. Bull.* **70**, 254–76.

LEVINSON, B. and REESE, H. W. (1963) *Patterns of Discrimination Learning Set in Preschool Children, Fifth Graders, College Freshers, and the Aged*, Final report, Cooperative Research Project, No. 1059, U.S. Dept. of Hth, Educ. and Welf.

LIPSITT, L. P. (1958) The systematic study of variables affecting children's discrimination learning. Paper read at APA, Washington D. C.

LIPSITT, L. P. and SPIKER, C. C. (eds.) (1963) *Advances in Child Development and Behaviour*, Vol. 1, London, Academic Press.

LIPSITT, L. P. and SPIKER, C. C. (eds.) (1965) *Advances in Child Development and Behaviour*, Vol. 2, London, Academic Press.

LONG, L. (1940) Conceptual relationships in children: the concept of roundness, *J. genet. Psychol.* **57**, 289–315.

LUCHINS, A. S. (1942) Mechanisation in problem solving. The effect of Einstellung, *Psychol. Monogr.* **54**, No. 248.

LUMSDAINE, A. A. and GLASER, R. (eds.) (1960) *Teaching Machines and Programmed Learning: A Source Book*, Washington D.C., Natl. Educ. Assn.

LURIA, A. R. (1957) The role of language in the formation of temporary connexions, in B. Simon (ed.), *Psychology in the Soviet Union*, Routledge & Kegan Paul, pp. 115–30.

LURIA, A. R. (1961a) *The Role of Speech in the Regulation of Normal and Abnormal Behaviour*, ed. J. Tizard, Oxford, Pergamon.

LURIA, A. R. (1961b) The genesis of voluntary movements, in N. O'Connor (ed.), *Recent Soviet Psychology*, Pergamon, 165–85.

LYNN, R. (1966) *Attention, Arousal and the Orientation Reaction*, Oxford, Pergamon.

MACGILLIVARY, M. E. and STONE, C. P. (1930) Suggestions towards an explanation of systematic errors made by albino rats in a multiple discrimination apparatus, *J. genet. Psychol.* **38**, 484–9.

MACH, E. (1914) *The Analysis of Sensations*. Trans. C. M. Williams. Rev. by S. Waterlow. London, Open Court Publ. Co.

MACKINTOSH, N. J. (1962) The effects of overtraining on a reversal and a non-reversal shift, *J. comp. physiol. Psychol.* **55**, 555–9.

MACKINTOSH, N. J. (1963a) Extinction of a discrimination habit as a function of overtraining, *J. comp. physiol. Psychol.* **56**, 842–7.

MACKINTOSH, N. J. (1963b) The effect of irrelevant cues on reversal learning in the rat, *Brit. J. Psychol.* **54**, 127–34.

MACKINTOSH, N. J. (1964) Overtraining and transfer within and between dimensions in the rat, *Quart J. exp. Psychol.* **16**, 250–54.

MACKINTOSH, N. J. (1965a) Overtraining, reversal, and extinction in rats and chicks, *J. comp. physiol. Psychol.* **59**, 31–36.

MACKINTOSH, N. J. (1965b) Overtraining, transfer to proprioceptive control and position reversal, *Quart. J. exp. Psychol.* **17**, 26–36.

MACKINTOSH, N. J. (1965c) Selective attention in animal discrimination learning, *Psychol. Bull.* **64**, 124–50.

MACKINTOSH, N. J. and MACKINTOSH, J. (1963) Reversal learning in *Octopus vulgaris* (Lamarck) with and without irrelevant cues, *Quart. J. exp. Psychol.* **15**, 236–42.

MACKINTOSH, N. J. and MACKINTOSH, J. (1964) Performance of octopus over a series of reversals of a simultaneous discrimination, *Animal Behav.* **12**, 321–4.

MACKINTOSH, N. J. and SUTHERLAND, N. S. (1963) Visual discrimination by the goldfish: the orientation of rectangles, *Animal Behav.* **11**, 135–41.

MAGOUN, H. W. (1963) *The Waking Brain*, 2nd ed., Springfield, Illinois, Thomas.

MAIER, N. R. F. (1949) *Frustration: The Study of Behaviour without a Goal*, New York, McGraw-Hill.

MALMQUIST, E. (1958) *Factors Relating to Reading Disabilities in the First Grade of the Elementary School*, Stockholm, Almquist & Wiksell.

MARSHALL, W. H. and TALBOT, S. A. (1942) Recent evidence for neural mechanisms in vision leading to a general theory of sensory activity. In H. Klüver (ed.), *Visual Mechanisms*. Lancaster, Pa, Cattell. 117–64.

MASLOW, P., FROSTIG, M., LEFEVER, D. W. and WHITTLESEY, J. R. B. (1964) The Marianne Frostig developmental test of visual perception, 1963 standardisation, *Percept. mot. Skills*. **19**, 463–99, Monogr. Supplem. 2–V19.

MAX, L. W. (1935) An experimental study of the motor theory of consciousness: III. Action—current responses in deaf-mutes during sleep, sensory stimulation and dreams, *J. comp. Psychol*. **19**, 469–86.

MAX, L. W. (1937) An experimental study of the motor theory of consciousness: IV. Action—current responses in the deaf during awakening, kinesthetic imagery and abstract thinking, *J. comp. Psychol.* **24**, 301–44.

McCARTHY, J. J. and KIRK, S. A. (1961) *Illinois Test of Psycholinguistic Abilities* (Experimental Edition), Institute for Research on Exceptional Children, Univ. of Illinois.

McCARTHY, J. J. and KIRK, S. A. (1963) *The Construction, Standardisation and Statistical Characteristics of the Illinois Test of Psycholinguistic Abilities*, Madison, Wisconsin, Photo Press Inc.

McCLEARN, G. E. and HARLOW, H. F. (1954) The effect of spatial contiguity on discrimination learning by rhesus monkeys, *J. comp. physiol. Psychol*. **47**, 391–94.

McFIE, J. (1952) Cerebral dominance in dyslexia, *J. Neurol. Neurosurg. Psychiat*. **15** 194–9.

McLEISH, J. (1955) Materials on Soviet Psychology, *Psychol. Bull*. **2**, 8–12.

MEREDITH, C. P. (1962) Psycho-physical aspects of word-blindness and kindred disorders, in A. W. Franklin (ed.), *Word Blindness or Specific Developmental Dyslexia*, London, Pitman Med. Publ. Co.

MEREDITH, C. P. (1963) Word Blindness, *Word Blind. Committee Bull*. **1**, 1–4.

MEYER, D. R., POLIDORA, V. J. and McCONNELL, D. G. (1961) Effects of spatial S–R contiguity and response delay upon discriminative performances by monkeys, *J. comp. physiol. Psychol*. **54**, 175–7.

MILLER, G. A., GALANTER, E. and PRIBRAM, K. H. (1960) *Plans and the Structure of Behaviour*, New York, Holt.

MILLER, N. E. (1948) Theory and experiment relating psychoanalytic displacement to stimulus-response generalisation, *J. abnorm. soc. Psychol*. **43**, 155–78.

MILLER, N. E. and DOLLARD, J. (1941) *Social Learning and Imitation*, New Haven, Yale Univ. Press.

MILLER, R. E. and MURPHY, J. V. (1964) Influence of the spatial relationship between the cue, reward and response in discrimination leaning, *J. exp. Psychol*. **67**, 120–23.

MINTZ, A. (1958) Recent Developments in the USSR, *Ann. Rev. Psychol*. **9**, 453–504.

MINTZ, A. (1959) Further developments in pyschology in the USSR, *Ann. Rev. Psychol*. **10**, 464.

MONROE, M. (1928) Specific reading disability, *Genet. Psychol. Monogr*. **4**, 332.

MONROE, M. (1939) *Children Who Cannot Read*, Univ. of Chicago Press.

MONROE, M. and BACKUS, B. (1937) *Remedial Reading*, Boston, Houghton Mifflin.

MOON, L. E. and HARLOW, H. F. (1955) Analysis of oddity learning by rhesus monkeys, *J. comp. physiol. Psychol.* **48**, 188–95.

MOUNTCASTLE, V. B. (ed.) (1962) *Interhemispheric Relations and Cerebral Dominance*, John Hopkins Press.

MUENZINGER, K. F. (1938) Vicarious trial and error at a point of choice. I. A general survey of its relation to learning efficiency, *J. genet. Psychol.* **53**, 75–86.

MURPHY, G. (1947) *Personality*, New York, Harper.

MURPHY, J. V. and MILLER, R. E. (1955) The effect of spatial contiguity of cue and reward in the object–quality learning of rhesus monkeys, *J. comp. physiol. Psychol.* **48**, 221–4.

MURPHY, J. V. and MILLER, R. E. (1958) Effect of the spatial relationship between cue, reward and response in simple discrimination learning, *J. exp. Psychol.* **56**, 26–31.

MURPHY, J. V. and MILLER, R. E. (1959) Spatial contiguity of cue, reward and response in discrimination learning by children, *J. exp. Psychol.* **58**, 485–9.

NEVIN, J. A., CUMMING, W. W. and BERRYMAN, R. (1963) Ratio reinforcement of matching behaviour, *J. exp. Anal. Behav.* **6**, 149–54.

NEWHALL, S. M. (1937) Identification by young children of differently oriented visual forms, *Child Develpm.* **8**, 105–11.

NEWSON, E. (1955) The Development of Line Figure Discrimination in Preschool Children, Ph.D. Thesis, Univ. of Nottingham.

NISSEN, H. W., BLUM, J. S. and BLUM, R. A. (1948) Analysis of matching behaviour in chimpanzee, *J. comp. physiol. Psychol.* **41**, 62–74.

NORCROSS, K. J. (1958) The effects on discrimination performance of the similarity of previously acquired stimulus names, *J. exp. Psychol.* **56**, 305–9.

NORCROSS, K. J. and SPIKER, C. C. (1957) The effects of type of stimulus pretraining on discrimination performance in preschool children, *Child Develpm.* **28**, 79–84.

O'CONNOR, N. (ed.) (1961) *Recent Soviet Psychology*, Pergamon.

ORLANDO, R. and BIJOU, S. W. (1960) Single and multiple schedules of reinforcement in developmentally retarded children, *J. exp. Anal. Behav.* **4**, 339–48.

ORTON, S. T. (1925) "Wordblindness" in school children. *Arch. Neurol. Psych.* **14**.

ORTON, S. T. (1929) The "sight reading" method of teaching reading disability, *J. educ. Psychol.* **20**, 135–43.

ORTON, S. T. (1937) *Reading, Writing and Speech Problems in Children*, London, Chapman & Hall.

OVER, R. (1967) Detection and recognition measures of shape discrimination, *Nature* **214**, 1272–3.

PAVLOV, I. P. (1927) *Conditioned Reflexes*, Oxford Univ. Press (1960), New York, Dover.

PAVLOV, I. P. (1928) *Lectures on Conditioned Reflexes*, New York, Liveright.

PFAFFLIN, S. M. (1960) Stimulus meaning in stimulus predifferentiation, *J. exp. Psychol.* **59**, 269–74.

PIAGET, J. (1947) *The Psychology of Intelligence*, Routledge & Kegan Paul.

PIAGET, J. (1961) *Les Méchanismes Perceptifs*, Presses Universitaires de France.

PIAGET, J. and INHELDER, B. (1956) *The Child's Conception of Space*, Routledge & Kegan Paul.

PICK, H. L. (1963) Some Soviet research on learning and perception in children, in J. C. Wright and J. Kagan (eds.), *Basic Cognitive Processes in Children*, Soc. Res. Child Develpm. **28**, No. 2, 185–90.

POLIDORA, V. J. and FLETCHER, H. J. (1964) An analysis of the importance of S–R spatial contiguity for proficient primate discrimination performance, *J. comp. physiol. Psychol.* **57**, 224–30.

POLIDORA, V. J. and THOMPSON, W. J. (1965) Orienting behaviour and the S–R spatial discontiguity effect in monkeys, *J. comp. physiol. Psychol.* **59**, 240–5.

PREYER, L. (1895) *Zur Psychologie des Schreibens.*

PRITCHARD, R. M. (1961) Stabilized images on the retina, *Sci. Amer.* **204**, 72–78.

PRITCHARD, R. M., HERON, W. and HEBB, D. O. (1960) Visual perception approached by the method of stabilized images, *Canad. J. Psychol.* **14**, 66–77.

Problems of Psychology (1960) 1, 2 (Translation of *Voprosy Psikhologii*) Pergamon.

PUBOLS, B. H. (1956) The facilitation of visual and spatial discrimination reversal by overlearning, *J. comp. physiol. Psychol.* **49**, 243–8.

RAZRAN, G. (1961) Recent Soviet phyletic comparisons of classical and operant conditioning: experimental designs, *J. comp. physiol. Psychol.* **54**, 357–65.

REESE, H. W. (1962) Verbal mediation as a function of age level, *Psychol. Bull.* **59**, 502–9.

REID, L. S. (1953) The development of non-continuity behaviour through continuity learning, *J. exp. Psychol.* **46**, 107–12.

RENSHAW, S. (1930) The errors of cutaneous localisation and the effect of practice on the localising movement in children and adults, *J. Gen. Psychol.* **38**, 223–38.

RESTLE, F. (1955a) Axioms of a theory of discrimination learning, *Psychometrika* **20**, 201–8.

RESTLE, F. (1955b) A theory of discrimination learning, *Psychol. Rev.* **62**, 11–19.

REVÈSZ, G. (1950) *The Psychology and Art of the Blind*, Longmans.

RICE, C. (1930) The orientation of plane figures as a factor in their perception by children, *Child Develpm.* **1**, 111–43.

RIESS, B. F. (1946) Genetic changes in semantic conditioning, *J. exp. Psychol.* **36**, 143–52.

RIGGS, L. A., RATLIFF, F., CORNSWEET, J. C. and CORNSWEET, T. N. (1953) The disappearance of steadily fixated visual test objects, *J. Opt. Soc. Amer.* **43**, 495–501.

RIOPELLE, A. J., RAHM, U., ITOIGAWA, N. and DRAPER, W. A. (1964) Discrimination of mirror image patterns by rhesus monkeys, *Percept. mot. Skills* **19**, 383–9.

ROBINSON, J. S. (1955) The effect of learning verbal labels for stimuli on their later discrimination, *J. exp. Psychol.* **49**, 112–14.

ROSSMAN, I. L. and GOSS, A. E. (1951) The acquired distinctiveness of cues: the role of discriminative verbal responses in facilitating the acquisition of discriminative motor responses, *J. exp. Psychol.* **42**, 173–82.

RUDEL, R. G. (1963) Cross modal transfer effects in children and adults. Paper given at APA Meeting, Philadelphia, Aug. 1963.

RUDEL, R. G. and TEUBER, H. L. (1963) Discrimination of direction of line in children, *J. comp. physiol. Psychol.* **56**, 892–8.

RUZSKAIA, A. G. (1958) Orienting-investigatory activity in the formation of elementary generalisations in the child, in L. G. Voronin *et al.* (eds.), *The Orienting Reflex and Exploratory Behaviour*, Moscow, Acad. Pedag. Sci.

SCHLOSBERG, H. and SOLOMON, R. L. (1943) Latency of response in a choice discrimination, *J. exp. Psychol.* **33**, 22–39.

SCHONELL, F. J. (1942) *Backwardness in the Basic Subjects*, Edinburgh, Oliver & Boyd.

SCHOPLER, E. (1964) Unpublished dissertation research. Univ. of Chicago. Quoted by S. H. White, 1964a.

SCHRIER, A. M., STOLLNITZ, F. and GREEN, K. F. (1963) Titration of spatial S–R separation in discrimination by monkeys (*Macaca mulatta*), *J. comp. physiol. Psychol.* **56**, 848–51.

SHUCK, J. R. (1960) Pattern discrimination and visual sampling by the monkey, *J. comp. physiol. Psychol.* **53**, 251–5.

SHEPARD, R. N. (1957) Stimulus and response generalisation: a stochastic model relating generalisation to distance in psychological space, *Psychometrika*, **22**, 325–45.

SHEPARD, R. N. (1958) Stimulus and response generalisation: tests of a model relating generalisation to distance in psychological space, *J. exp. Psychol.* **55**, 509–23.

SHEPARD, W. O. (1956) The effect of verbal training on initial generalisation tendencies, *Child Develpm.* **27**, 311–16.

SIMON, B. (ed.) (1957) *Psychology in the Soviet Union*, Routledge & Kegan Paul.

SKINNER, B. F. (1950) Are theories of learning necessary? *Psychol. Rev.* **57**, 193–216. Also in *Cumulative Record*, Methuen, 1961, 39–69.

SKINNER, B. F. (1953) *Science and Human Behaviour*, New York, MacMillan.

SKINNER, B. F. (1961a) *Cumulative Record*. Enlarged edition. Methuen.

SKINNER, B. F. (1961b) Teaching machines, *Sci. Amer.* **205**, 90–102.

SMITH, K. U. (1945) The role of the commissural systems of the cerebral cortex in the determination of handedness, eyedness and footedness in man, *J. Gen. Psychol.* **32**, 39–80.

SMITH, N. B. (1928) Matching ability as a factor in first grade reading, *J. educ. Psychol.* **19**, 560–71.

SPENCE, K. W. (1936) The nature of discrimination learning in animals, *Psychol. Rev.* **43**, 427–49.

SPENCE, K. W. (1937a) The differential response in animals to stimuli varying within a single dimension, *Psychol. Rev.* **44**, 330–44.

SPENCE, K. W. (1937b) Analysis of formation of visual discrimination habits in chimpanzee, *J. comp. Psychol.* **23**, 77–100.

SPENCE, K. W. (1939) A reply to Dr. Razran on the transposition of response in discrimination experiments, *Psychol. Rev.* **46**, 88–91.

SPENCE, K. W. (1940) Continuous vs. noncontinuous interpretations of discrimination learning, *Psychol. Rev.* **47**, 271–88.

SPENCE, K. W. (1941) Failure of transposition in size discrimination of chimpanzee, *Amer. J. Psychol.* **54**, 223–9.

SPENCE, K. W. (1945) An experimental test of the continuity and noncontinuity theories of discrimination learning, *J. exp. Psychol.* **35**, 253–66.

SPENCE, K. W. (1951) Theoretical interpretations of learning, in S. S. Stevens (ed.), *Handbook of Experimental Psychology*, New York, Wiley, pp. 690–729.

SPENCE, K. W. (1952) The nature of the response in discrimination learning, *Psychol. Rev.* **59**, 89–93.

SPENCE, K. W. (1955) *Behaviour Theory and Conditioning*, Yale Univ. Press.

SPENCE, K. W. (1960) *Behaviour Theory and Learning*, Englewood Cliffs, N. J., Prentice-Hall.

SPERRY, R. W. (1961) Cerebral organisation and behaviour, *Sci.* **133**, 1749–57.

SPERRY, R. W. (1964) The great cerebral commissure, *Sci. Amer.* **210**, 42–52.

SPIKER, C. C. (1956) Stimulus pretraining and subsequent performance in the delayed reaction experiment, *J. exp. Psychol.* **52**, 107–11.

SPIKER, C. C. (1959) Performance on a difficult discrimination following pretraining with distinctive stimuli, *Child Develpm.* **30**, 513–21.

SPIKER, C. C. (1963) Verbal factors in the discrimination learning of children, in J. C. Wright and J. Kagan (eds.), *Basic Cognitive Processes in Children*, Monogr. Soc. Res. Child Develpm. **28**, No. 2, 53–71.

SPIKER, C. C. and NORCROSS, K. J. (1962) Effects of previously acquired stimulus names on discrimination performances, *Child Develpm.* **33**, 859–64.

STAATS, A. W. and STAATS, C. K. (1963) *Complex Human Behaviour*, Holt, Rinehart & Winston.

STERN, W. L. (1909) Ueber Verlagerte Raumformen, *Zeitsch. f. Angew. Psychol. u. Psych. Sammelforschung.* 498–526.

STERN, W. L. (1926) *The Psychology of Early Childhood.* Transl. from 3rd ed. by Banwell, New York, Holt.

STEVENSON, H. W. (ed.) (1963) *Child Psychology*, 62nd Yearbook, of the National Society for the Study of Education, part 1, Univ. of Chicago Press.

STEVENSON, H. W. and ISCOE, I. (1955) Transposition in the feebleminded, *J. exp. Psychol.* **49**, 11–15.

STOLLNITZ, F. and SCHRIER, A. M. (1962) Discrimination learning by monkeys with spatial separation of cue and response, *J. comp. physiol. Psychol.* **55**, 876–81.

SUTHERLAND, N. S. (1957a) Visual discrimination of orientation by octopus, *Brit. J. Psychol.* **48**, 55–71.

SUTHERLAND, N. S. (1957b) Visual discrimination of orientation and shape by octopus, *Nature* **179**, 11.

SUTHERLAND, N. S. (1958a) Visual discrimination of the orientation of rectangles by *Octopus Vulgaris* (Lamarck), *J. comp. physiol. Psychol.* **51**, 452–8.

SUTHERLAND, N. S. (1958b) Visual discrimination of shape by octopus: squares and triangles, *Quart. J. exp. Psychol.* **10**, 40–47.

SUTHERLAND, N. S. (1959a) Stimulus analysing mechanisms, in *Proceedings of a Symposium on the Mechanisation of Thought Processes*, Vol. 2, London, H.M.S.O., pp. 575–609.

SUTHERLAND, N. S. (1959b) Visual discrimination of shape by octopus. Circles and squares, and circles and triangles. *Quart. J. exp. Psychol.* **11**, 24–32.

SUTHERLAND, N. S. (1959c) A test of a theory of shape discrimination in *Octopus vulgaris* (Lamarck) *J. comp. physiol. Psychol.* **52**, 135–41.

SUTHERLAND, N. S. (1960a) Visual discrimination of orientation by octopus: mirror-images, *Brit. J. Psychol.* **51**, 9–18.

SUTHERLAND, N. S. (1960b) Theories of shape discrimination in octopus, *Nature* **186**, 840–4.

SUTHERLAND, N. S. (1960c) Visual discrimination of shape by octopus: squares and rectangles, *J. comp. physiol. Psychol.* **53**, 95–103.

SUTHERLAND, N. S. (1960d) Visual discrimination of shape by octopus: open and closed forms, *J. comp. physiol. Psychol.* **53**, 104–112.

SUTHERLAND, N. S. (1961a) Shape discrimination by animals, *Exp. Psychol. Soc. Monogr.* No. 1.

SUTHERLAND, N. S. (1961b) Discrimination of horizontal and vertical extents by octopus, *J. comp. physiol. Psychol.* **54**, 43–48.

SUTHERLAND, N. S. (1961c) Discrimination of horizontal and vertical rectangles by rats in a new discrimination training apparatus, *Quart. J. exp. Psychol.* **13**, 117–21.

SUTHERLAND, N.S. (1962) Visual discrimination of shape by octopus: squares and crosses, *J. comp. physiol. Psychol.* **55**, 939–43.

SUTHERLAND, N. S. (1963a) Shape discrimination and receptive fields, *Nature* **197**, 118–22.

SUTHERLAND, N. S. (1963b) The shape-discrimination of stationary shapes by octopuses, *Amer. J. Psychol.* **76**, 177–90.

SUTHERLAND, N. S. (1963c) Visual acuity and discrimination of stripe width in *Octopus Vulgaris* (Lamarck), *Publ. staz, zool. Napoli* 33, 92–109.

SUTHERLAND, N. S. (1963d) Cat's ability to discriminate oblique rectangles, *Sci.* 139, 209–10.

SUTHERLAND, N. S. (1963e) *Switching in Stimulus Analysing Mechanisms*, Report of project on Stimulus Analysing Mechanisms.

SUTHERLAND, N. S. (1964) Visual discrimination in animals, *Brit. Med. Bull.* 20, 54–59.

SUTHERLAND, N. S. and CARR, A. E. (1962) Visual discrimination of open and closed shapes by rats. II. Transfer tests, *Quart. J. exp. Psychol.* 14, 140–56.

SUTHERLAND, N. S. and CARR, A. E. (1963) The visual discrimination of shape by octopus: the effects of stimulus size, *Quart. J. exp. Psychol.* 15, 225–35.

SUTHERLAND, N. S., CARR, A. E. and MACKINTOSH, J. A. (1962) Visual discrimination of open and closed shapes by rats. I. Training, *Quart. J. exp. Psychol.* 14, 129–39.

SUTHERLAND, N. S., MACKINTOSH, N. J. and MACKINTOSH, J. (1963a) Simultaneous discrimination training of octopus and transfer of discrimination along a continuum, *J. comp. physiol. Psychol.* 56, 150–6.

SUTHERLAND, N. S. MACKINTOSH, N. J. and MACKINTOSH, J. (1963b) Shape and size discrimination in octopus: the effects of pretraining along different dimensions, *Brit. J. Psychol.*

SUTHERLAND, N. S., MACKINTOSH, J. and MACKINTOSH, N. J. (1963c) The visual discrimination of reduplicated patterns by octopus, *Animal Behav.* 11, 106–10.

TERRACE, H. S. (1963a) Discrimination learning with and without errors, *J. exp. Anal. Behav.* 6, 1–27.

TERRACE, H. S. (1963b) Errorless transfer of a discrimination across two continua, *J. exp. Anal. Behav.* 6, 223–46.

THORNDIKE, E. L. (1898) *Animal Intelligence*, New York, McMillan.

THORNDIKE, E. L. (1903) *Educational Psychology*, New York, Lemcke & Buechner.

THORNDIKE, E. L. (1913) *Educational Psychology. Vol. 2. The Psychology of Learning*, New York Teachers College.

THORNDIKE, E. L. (1932) *The Fundamentals of Learning*, New York Teachers College.

THORNDIKE, E. L. (1935) *The Psychology of Wants, Interests and Attitudes*, New York, Appleton–Century.

THORNDIKE, E. L. (1949) *Selected Writings from a Connectionist's Psychology*, New York, Appleton–Century–Crofts.

THORNDIKE, E. L. and WOODWORTH, R. S. (1901) The influence of improvement in one mental function upon the efficiency of other functions, *Psychol. Rev.* 8, 247–61.

TOLMAN, E. C. (1932) *Purposive. Behaviour in Animals and Man*, New York, Appleton–Century–Crofts.

TOLMAN, E. C. (1939) Prediction of vicarious trial and error by means of the schematic sow-bug, *Psychol. Rev.* 46, 318–36.

TOLMAN, E. C. (1948) Cognitive maps in rats and men, *Psychol. Rev.* 55, 189–208.

TOLMAN, E. C. and MINIUM, E. (1942) V.T.E. in rats: overlearning and difficulty of discrimination, *J. comp. Psychol.* 34, 301–6.

TOLMAN, E. C. and RICHIE, B. F. (1943) Correlation between V.T.E.'s on a maze and on a visual discrimination apparatus, *J. comp. Psychol.* 36, 91–98.

TOWNSEND, E. A. (1951) A study of copying ability in children, *Genet. Psycho. Monogr.* 43, 3–51.

UTTLEY, A. M. (1956) A theory of the mechanism of learning based on the computation of conditional probabilities, *Proc. First Internat. Congress on Cybernetics*, Namur.

UTTLEY, A. M. (1958) Conditioned probability computing in a nervous system, in *The Mechanisation of Thought Processes*, London, H.M.S.O.

UTTLEY, A. M. (1959) The design of conditional probability computers, *Information and Control* 2, 1–24.

VERNON, M. D. (1954) *A Further Study of Visual Perception*, Cambridge Univ. Press.

VERNON, M. D. (1957) *Backwardness in Reading*, Cambridge Univ. Press.

VYGOTSKY, L. S. (1962) *Thought and Language*, M.I.T., Wiley.

WALLIN, J. W. E. (1921) Congenital word blindness, *Lancet* 200, 890–92.

WATSON, J. B. (1914) *Behaviour: An Introduction to Comparative Psychology*, New York, Holt.

WEINSTEIN, B. (1941) Matching from sample by Rhesus monkeys and by children, *J. comp. Psychol.* 31, 195–213.

WEINSTEIN, B. (1945) The evolution of intelligent behaviour in rhesus monkeys, *Genet. Psychol. Monogr.* 31, 3–48.

WERTHEIMER, M. (1923) Principles of perceptual organisation, in D. Beardslee and M. Wertheimer (eds.), *Readings in Perception*, Princeton, Van Nostrand, 1958, pp. 115–35.

WERTHEIMER, M. (1945) *Productive Thinking*, New York, Harper.

WHITE, S. H. (1958) Generalisation of an instrumental response with variation in two attributes of the CS, *J. exp. Psychol.* 56, 339–43.

WHITE, S. H. (1962) *Research on Attentional Processes in Learning*, Progress Report, USPHS Grant M–3639.

WHITE, S. H. (1963) Learning, in H. W. Stevenson (ed.), *Child Psychology*, 62nd Year. Nat. Soc. Stud. Educ., part I, Chicago, U. Chicago.

WHITE, S. H. (1964a) Age differences in reaction to stimulus variation. Paper given at ONR Conference on Adaptation to Complex and Changing Environments at Boulder, Colorado. March, 1964.

WHITE, S. H. (1964b) Training and timing in the generalisation of a voluntary response, *J. exp. Psychol.* 69, 269–75.

WHITE, S. H. (1964c) Evidence for a hierarchical arrangement of learning processes, in L. P. Lipsitt and C. C. Spiker (eds.), *Advances in Child Psychology*, Vol. 2.

WHITE, S. H. and GRIM, P. F. (1962) Investigation of a voluntary generalisation paradigm, *Amer. Psychol.* 17.

WHITE, S. H. and PLUM, G. (1962) Child's eye movements during a discrimination series, *Amer. Psychol.* 17, 367.

WILSON, F. T. and FLEMING, C. W. (1938) Reversals in reading and writing made by pupils in the kindergarten and primary grades, *J. genet. Psychol.* 53, 3–31.

WITKIN, H. A. (1959) The perception of the upright, *Sci. Amer.* 200, 50–70.

WODINSKY, J. and BITTERMAN, M. E. (1953) The solution of oddity and non-oddity problems by the rat, *Amer. Psychol.* 8, 458 (Abstract).

WOODWORTH, R. S. and SCHLOSBERG, H. (1954) *Experimental Psychology*, London, Methuen.

WORTIS, J. (ed.) (1950) *Soviet Psychiatry*, Baltimore, Williams & Wilkins.

WRIGHT, J. C. and KAGAN, J. (eds.) (1963) *Basic Cognitive Processes in Children*, Soc. Res. Child Develpm., 28, No. 2.

WUNDERLICH, R. A. and DORFF, J. E. (1965) Contiguity relationships of stimulus, response and reward as determinants of discrimination difficulty, *J. comp. physiol. Psychol.* 59, 147–9.

WYCKOFF, L. B. (1951) The role of observing responses in discrimination learning. Unpubl. Ph.D. Thesis. Indiana Univ.

WYCKOFF, L. B. (1952) The role of observing responses in discrimination learning, *Psychol. Rev.* **59**, 431–42.

WYCKOFF, L. B. (1954) A mathematical model and an electronic model for learning, *Psychol. Rev.* **61**, 89–97.

YERKES, R. M. (1916) The mental life of monkeys and apes: a study of ideational behaviour, *Behav. Monogr.* **3**, No. 1, Serial No. 12.

YOUNG, J. Z. (1960) Regularities in the retina and optic lobes in relation to form discrimination, *Nature* **186**, 836–9.

YOUNG, J. Z. (1962) The retina of cephalopods and its degeneration after optic lobe section, *Philos. Trans.* **245**, 1–18.

YOUNG, J. Z. (1964) *A model of the Brain*, Oxford, Clarendon Press.

YOUNG, M. L. and HARLOW, H. F. (1943) Generalisation by rhesus monkeys of a problem involving the Weigl principle using the oddity method, *J. comp. Psychol.* **36**, 201–16.

ZANGWILL, O. L. (1960) *Cerebral Dominance and its Relation to Psychological Function*, Edinburgh, Oliver & Boyd.

ZAPOROZHETS, A. V. (1957) The development of voluntary movements, in B. Simon (ed.), *Psychology in the Soviet Union*, Routledge & Kegan Paul, pp. 108–14.

ZAPOROZHETS, A. V. (1961) The origin and development of the conscious control of movements in man, in O'Connor (ed.), *Recent Soviet Psychology*, Pergamon, pp. 273–389.

ZEAMAN, D. and HOUSE, B. J. (1963) The role of attention in retardate discrimination learning, in N. R. Ellis (ed.), *Handbook of Mental Deficiency*, New York, McGraw-Hill, pp. 159–223.

ZEAMAN, D., HOUSE, B. J. and ORLANDO, R. (1958) Use of special training conditions in visual discrimination learning with imbeciles, *Amer. J. ment. Defic.* **63**, 453–9.

ZINCHENKO, V. P. and LOMOV, B. F. (1960) The function of hand and eye movements in the process of perception, *Prob. Psychol.* **1**, 12–25.

ZIPF, G. K. (1949) *Human Behaviour and the Principle of Least Effort*, Cambridge, Mass. Addison-Wesley.

AUTHOR INDEX

Alberts, E.   47, 77
Arnheim, R.   163
Arnoult, M. D.   62
Atkinson, R. C.   20

Backus, B.   123, 132
Baer, D. M.   8–10, 177
Baker, K. E.   62
Baker, R. A.   60
Bartlett, F.   168
Beck, H. S.   149, 152
Bekhterev, V. M.   38
Belmont, L.   149
Berlyne, D. E.   4, 20, 23, 29, 34, 38, 113
Bernstein, L.   169
Berryman, R.   91
Betts, E. A.   152
Bijou, S. W.   8–10, 37, 47, 61–62, 140–4, 177
Bingham, H. C.   12, 116, 153
Birch, H. G.   32, 33, 149
Bitterman, M. E.   92
Blakemore, C. B.   55
Blum, J. S.   90
Blum, R. A.   90
Bowman, R. E.   183–4
Broadbent, D. E.   65, 98
Brown, J.   98
Brown, R. W.   132
Brozek, J.   38
Bruner, J. S.   3
Bush, R. R.   33, 56

Cantor, G. N.   26
Cantor, J. H.   62
Capaldi, E. J.   53
Carr, A. E.   159
Carr, H. A.   40
Clarke, A. D. B.   55, 56
Cohen, L. B.   46
Coleman, R. I.   149
Cookson, M.   56

Cornsweet, J. C.   4
Cornsweet, T. N.   4
Critchley, M.   148–9
Cumming, W. W.   91

Deutsch, C. P.   149
Deutsch, J. A.   1, 155, 164
Diack, H.   119, 149
Ditchburn, R. W.   4
Dodwell, P. C.   8, 17, 55, 155, 164
Dollard, J.   41, 63, 134
Dorff, J. E.   45
Draper, W. A.   151, 155

Edfeldt, A. W.   69
Ehrenfreund, D.   17, 45, 47, 74, 91, 154
Eriksen, C. W.   64
Evans, C. R.   4

Fellows, B. J.   9, 10, 35, 74, 80–81, 121–2, 127, 131, 138–9, 187–90
Fernald, G. M.   123, 133
Ferster, C. B.   44, 46, 90, 96, 113
Fields, P. E.   12, 153
Fleming, C. W.   121
Fletcher, H. J.   46–48, 82
Forgus, R. H.   6
Fowler, W.   177
Frank, H.   121, 127
Franklin, A. W.   148
Frostig, M.   56

Gagne, R. M.   62
Galanter, E.   2, 3, 43–44, 133
Gellerman, L. W.   8, 33, 45, 163, 188
George, F. H.   55
Ghent, L.   128–9, 165, 166–9
Gibson, E. J.   57, 74, 88, 121, 125–7, 130–2
Gibson, J. J.   125–7, 128, 130–2

SUBJECT INDEX

Pergamon Press Ltd., Headington Hill Hall, Oxford
4 & 5 Fitzroy Square, London W.1
Pergamon Press (Scotland) Ltd., 2 & 3 Teviot Place, Edinburgh 1
Pergamon Press Inc., Maxwell House, Fairview Park,
Elmsford, New York 10523
Pergamon of Canada Ltd., 207 Queen's Quay West, Toronto 1
Pergamon Press (Aust.) Pty. Ltd., 19a Boundary Street,
Rushcutters Bay, N.S.W. 2011, Australia
Pergamon Press S.A.R.L., 24 rue des Écoles, Paris 5ᵉ
Vieweg & Sohn GmbH, Burgplatz 1, Braunschweig

First edition 1968

Reprinted 1969

Library of Congress Catalog Card No. 67–31016

PRINTED IN GREAT BRITAIN BY A. WHEATON AND CO. LTD., EXETER
08 012521 2

The Discrimination Process and Development

BY

BRIAN J. FELLOWS

1966

PERGAMON PRESS

OXFORD · LONDON · EDINBURGH · NEW YORK

TORONTO · SYDNEY · PARIS · BRAUNSCHWEIG

OTHER TITLES IN THE SERIES IN EXPERIMENTAL PSYCHOLOGY

INTERNATIONAL SERIES OF MONOGRAPHS IN
EXPERIMENTAL PSYCHOLOGY
GENERAL EDITOR: H. J. EYSENCK

Volume 5

THE DISCRIMINATION PROCESS
AND DEVELOPMENT

TO JEAN, WILLIAM AND DANIEL